WILDFLOWERS AND OTHER PLANTS OF IOWA WETLANDS

Wildflowers

and Other Plants of **Iowa Wetlands**

BY SYLVAN T. RUNKEL AND DEAN M. ROOSA

IOWA STATE UNIVERSITY PRESS AMES

© 1999 Iowa State University Press
All rights reserved

Iowa State University Press
2121 South State Avenue, Ames, Iowa 50014

Orders: 1-800-862-6657
Office: 1-515-292-0140
Fax: 1-515-292-3348
Web site: www.isupress.edu

Cover photo: Blue flag iris by Carl Kurtz

∞ Printed on acid-free paper in Hong Kong

First edition, 1999

Library of Congress Cataloging-in-Publication Data

Runkel, Sylvan T.
    Wildflowers and other plants of Iowa wetlands / by Sylvan T. Runkel and Dean M. Roosa
        p.   cm.
    Includes bibliographical references (p.   ) and index.
    ISBN 0-8138-2174-6
    1. Wild flowers—Iowa—Identification. 2. Wetland plants—Iowa—Identification. 3. Plants, Useful—Iowa—Identification.
    I. Roosa, Dean M.   II. Title.
    QK160.R85   1999
    581.7′68′09777—dc21   99-10922

The last digit is the print number: 9 8 7 6 5 4 3 2 1

To John D. Dodd,
longtime professor of botany
at Iowa State University,
who, with his gentle humor
and compassion, touched
so many lives. It was
an honor for both authors
to know and work with John
on various professional levels.

John Dodd, shown here with an algology class at Pilot Knob bog—one of his favorite Iowa haunts—contributed greatly to our understanding of the algal flora, particularly of diatoms.

CONTENTS

FOREWORD

In the more than 25 years that I have been working on wetlands, an amazing transformation has occurred. They have gone from being perceived universally as wastelands to being touted, at least in some circles, as wonderlands. As is so often the case, the value of wetlands in our landscapes was not understood or appreciated until they were nearly all gone. The legacy of wetland drainage in Iowa and the rest of the Midwest ranges from polluted lakes and rivers, increased flooding, calamitous population declines in many game and non-game animal species to a homogenization of our landscapes that has robbed them of much of their inherent beauty.

An interest in wetland preservation, which came too late to have much impact on Iowa wetlands, was soon followed by an interest in wetland restoration in order to recapture some of the benefits of having wetlands in our landscapes. In the last ten years, the dismal trend of ever fewer acres of wetlands in Iowa was finally reversed. The restoration in recent years of hundreds of prairie potholes in northern Iowa and of floodplain wetlands along rivers in eastern Iowa has resulted in a net increase in wetland acreage. Although wetlands have come to be appreciated by more and more people, there has been relatively little in the way of accessible information about them, especially information that is intelligible and useful to non-experts. Fortunately, this too has finally begun to change. Last year saw the publication of Michael Lannoo's *Okoboji Wetlands* by the University of Iowa Press, the first account of the wetlands of any region of Iowa. Now we have this important new book on the wetland plants of Iowa.

"In the end we will conserve only what we love, we will love only what we understand, and we will understand only what we are taught," says Baba Dioum. There are none better suited and better qualified to teach us about Iowa's aquatic plants and wetlands than Dean Roosa and the late Sylvan Runkel. Sy Runkel was one of Iowa's best-known and respected naturalists. Through his previous books (*Wildflowers of Iowa Woodlands* and *Wildflowers of the Tallgrass Prairie*), he has done more to familiarize people with Iowa's rich natural heritage than anyone else. Dean Roosa, who co-authored *Wildflowers of the Tallgrass Prairie*, was for many years the State Ecologist of Iowa.

Dean was trained as a wetland ecologist at Iowa State University and has been working with wetlands for over thirty years. Both are distinguished embodiments of the environmental philosophy of Baba Dioum and have spent their lives helping Iowans to understand and appreciate their natural heritage.

Wildflowers and Other Plants of Iowa Wetlands does for Iowa wetlands what the previous two volumes in this series did for its forests and prairies. They made these scarce and important ecosystems accessible and understandable to the lay person. This book is similar to its two predecessors in many ways. It contains not only descrip-

tions and photographs of all major wetland species in the state, but also much useful information about how these species have been used historically by people and about Iowa wetlands in general. In short, this book is a splendid introduction to the different types of wetlands in Iowa and their beautiful and varied flora. By enabling more people to become familiar with our wetlands, this book will help ensure that those wetlands that remain and are being restored will not disappear. It is a fitting capstone to Sy Runkel's long and productive career.

—Arnold van der Valk
Ames, Iowa

PREFACE

As many images come to mind when "wetland" is spoken as there are people hearing the word. Some think of the beautiful marshes of northern Iowa; some think of backwater areas along the Mississippi; some think of that wet place in the field they can't farm certain years; some think of a place to hunt ducks; some think of a mosquito-infested swamp they visited at camp; some think of an area going to waste unless it can be drained.

We slowly caught on to the fact that wetlands have great ecologic and economic value and began to pass laws to protect them against further loss. As our understanding deepened, we even began to restore wetlands, to bring back places of recreation, of water storage, of wildlife habitat—of beauty.

With the increasing awareness of the importance of wetlands, a book was needed to help the non-specialist understand how wetlands are classified and to aid in the identification of wetland plants. There are wonderful taxonomic books available, however, they are often so technical that all but professional taxonomists become discouraged. These manuals are often regional in scope and contain many plants that do not occur in the local area. This tends to frustrate many users, particularly beginners. We think wetlands are grand places. We want you to enjoy them as we do. Hence, we offer this book as a starting place for those who wish to learn more about Iowa's wetlands and wetland plants.

Wetlands are a valuable resource, but one which many people do not visit. They possess a beauty often not appreciated by anyone but hunters, trappers, a few photographers, or recreationists on the larger lakes. This book is designed to point out the diversity of wetland types in our state. It also may be of value in assisting those persons involved in implementing the regulatory aspects of wetland protection—specifically Section 404 of the Clean Water Act and Section 10 of the Rivers and Harbors Act. We hope environmental consultants will find it useful in their task of wetland delineation.

Plant descriptions are presented by habitat (terrestrial or aquatic), then refined by habit (e.g., floating or submerged) or by taxonomic group (e.g., ferns and allies or trees and shrubs). Common names vary throughout the country, so we have included those in frequent use, although others may be used regionally or locally. We have also included the plant's Latin name, along with the authority.

While knowledge of this two-name system of naming plants is not necessary for the enjoyment of wetland plants, the system is useful and practical. The first name, the genus name (plural: genera), applies to a group of closely related species. The family name (example: *Cyperaceae*) indicates a group of closely related genera. The scientific name, generally derived from Latin or Greek, is often descriptive of the plant.

We hope the pictures, contributed by many photographers, along with the description of the plant and some information about its uses will increase the enjoyment of visitors to Iowa's wetlands and will entice newcomers to get to know these priceless areas. We further hope that teachers will use this book to become acquainted with wetlands and wetland plants and gain the confidence to visit wetlands with their classes. With the resurgence of interest in uses of native plants for medicines, we felt it important to include information on uses of wetland plants by Native Americans and early pioneers.

A wetland experience can be exhilarating with proper preparation; it can also be disappointing and uncomfortable without proper attire or with bad timing. Mosquitos do like wetlands, the humidity can be high and uncomfortable, and you can sink up to your knees in muck. But wetlands can also be among the most treasured places on earth. They are incomparably beautiful at dawn when the grebes and yellow-headed blackbirds are calling, the lotus is in bloom, the iris is at its peak, and hardly a ripple on the surface of the water. Or, just at sunset a fog may settle over the marsh and the cool damp air envelopes you and the distinctive smell pervades the air. Experience this and you will agree with us—these are grand places.

ARRANGEMENT OF THE BOOK

Nomenclature and common names follow Eilers and Roosa (1994), except for some cases wherein common names were taken from *A Flora of the Great Plains* (1986).

A description of Iowa's wetlands, along with illustrations, serves to introduce readers to the topic of wetland botany. An attempt was made to include a photograph of each type of wetland found in Iowa so users can affix a name to a wetland they may be visiting.

Species' descriptions are grouped by the habitat in which they occur, or by the separation of a major group of plants. Species appear in alphabetic order for smaller groups, like the ferns and trees; they appear in the approximate order of flowering in the section on terrestrial herbs.

Terrestrial habitats

• Herbs
• Ferns and allies
• Trees and shrubs

Aquatic habitats

• Plants growing in water (emergent, floating, submerged)

Examples: Duckweeds are found in the section on floating plants; silver maples are found in the section on trees and shrubs; marsh marigold is found early in the sections on herbs of terrestrial habitats; bottle gentian is found late in this same section.

ACKNOWLEDGMENTS

Many people encouraged us to compile a guide to the wetlands and wetland flora of Iowa. These include professional botanists, teachers, photographers, naturalists—all good friends of the authors. If we haven't told you individually, let us take this opportunity to express our gratitude.

We thank Bill Pusateri, Des Moines, and Jim Peck of the University of Arkansas, Little Rock, who read portions of the book and offered suggestions.

We also thank the many photographers who willingly shared their photographs with us—without them, this book could not be a reality.

Scott Zager of the Minnesota Department of Natural Resources was very helpful in undertaking the difficult task of identifying members of the genus *Carex*. John Pearson, Iowa Department of Natural Resources, provided information on wetland types as used by the Natural Areas Inventory.

The roles played by our wives, Bernie Runkel and Carol Jacobs, were especially important. Without their encouragement and sacrifice, this book would not have been possible.

WILDFLOWERS AND OTHER PLANTS OF IOWA WETLANDS

The ripple of the murky water
Rocks the canoe both fore and aft.
The grebe raises his beak and yodels,
A stirring from the distant past.

The cattails nod their heads in greeting,
Blackbirds adorn the marshland sky,
The muskrat stops his busy eating,
As the canoe glides silently by.

The marshland peace is so fulfilling,
The busy pace of life subsides.
This is Iowa primeval,
A beauty that so often hides.

These are marshes—loved and hated,
Here's where Errington did thrive.
In twelve millennia they were created,
Here's where feelings come alive.

Here's where Dodd and Weller studied,
Here's where Hayden often trod,
Here's where Pammel took his classes,
Here's where one feels close to God.

The place we now call "Iowa" surely was, prior to settlement, a world-class treasure. With its 28 million acres of prairie, its 3 to 4 million acres of woodland, and its 1.5 million acres of wetlands, it represented a seemingly unconquerable landscape to the early settlers. But conquer it we did. An onslaught of the plow, the cow, the dredge, and the saw changed the face of Iowa to what it is today—the most heavily modified landscape in the continental United States. Only 4 percent of the land still shows some native character.

The settlers had mixed emotions about the new landscape. Much was treeless when they were accustomed to many trees; much was water-logged and boggy when they were accustomed to dry land. But wildlife abounded, and it was a landscape that gave a sense of freedom and beauty they couldn't previously have imagined.

WHAT WE LOST

The wetlands were an impediment to westward travel—probably second only to the major rivers that had to be crossed on ice or by barge. Yet those wetlands, cursed and admired, teemed with life—from a rich array of plants to flocks of waterfowl and stately cranes. The associated prairie grasses cleansed and slowed the flow of water into the streams, leaving them crystal clear. They teemed with life and also teemed with a commodity so valuable that legislative acts were passed so these bountiful areas could be "reclaimed" and the deep rich soil converted to crop fields. And reclaim them we did.

Drainage districts were formed to finance drainage projects and to ensure that one landowner could not stand in the way of "progress." Counties put in tile drains and dredge ditches and the land dried out. After clay tiles were invented, tiling machines made fast work of tiling fields. The million plus acres of wetlands dwindled, agriculture prospered, the rich wetland flora was pushed to remote corners and the stately crane left.

When Iowa achieved statehood, it was granted 1,196,392 acres of public domain wetlands for swamp reclamation. This land was then transferred to the counties where it was bartered for public utilities or sold cheaply to immigration companies, with the provision they install set-

Dredge ditches are common in the young landscape of the Des Moines Lobe. They need to be dredged of silt periodically, but can be refuges for some wetland plants.

tlers. Some was given to railroad companies as an inducement to build roadbeds. Inventories in 1906 listed 930,000 acres of wetlands; by 1922 it was 368,000 acres. As agriculture became a way of life, wetland draining accelerated. In 1955, the wetland acreage was estimated to be around 155,000 (Mann 1955). By 1980, as few as 26,470 acres of natural marshes were all that remained on the Des Moines Lobe (Bishop 1981). Bishop and van der Valk (1982) estimated a statewide wetland area of around 110,000 acres.

There are no reliable means of comparing estimates because historically no generally accepted definition of a wetland has existed. The discrepancy in the figures reflects the fact that one estimate may have counted oxbows, seeps, and forested wetlands, while the others did not. Recently, guidelines have been proposed to assist in delineating wetlands to aid in compliance of the Clean Water Act. These guidelines include the presence of hydric soils, hydrophytic vegetation and wetland hydrology.

It is estimated that the United States loses some 300,000 acres of wetlands each year, and that the lower forty-eight states have lost about 50 percent of their wetlands since European settlement began (Conservation Foundation 1988). When floods and severe soil erosion occur, we scratch our heads and wonder why. We channelize and dike a river and drain the oxbows and the people of

St. Louis and New Orleans are recipients of the outcome of these unsound measures.

A RESURGENCE

Iowa's wetlands, after over a century of being considered an enemy of the settler, the farmer, the citizen—in fact nearly everyone—have come into their own. We are finally caring for these important habitats. Wetlands, to our amazement, have been shown to be an important cog in the wheel of our existence—both ecologic and economic. After rains, they provide a natural reservoir for temporary storage of water, which is released slowly, thus easing the threat of flooding. We pursue many of our recreational endeavors in wetlands, from waterfowl hunting, trapping, and fishing to the gentler pursuits of canoeing, photography, and simple appreciation of nature. Wetlands provide the potential for cleansing polluted waters and so may assist in waste treatment facilities. They also provide habitat for an array of both common and rare plants and animals. On a federal and state level, initiatives have been taken to reverse the loss of wetlands and to restore some of those long drained.

The federal government has teamed up with state agencies to establish a program termed the Prairie Pothole Joint Venture (PPJV), the Iowa Natural Heritage Foundation has established a Wetlands for Iowans program, and the Corps of Engineers has been assigned regulatory oversight of wetlands through provisions of the Clean Water Act. The Environmental Protection Agency (EPA) has designated May as American Wetlands Month.

Relatively new programs are adding significantly to our wetland heritage. These include the Wetland Reserve Program and the Emergency Wetland Reserve Program. The Wetland Reserve Program was established under the Food Security Act of 1985 and renewed in the 1990 and 1996 Farm Bills. The Natural Resources Conservation Service (NRCS), formerly the Soil Conservation Service, administers the Wetland Reserve Program, where lands or easements are purchased from private landowners and wetlands restored on a cost-shared basis. The "swampbuster" provisions of the Food Security Act and the 1986 Farm Bill were designed to prevent the conversion of lands unsuitable for agriculture and include drainage prevention of some wetlands. This is administered by the Natural Resources Conservation Service. The Department of the Interior administers the Emergency Wetland Reserve Program which is designed to purchase or obtain easements on flood-prone lands. Land has been purchased or easements obtained under this program for approximately 2,500 acres in Louisa County, and over 10,000 acres in Benton,

PHOTO BY DEAN ROOSA

The broad floodplain of the Iowa River in Louisa County. Land like this has been diked and farmed but remains flood-prone. The flood of 1993 caused such extensive damage to the levee system that many owners enrolled their land in the Emergency Wetland Reserve Program or sold it to the Fish and Wildlife Service.

Iowa, and Tama counties, along the Iowa River under the Iowa River Corridor Project. By late 1995, these two programs had protected over 65,000 acres of wetlands in Iowa, which has become a national leader in wetland restoration. A recent initiative, spearheaded by the Polk County Conservation Board, with participation of numerous groups, including various chapters of Ducks Unlimited and Pheasants Forever, the Iowa Natural Heritage Foundation, the Department of Natural Resources, the Des Moines Izaak Walton League and the Jasper County Conservation Board, has protected wetlands along the Skunk River in Polk County.

In short, wetlands are getting long-overdue respect. Within the last two decades we have begun to realize our folly, and it may not be too late. We are fortunate in Iowa in having a statewide system of County Conservation Boards to promote conservation measures on a local level. Many of these boards have purchased wetlands, or have assisted in management of wetlands on private lands. The various chapters of Ducks Unlimited have helped acquire wetlands for waterfowl habitat.

Politics figures into the fate of wetlands. In recent years, Congress has been involved in wetland protection—attempting to determine how to preserve wetlands without abridging private landowner rights. Presidential orders have been issued on behalf of wetland protection. Departments of Transportation are instructed to protect wetlands during construction of roadways—either by mitigation or highway design. The EPA and the U.S. Army Corps of Engineers team up with Departments of Natural Resources to oversee compliance with federal and state laws.

In fact, the state had already been acquiring existing wetlands. Two important federal initiatives did much to protect many of the wetlands under state ownership today. The first was during the original land office surveys when 65 lands and marshes were designated sovereign lands. The second was the enactment of the Pittman-Robertson Act of 1937 wherein an excise tax of 11 percent was placed on sporting arms and ammunition. These funds permitted the state to acquire marshes in northcentral Iowa for waterfowl hunting purposes. This program continues today.

STUDIES OF IOWA WETLANDS

While there have been numerous studies of Iowa's wetland plants, virtually nothing has been published for the beginner or lay person. Hayden (1943), published a botanical survey of the lakes region of Clay and Palo Alto counties; Beal (1954) studied the distribution of aquatic monocotyledons in Iowa; Beal and Monson (1954) presented a set of keys and distribution maps of wetland plants. They defined wetland plants narrowly, tending toward those of pure aquatic habitats. Lammers and van der Valk (1977, 1979) expanded the definition beyond what Beal and Monson used and published distribution maps and an annotated list of wetland plants. Recent research into Iowa fens resulted in distribution information, species lists, and geology of these unusual habitats (See Nekola 1990; Pearson and Leoschke, 1992; Thompson et al. 1992). Most recently, Eilers and Roosa (1994) published an annotated list of all Iowa plants and excluded certain records believed to be in error.

There have been a series of studies that investigated the technical aspects of wetlands (e.g. Clambey and Landers 1978; Currier, Davis and van der Valk 1978; Roosa 1981; Van Dyke 1972; van der Valk and Davis 1976a, 1976b, 1978a, 1978b). Peck and Roosa (1983) presented an extensive bibliography of the literature on Iowa's wetlands. Two other books that include information on Iowa's wetlands are Weller (1981) and van der Valk (1989). Weller and Spatcher (1965) did some pioneering work in the cycling of marsh vegetation, how it is impacted by muskrat populations, and how it relates to the distribution of marsh birds. Errington (1960a, 1960b, 1961, 1963) did much to create public awareness of wetlands and established a link between muskrat populations and marsh vegetation cycles.

IOWA WETLAND TYPES

A wetland defined: *An area inundated or saturated by surface or ground water at a frequency and duration sufficient for hydrophytic vegetation to develop.*

There are many ways to classify wetlands—probably about as many ways as there are wetland ecologists, but there is a movement to develop a regional or national system. For people interested in wetland classification, sources to consult include Shaw and Fredine (1971); Cowardin et al. (1979); or the Natural Areas Inventory, Wallace State Office Building, Des Moines, Iowa 50319. Recently the Department of Interior has adopted Cowardin et al. as their official classification methodology.

Below is a list of wetland habitat types in Iowa as used by the Natural Areas Inventory of the Department of Natural Resources, simplified for non-professional readers, and with some additions based on personal preferences:

- Marsh (including deep and shallow marshes)
- Floodplain forest (also termed a bottomland forest)
- Alder thicket (also termed an alder swamp)
- Rich fen (or simply fen or alkaline fen)
- Bog (also termed a nutrient-poor fen)
- Coldwater stream
- Open water lake
- Oxbow
- Seep
- Ephemeral pond
- Wet prairie
- Willow thicket
- Sedge meadow (also called a wet meadow or Carex swale)
- Farm ponds and impoundments

MARSHES

These are what most people visualize when they hear the word "wetland". They are areas of open water with a peripheral zone normally dominated by cattails (*Typha* sp.), hard-stemmed bulrush (*Scirpus acutus*), water plantain (*Alisma plantago-aquatica*), and arrowheads (*Sagittaria* sp.), often with leaves of pondweeds (*Potamogeton* sp.) floating on the surface. Some marshes contain large populations of water lilies (*Nymphaea tuberosa* and *Nuphar advena*). These marshes are also called prairie potholes or prairie glacial marshes and in Iowa are restricted to the Des Moines Lobe in the northcentral portion.

Marshes go through vegetation cycles, dependent on moisture and the presence of herbivores like muskrats.

Many have their water levels manipulated by structures which allow biologists to drain them to stimulate the germination of seeds of annuals like smartweeds (*Polygonum* sp.), nut rushes (*Cyperus* sp.), and stick-tights (*Bidens* sp.) to serve as food for migrating waterfowl. These marshes are often divided into "deep marshes" and "shallow marshes", the distinction being that shallow marshes have standing water up to 6 inches in depth most of the growing season, and deep marshes have water 6 inches to 3 feet or more most of the growing season.

Deep marshes have dominants of hard stemmed bulrush (*Scirpus acutus*), cattails (*Typha* sp.), water lilies (*Nuphar* sp. and *Nymphaea* sp.), pondweeds (*Potamogeton* sp.), coontail (*Ceratophyllum demersum*), milfoil (*Myriophyllum exalbescens*), and often beds of muskgrass (*Chara* sp.), a macroscopic alga. Shallow marshes have dominants which include river bulrush (*Scirpus fluviatilis*), bur-reed (*Sparganium eurycarpum*), arrowhead (*Sagittaria* sp.), lesser duckweed (*Lemna minor*), and slough sedge (*Carex atherodes*). In short, deep marshes have floating, emergent and submerged plants; shallow marshes have only small floating and emergent plants.

FLOODPLAIN FORESTS

Floodplain forests are associated with riverine systems and grow on alluvial soils deposited by floodwaters. The dom-

PHOTO BY DEAN ROOSA

This deep marsh, Cheever Lake in Emmet County, is ringed by cattails; emergent plants are near the edge with floating plants and submerged plants in deeper water.

11

inant trees are silver maple (*Acer saccharinum*), cottonwood (*Populus deltoides*), green ash (*Fraxinus pennsylvanica* var. *lanceolata*), black willow (*Salix nigra*), and in southern Iowa, sycamore (*Platanus occidentalis*). These floodplains include forested wetlands, where woody vegetation grows in standing water that is present much of the year. Along the Mississippi River in southeast Iowa, some of these floodplains have areas dominated by shrubs, mainly buttonbush (*Cephalanthus occidentalis*), which emerge from standing water. Such an area may be called a shrub swamp, or a shrub carr. Other characteristic plants include halberd-leaved rose mallow (*Hibiscus laevis*), Gray's sedge (*Carex grayii*), hop sedge (*Carex lupulina*), squarrose sedge (*Carex squarrosa*), wild grape (*Vitis riparia*), and river birch (*Betula nigra*).

ALDER THICKETS

These areas are normally found along small streams in peaty depressions. The soil is permanently wet and the alders form a closed canopy. The dominant species is speckled alder (*Alnus rugosa*). Herbs found growing beneath the alder and on the edges include spinulose wood fern (*Dryopteris spinulosa*), goldie's fern (*Dryopteris goldiana*), purple fringed orchid (*Platanthera psycodes*), ironweed (*Vernonia fasciculata*), river bulrush (*Scirpus fluviatilis*), and woolly bulrush (*Scirpus cyperinus*).

12

PHOTO BY DEAN ROOSA

A floodplain or forested wetland in Muscatine County.

These thickets are very rare in Iowa and, when found, are generally small. The best example known to us is in Mitchell County and was recently purchased by the Mitchell County Conservation Board.

FENS

Fens may be defined as small, boggy, spring-fed wetlands which often harbor rare plant species (Pearson and Leoschke 1992), or as peatlands dependent on a source of water in addition to atmospheric precipitation and with a minero- or mesotrophic status (Thompson et al. 1992). Recent research has led to the conclusion that fens are more common and widespread than we had believed. Traditionally, those fens near the western edge of the Des Moines Lobe in Dickinson and Emmet counties were assumed to be the only ones extant in Iowa. Fens are now known to be present in virtually all of Iowa's landforms, though they are common only on the Iowan Surface and the Des Moines Lobe regions (Thompson et al. 1992). Research by the Natural Areas Inventory staff of the Department of Natural Resources (see Pearson and Leoschke 1992) and Jeff Nekola, now of the University of Wisconsin, has led to the location and description of many fens in northeast Iowa, mainly on the Iowan Surface. Research by Thompson et al. (1992) has elaborated the geology and hydrology of these areas. The vegetation is distinctive, reflecting the nature of the water chemistry.

PHOTO BY DEAN ROOSA

Silver Lake Fen State Preserve, Dickinson County. Several plants in Iowa are restricted to fens, due to the nature of the water chemistry.

13

Plants characteristic of fens, or which are restricted to fens, include arrowgrass (*Triglochin* sp.), grass of Parnassus (*Parnassia glauca*), hooded ladies' tresses (*Spiranthes romanzoffiana*), leafy northern green orchid (*Platanthera hyperborea*), and small bladderwort (*Utricularia minor*). The vegetation of those eastern Iowa fens is different in some respects from that of the fens in northwest Iowa (see Pearson and Leoschke, 1992). Fens in northeast Iowa often have a shrub component, with dwarf birch (*Betula pumila*) and bog willow (*Salix candida*) being two important woody taxa. Those in northwest Iowa are more likely to have orchids, such as leafy green orchid (*Platanthera hyperborea*), and hooded ladies' tresses (*Spiranthes romanzoffiana*).

BOGS

Bogs are peatlands which are fed by surface water and are principally restricted in North America to regions north of Iowa.

Discovery of a sphagnum bog in Hancock County was described by Grant and Thorne (1955). This is a floating mat dominated by several species of the moss in the genus *Sphagnum*. More recently this area has been described as a nutrient-poor fen or simply "poor fen" because it may be fed by groundwater rather than runoff of rainfall. A number of plants rare to Iowa are found here. Grant and Thorne (1955) reported the first valid record of the insectivorous plant sundew (*Drosera rotundifolia*) in Iowa, and it is also the only site currently known for several species of sedges. This small area has been the subject of numerous studies by botanists (e.g., Smith, 1962; Smith and Bovbjerg, 1958, Grant and Thorne, 1955). This site has apparently existed as a *Sphagnum*-dominated mat since the end of the Pleistocene (Dick Baker, pers. comm.); the wonder is that it escaped detection until the mid 1950s.

COLDWATER STREAMS

In northeast Iowa, principally in the Paleozoic Plateau, erosional deepening of valleys often has proceeded to a depth where the groundwater flow is intercepted. This results in springs, generally along steep sides of valleys. The subterranean flow of water is a result of the karst topography, where the limestone permits precipitation to percolate underground. The springs eventually flow together, forming a coldwater stream. Because the water of these streams originates from a bedrock aquifer, it is a constant temperature throughout the year. Many of these streams, and the associated property, have been purchased by the State of Iowa for trout fishing. They are thus protected from cattle and provide habitat for a complex of wetland and aquatic

Pilot Knob Bog, situated at the base of a glacial kame. Dominated by Sphagnum *moss, it is habitat for a complex of rare wetland plants.*

Coldwater streams, also called trout streams, are restricted to northeast Iowa. Wetland plant species, adapted to cool-water conditions and flowing water, are found in most of these streams.

15

plants. The vascular plants which are regularly found in or at the edge of these coldwater streams include waterweed (*Elodea canadensis*), manna grass (*Glyceria grandis*), water cress (*Nasturtium officinale*), pondweed (*Potamogeton foliosus*), curly-leaved pondweed (*Potamogeton crispus*), horned pondweed (*Zannichellia palustrus*), and white water crowfoot (*Ranunculus aquatilis* var. *capillaceus*).

OPEN WATER LAKES

The natural open water lakes in Iowa occur on the Des Moines Lobe, a reminder of the relatively recent retreat of a glacier. Good examples are Lake Okoboji and Spirit Lake in Dickinson County, and Clear Lake in Cerro Gordo County. In shallow, protected coves of these lakes you find a wonderful, diverse array of submersed aquatic plants. In West Lake Okoboji there are large populations of coontail (*Ceratophyllum demersum*), milfoil (*Myriophyllum exalbescens*), waterweed (*Elodea canadensis*), Naiad (*Najas flexilis*), as well as a half-dozen species of pondweeds (*Potamogeton* sp.), and wild celery (*Vallisneria americana*). In Spirit Lake, shallow water near the shore provides the only known site in Iowa for widgeon grass (*Ruppia maritima*).

Bays and coves on the margin of West Lake Okoboji provide excellent habitat for a variety of submerged plants. Little Miller's Bay, adjacent to Iowa Lakeside Laboratory,

PHOTO BY DEAN ROOSA

Spirit Lake, Dickinson County. Near the edge are beds of aquatic plants including the only known Iowa site for widgeon grass.

Bays or coves, like Little Miller's Bay, Lake Okoboji, provide excellent habitat for a diverse array of aquatic plants. This is the only known extant site in Iowa for water marigold.

a field teaching and research station owned jointly by Iowa's three public universities, is particularly rich in the aquatic plant flora. This is the only known Iowa location for water marigold (*Megalodonta beckii*).

OXBOWS

Occasionally a bend in a river is cut off from the main channel by erosion, resulting in an abandoned streambed with stagnant or slowly flowing water. These oxbows provide protected habitat for wetland plants. The quiet water surface is an excellent habitat for several species of wetland plants including duckweeds (*Lemna* sp.; *Spirodela polyrhiza*) and water meal (*Wolffia* sp.). Oxbows are found throughout the state but are most common along larger streams, such as the Des Moines, Cedar, Iowa, and Wapsipinicon rivers. Along the Missouri River in far western Iowa, these oxbows provide good habitat for a large complex of aquatic and wetland plants such as cattails (*Typha* sp.), boneset (*Eupatorium perfoliatum*), bulrushes (*Scirpus* sp.), three square (*Scirpus americanus*), and American lotus (*Nelumbo lutea*).

SEEPS

Seeps are common on the Southern Iowa Drift Plain which covers approximately the south half of the state. These seeps seem to issue from the hillside where an ancient

An oxbow of the Iowa River located in Horseshoe Bend Division of Mark Twain National Wildlife Refuge, Louisa County. These sites provide quiet water and a protected habitat for a wide array of wetland plants.

Seeps, found in woodlands in the eastern half of Iowa, provide habitat for a complex of wetland plants and may contain skunk cabbage. Hardin County.

buried soil (paleosol) is found. The seeps often form long shallow ditches that run downslope to a small stream. In these wet troughs a variety of wetland plants occur, including fox sedge (*Carex vulpinoidea*), deep green bulrush (*Scirpus atrovirens*), stick-tights (*Bidens* sp.), cinnamon willow-herb (*Epilobium coloratum*), Torrey's rush (*Juncus torreyi*), and blue flag (*Iris shrevei*).

EPHEMERAL PONDS

Ephemeral ponds are depressions that are wet or water-filled from rain or meltwater during the wet spring and fall seasons. They provide temporary storage for precipitation that seeps out of the surrounding landscape, acting as a buffer between the wet and dry seasons. The ponds offer valuable resting and feeding sites for migrating birds. Many of the plants that grow here are annuals or short-lived perennials and may include pigweeds (*Amaranthus rudis, A. tuberculatus*), foxtail (*Alopecurus aequalis*), smartweeds (*Polygonum* sp.), and barnyard grass (*Echinochloa crusgalli*). Some ephemeral ponds are situated in a deposit of eolian sand, especially along the Iowa and Cedar rivers, and also along the lower Des Moines River. These deposits were laid down by prevailing westerly winds moving sand from the floodplains during the late Wisconsinan.

An underlying impervious layer may cause lateral transport of the water, forming springs, seeps, or marshes.

PHOTO BY DEAN ROOSA

Ephemeral ponds are important for migrating waterfowl, retention of precipitation, and as habitat for annual wetland plants. The ponds are often in agricultural fields. If several successive wet years occur, perennial wetland plants such as cattails will become established. Webster County.

This pond, near Eddyville in Mahaska County, is perched on an eolian sand dune. It provides habitat for a wetland flora including buttonweed, buttonbush, bluejoint, and, on the wet sands nearby, tubercled orchid.

Emphemeral sandy ponds, like this one in Linn County, provide habitat for a variety of rare wetland plants.

20

These marshes are perched above the surrounding landscape and may become dry late in the summer or in periods of drought. Examples are the Greiner Nature Preserve, Muscatine County, Behrens Ponds, Linn County, both owned by the Nature Conservancy, and ponds on the edge of the Calvin Basin in Louisa County. These may harbor some of our rare wetland plants, such as Smith's bulrush (*Scirpus smithii*), Hall's bulrush (*Scirpus hallii*), hair sedge (*Bulbostylis capillaris*), meadow beauty (*Rhexia virginica*), yellow-eyed grass (*Xyris torta*), buttonweed (*Dioda teres*), royal fern (*Osmunda regalis*) and mosquito fern (*Azolla mexicana*).

WET PRAIRIES

These sites often form a transition zone from the Carex swale to a mesic prairie. Dominants or those of frequent occurrence are bluejoint (*Calamagrostis canadensis*), slough grass (*Spartina pectinata*), fox sedge (*Carex vulpinoidea*), fragrant coneflower (*Rudbeckia subtomentosa*), sawtooth sunflower (*Helianthus grosseserratus*), compass plant (*Silphium laciniatum*), prairie blazing star (*Liatrus pycnostachya*), golden ragwort (*Senecio aureus*), Riddell's goldenrod (*Solidago ridellii*), New England aster (*Aster novae-angliae*), and big bluestem (*Andropogon gerardii*).

PHOTO BY DEAN ROOSA

A bluejoint-dominated wet prairie in Polk County, with an ephemeral pond in the foreground. Wet prairies occur between mesic prairies and marshes. Wetland species present include sawtooth sunflower, several sedges, violets, and several asters.

21

WILLOW THICKETS

Along streams and in marshes, willows, usually the peach-leaved willow (*Salix amygdaloides*) or the sandbar willow (*Salix exigua* spp. *interior*), grow in dense, nearly mono-dominant stands. These thickets often result from the spreading of underground structures and crowd out most other vegetation. The thickets are excellent soil binders and offers good wildlife habitat, generally along streams, on islands in streams, or on floodplains where they may be associated with an oxbow or seep.

SEDGE MEADOW (CAREX SWALE)

Sedge meadows usually occur on the edges of marshes and may be dominated by a single species of sedge such as slough sedge (*Carex atherodes*). Or, such a habitat may occupy a broad drainage way and consist of a diverse array of members of the genus *Carex*—as in the case of Engeldinger Marsh in Polk County, where 17 species were identified. The assemblage of plants in the marsh included dark green bulrush (*Scirpus atrovirens*), spring cress (*Cardamine bulbosa*), marsh cress (*Rorippa palustris*), marsh skullcap (*Scutellaria galericulata*), mountain mint (*Pycnanthemum virginianum*), blue flag (*Iris shrevei*), fog fruit (*Phyla lanceolata*), and bog willowherb (*Epilobium leptophyllum*). This habitat has been particularly hard hit by drainage and heavy trampling by livestock.

PHOTO BY DEAN ROOSA

A fairly intact example of sedge meadow from Polk County. Sedge meadows often suffer disturbance through grazing and trampling. This disturbance may permit invasion by more-aggressive plants.

FARM PONDS AND IMPOUNDMENTS

Where marshes or prairie potholes have been filled or drained by erosional processes over a long time, farm ponds and impoundments become increasingly important as habitat for wetland plants. The shallow portions become rapidly colonized by plants from propagules transported in by wind or waterfowl. These ponds are often ringed by cattails and bulrushes, with duckweeds usually floating at the edge. Frequently pondweeds (*Potamogeton* sp.) are found in deeper water.

In recent decades, three large reservoirs have been constructed—Red Rock and Saylorville on the Des Moines River and Rathbun on the Chariton River. The reservoirs inundated floodplain forests during construction and filling and also created large areas of shallow backwater, which harbor a vast array of wetland plants. Depending on the quality of the stream, some of these shallows may become partially filled with silt, which will create areas conducive to the establishment of wetland plants. These backwaters have not been analyzed for the dynamics of vegetational change since their inception.

WETLANDS AND IOWA'S NATURAL REGIONS

As a basis for understanding Iowa's wetlands and how they vary with changes in the landscape, we will describe the most characteristic wetland types in each of Iowa's natural regions as defined by Prior (1991). We make no attempt to be exhaustive in the following sections. For example, oxbows and willow thickets occur on all landforms except the Loess Hills and may not be described for each one.

DES MOINES LOBE

The youngest landform in Iowa is the Des Moines Lobe, tongue-shaped and stretching from the northern border to the city of Des Moines, and from Dickinson County on the west to Cerro Gordo County on the east. This landform is 12,000–14,000 years old, young by geological standards, and has not had sufficient time to develop well-defined drainage patterns. The landscape still shows the influence of the recent glacial episode, with moraines, eskers, kames, and kettleholes being the most obvious. The Raccoon River forms part the western and the southern boundary. All the state's natural lakes are in this landform. Clear Lake, Storm Lake, Lake Okoboji, Spirit Lake, and numerous smaller lakes, marshes, and prairie swales are characteristic of a young, postglacial landscape. It once abounded

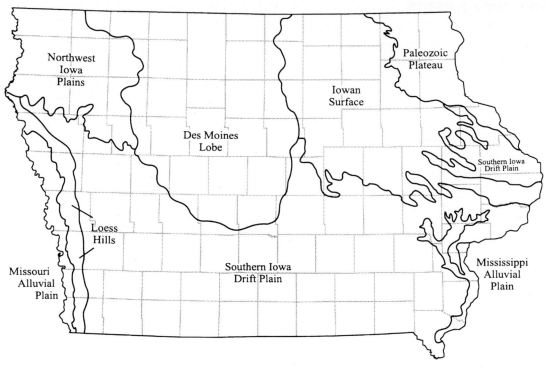

Northwest
Iowa
Plains

Paleozoic
Plateau

Iowan
Surface

Des Moines
Lobe

Southern Iowa
Drift Plain

Loess
Hills

Missouri
Alluvial
Plain

Southern Iowa
Drift Plain

Mississippi
Alluvial
Plain

LANDFORM REGIONS OF IOWA

MAP BY JEAN PRIOR, GEOLOGICAL SURVEY OF IOWA

in wetlands—prairie potholes, marshes, prairie streams, oxbows, and fens. At the time of settlement, this spongy landscape consisted of around 7.6 million acres—6 million of which were a mix of prairies and wetlands.

MARSH (PRAIRIE POTHOLES, PRAIRIE GLACIAL MARSH)

The most common wetland type on the Des Moines Lobe is the prairie pothole. These are what most people think of when they hear the word "wetland" or "marsh". They are most abundant in the northwest part of the lobe where the rumpled terrain is described as "knob and kettle" topography. Excellent examples of these potholes are Jemmerson Slough, Dickinson County; Cheever Lake, Emmet County; Goose Lake and Big Wall Lake, Hamilton County; Engeldinger Marsh, Polk County; Doolittle Potholes, Story County; Dewey's Pasture, Clay County; and Kalsow Prairie, Pocahontas County.

FENS

Fens are unusual wetland types. They are peatlands which are dependent on a source of water in addition to atmospheric precipitation and with a minero- or mesotropic status (Thompson et al. 1992). As water is transported laterally through glacial till, it often becomes high in carbonate concentration. The high carbonate levels limit the occurrence of certain plants and permit others to flourish. The

PHOTO BY DEAN ROOSA

Jemmerson Slough, Dickinson County, an excellent example of a deep marsh.

result is a complex of plants found on these peatlands as their only Iowa habitat: arrow grasses (*Triglochin* sp.), grass of Parnassus (*Parnassia glauca*), hooded ladies' tresses (*Spiranthes romanzoffiana*), leafy northern green orchid (*Platanthera hyperborea*), small bladderwort (*Utricularia minor*), nut rush (*Scleria verticillata*), beaked rush (*Rhynchospora capillacea*), and Kalm's lobelia (*Lobelia kalmii*).

Fens located on the Des Moines Lobe are mostly found near the interface of the lobe and the Northwest Iowa Plains; fewer near the interface with the Iowan Surface. The most famous is Silver Lake Fen on the south shore of Silver Lake, Dickinson County. This site, first surveyed by Anderson (1943), has been the subject of research from Iowa Lakeside Laboratory. Holte (1966) discovered and described a complex of fens in Excelsior Township, Dickinson County. Recently these were added to state ownership.

Peatlands which occur near the interface of the Des Moines Lobe and the Iowan Surface differ in lacking zonation and having a higher incidence of woody shrubs. Buffalo Slough, a peatland which lies in the ancient channel of the Winnebago River near Mason City, has a rich history and flora. This site was a favorite study and collecting site for Bohumil Shimek, noted naturalist from the University of Iowa. A complex of rare plants is found there including

PHOTO BY DEAN ROOSA

Buffalo Slough, in an ancient channel of the Winnebago River, Cerro Gordo County, is a peatland which has a rich flora of rare wetland plants.

bogbean (*Menyanthes trifoliata*), sage willow (*Salix candida*), northern bedstraw (*Galium labradoricum*), five-finger (*Potentilla palustris*), and angelica (*Angelica atropurpurea*).

BOGS (NUTRIENT-POOR FEN)
A bog is a peatland which has only surface water as a source of moisture and generally has a floating mat, or mass of vegetation. One bog appears frequently in Iowa's natural history literature. Located in Pilot Knob State Park and Preserve, Hancock County, it is dominated by *Sphagnum* and provides good habitat for several unusual plants, including sundew (*Drosera rotundifolia*). Some researchers refer to this as a nutrient-poor fen, or simply a "poor fen", as it may have a source of water other than from the land surface. The bog escaped detection until the mid-1950s, when Grant and Thorne (1955), acting on a tip from Henry Conard, surveyed the area. This site has been the subject of several general studies, a number of which describe the algal flora, particularly diatoms.

SEDGE MEADOWS OR CAREX SWALES
Often associated with prairie potholes, Carex swales are also called sedge meadows. These are shallow, permanently saturated areas between a marsh and a wet prairie. The areas are dominated by members of the *Carex* genus. Good

PHOTO BY DEAN ROOSA

A natural history class standing on the bog at Pilot Knob State Preserve. The bog is dominated by Sphagnum *moss and is the only Iowa site for sundew, an insectivorous plant. Adjacent Dead Man's Lake is one of only a few known extant sites in Iowa for the large-leaved pondweed (*Potamogeton amplifolius*).*

examples are found in the Lakes Area in association with marshes or prairies. Another good example is Engeldinger Marsh, Polk County—unusual because it is located at the southern terminus of the Des Moines Lobe. This is a largely under-studied habitat in Iowa—partly because it is often dominated by a single genus of plant with numerous species difficult to distinguish, and often is degraded by years of grazing.

Carex swales form a transition from prairie to marsh and contain species which are resilient—being able to withstand both some inundation and periodic droughts. In addition to the common dominant sedges such as *Carex atherodes, C. stricta, C. vulpinoidea*, these swales provide good habitat for such interesting wetland plants as spring cress (*Cardamine bulbosa*), great lobelia (*Lobelia siphilitica*), and the more common plants bluejoint (*Calamagrostis canadensis*), fowl manna grass (*Glyceria striata*), stick-tight (*Bidens* sp.), and several species of bulrush (*Scirpus* sp.).

OXBOWS

Oxbows appear along the major rivers on the lobe: the Des Moines, the Boone, and the Skunk. Once the main channel, oxbows are now cut off and lie with standing water. They form ideal habitat for a variety of quiet-water species, such as duckweed (*Lemna* sp., *Spirodela polyrhiza*), water-

28

PHOTO BY DEAN ROOSA

A Carex swale (sedge meadow) in Polk County in the terminal moraine of the Des Moines Lobe. It is unusual in its location at the very edge of the lobe and its diversity of sedges.

meal (*Wolffia* sp.), and those which thrive on mud banks, such as stick-tight (*Bidens* sp.), stinging nettle (*Urtica dioica*), and wood nettle (*Laportea canadensis*). Trees, such as cottonwood (*Populus deltoides*), Sycamore (*Platanus occidentalis*), Black willow (*Salix nigra*), and silver maple (*Acer saccharinum*) thrive at the edges of oxbows.

FLOODPLAINS

Along the major rivers, floodplains harbor a variety of wetland plants. These are normally dominated by silver maple (*Acer saccharinum*), green ash (*Fraxinus pennsylvanica*), cottonwood (*Populus deltoides*), black walnut (*Juglans nigra*) and box elders (*Acer negundo*). Sycamores (*Platanus occidentalis*) are found in the southern part of the lobe. Floodplains also provide excellent habitat for stinging nettle (*Urtica dioica*), wood nettle (*Laportea canadensis*), and wood reed (*Cinna arundinacea*).

Some streams, particularly in the south of the lobe, have very wide floodplains in relation to their size—a result of carrying meltwater from the Wisconsinan glacier. The Skunk River, south of Ames, has one such wide floodplain. Although drained now, it was once a large, spongy wetland which impeded settlers on their way west. This particular site gained the name "slough of despond" because of the difficulty it presented to prairie schooners.

PHOTO BY DEAN ROOSA

An oxbow of the Des Moines River in Emmet County. These areas provide excellent habitat for a wide variety of wetland plants, such as duckweeds and watermeal.

WILLOW THICKETS

On the lower portions of long slopes willow thickets are often found. These are much like those described in the general discussion of communities.

PALEOZOIC PLATEAU

This rugged terrain, deeply dissected by valleys which often have eroded so far they intercept the groundwater flow, covers the extreme northeast corner of Iowa—portions of Allamakee, Clayton, Dubuque, Fayette, Howard, Jackson, and Winneshiek counties. Hartley (1966) and Pusateri, Roosa, and Farrar (1994) have discussed the vegetation of this area. The wetland types include the following.

COLD, SPRING-FED STREAMS

These streams, fed by springs, have a constant flow and constant temperature. Aquatic plants found growing in these fast-flowing streams include water cress (*Nasturtium officinale*), water crowfoot (*Ranunculus aquatilis* var. *capillaceus*), horned pondweed (*Zanichellia palustris*), waterweed (*Elodea canadensis*), and wavy-leaved pondweed (*Potamogeton crispus*).

FLOODPLAINS (BOTTOMLANDS)

Floodplains or floodplain forests typically include flood-tolerant species, such as silver maples (*Acer saccharinum*),

PHOTO BY DEAN ROOSA

Coldwater streams are common in the Paleozoic Plateau. Many are now owned by the state and were acquired for public fishing. Dubuque County.

cottonwoods (*Populus deltoides*), green ash (*Fraxinus pennsylvanica*), black walnut (*Juglans nigra*), and several willows (*Salix* sp.). Common herbaceous species include over a dozen sedges (*Carex* sp.), bluejoint (*Calamagrostis canadensis*), wood reed (*Cinna arundinacea*), wild madder (*Galium obtusum*), wood nettle (*Laportea canadensis*), rice cut grass (*Leersia oryzoides*), fringed loosestrife (*Lysimachia ciliata*), moneywort (*Lysimachia nummularia*), jewel weed (*Impatiens capensis*), and jumpseed (*Polygonum virginianum*).

OXBOWS AND SHALLOW BACKWATERS
The backwaters of the Mississippi River often harbor wetland species, which include American lotus (*Nelumbo lutea*), pickerel weed (*Pontederia cordata*), waterweed (*Elodea* sp.), bur-reed (*Sparganium eurycarpum*), tape grass (*Vallisneria americana*), arrowheads (*Sagittaria* sp.), coontail (*Ceratophyllum demersum*), pondweeds (*Potamogeton crispus, P. foliosus*), horned pondweed (*Zannichellia palustris*), and an array of floating plants such as duckweeds (*Lemna* sp., *Spirodela polyrhiza*). Flood-tolerant woody species are found on the moist stream banks.

FLOODPLAIN MARSHES
Normally adjacent to streams and close to the water table, depressions in the floodplain retain water most of the year.

PHOTO BY JON STRAVERS

Bottomlands along the larger streams permit a large species of flood-adapted species to flourish. Soft maples, cottonwoods, stinging nettle, wood nettle, several species of bedstraw, and jewelweed all do well here. Allamakee County.

A floodplain marsh, Allamakee County, with a very large population of the hybrid horsetail (Equisetum X littorale).

Shallow backwater of the Mississippi River, Allamakee County.

They are a valuable habitat for the protection of wetland plants and as a feeding or hunting area for animals. These marshes have a fringe of silver maple, willow, cottonwood, river birch (*Betula nigra*), elderberry (*Sambucus canadensis*), dogwood (*Cornus* sp.), and horsetail (*Equisetum arvense, E. fluviatilis, E. X littorale*). In one such marsh in Allamakee County there is the largest known population of the hybrid horsetail (*E. X littorale*).

FENS

Fens have been recently discovered on the Paleozoic Plateau; seven were found on the fen survey conducted by the Department of Natural Resources in 1992. Bogbean (*Menyanthes trifoliata*), one of our rarest aquatic plants, and yellow-lipped orchid (*Spiranthes lucida*) were found on an Allamakee County fen.

IOWAN SURFACE

This large landform region is bounded on the west by the Des Moines Lobe, on the east by the Paleozoic Plateau, and on the south by the Southern Iowa Drift Plain. Encompassing all, or nearly all, of 27 counties in northcentral Iowa, the region is tongue-shaped, with the long axis oriented in a north-northwest to south-southeast direction. The southern terminus is deeply lobed with protrusions of upland areas between the valleys of large rivers. Eilers (1971) is an important botanical reference to this landform.

SEDGE MEADOWS

Along major streams, like the Wapsipinicon and Cedar rivers, are depressions which may be classed as marshes or sedge meadows. These are dominated by sedges such as *Carex atherodes, Carex stricta,* and several species of bulrushes (*Scirpus* sp.).

WET PRAIRIES

The low relief of this landform results in many poorly drained depressions. These, if they occur in an open area where grasses dominate, are called wet prairies or prairie swales. These transition areas between sedge meadows and mesic prairies are good habitat for a variety of wetland sedges: bluejoint (*Calamagrostis canadensis*), sneezeweed (*Helenium autumnale*), cordgrass (*Spartina pectinata*), dock (*Rumex* sp.), veiny pea (*Lathrus palustris*), skullcap (*Scutellaria galericulata*), New England aster (*Aster novae-angliae*), stick-tight (*Bidens cernua*), slough grass (*Spartina pectinata*), blazing star (*Liatris pycnostachya*), Riddell's goldenrod (*Solidago ridellii*), and big bluestem (*Andropogon gerardii*).

FLOODPLAINS AND FORESTED WETLANDS

This habitat occurs low on the landscape, close to streams, and often has depressions where water stands much of the year. The canopy consists of silver maple (*Acer saccharinum*), American elm (*Ulmus americana*), black walnut (*Juglans nigra*), green ash (*Fraxinus pennslyvanica*), and cottonwood (*Populus deltoides*). These wetlands provide good habitat for great lobelia (*Lobelia siphilitica*), cardinal flower (*Lobelia cardinalis*), marsh fern (*Thelypteris palustris*), bog hemp (*Boehmeria cylindrica*), Gray's sedge (*Carex grayii*), red-osier dogwood (*Cornus stolonifera*) in the extreme northern part of state, and touch-me-not (*Impatiens pallida*).

FENS

The incidence and importance of fens on the Iowan Surface was largely unknown until the early 1990s when the Iowa Natural Areas Inventory of the Iowa Department of Natural Resources and Jeff Nekola of Cedar Rapids conducted a fen survey (see Pearson and Leoschke, 1992 for location and species lists).

These are peatlands, composed largely of muck soils, fed by groundwater. Because the groundwater is transported through glacial till, it becomes high in carbonates prior to discharge. This water chemistry permits the growth of certain plants which are not found in other habi-

PHOTO BY CAROL THOMPSON

Kinney-Lindstrom Fen, Cerro Gordo County. Fens have suffered from grazing and trampling and many have been lost. Those that remain are precious refuges for a complex of wetland plants, many rare.

34

tats. Some plants restricted, or nearly so, to fens are sage willow (*Salix candida*), arrow grass (*Triglochin maritimum, T. palustris*), dwarf birch (*Betula pumila var. glandulifera*), bog bedstraw (*Galium labradoricum*), cottongrass (*Eriophorum angustifolium, E. gracile, E. virginicum*), beaked rush (*Rhynchospora capillacea*), and Kalm's lobelia (*Lobelia kalmii*). On the Iowan surface, these fens are found in Benton, Black Hawk, Bremer, Buchanan, Cerro Gordo, Chickasaw, Franklin, and Howard counties.

ALDER THICKETS
Alder thickets, described earlier, are nearly exclusive to this landform.

SOUTHERN IOWA DRIFT PLAIN

The Southern Iowa Drift Plain is a large landform, composing much of the southern half of the state. Since the last glaciation, some 500,000 years have allowed sufficient time for a mature landscape to form. The drainage patterns have taken a dendritic form and drained the postglacial wetlands. Slowly, erosion has erased the kames, filled the kettles and obliterated other signs of glacial activity. Wetlands now consist of oxbows, floodplains and floodplain wetlands, seeps, artificial lakes, and farm ponds.

FLOODPLAINS, FLOODPLAIN WETLANDS, AND OXBOWS
A number of streams flow across this landform toward the larger border rivers: the Boyer, Cedar, Des Moines, Iowa, and Skunk. Because these streams originate on the Des Moines Lobe and received massive amounts of meltwater as the glaciers wasted, some have extremely wide floodplains. The Skunk River was one such stream—small in size but with a formidable waterlogged floodplain. These floodplains were largely wetlands and as the waters changed course over the ages, many oxbows developed. These oxbows contain standing or stagnant water and often are surrounded by wetland vegetation.

Wetland plants which are found in this alluvial plain and associated wetlands include the following trees: sycamore (*Platanus occidentalis*), silver maple (*Acer saccharinum*), walnut (*Juglans nigra*), kingnut hickory (*Carya laciniosa*), river birch (*Betula nigra*), peach-leaved willow (*Salix amygdaloides*), black willow (*Salix nigra*), and Kentucky coffee tree (*Gymnocladus dioica*). Shrubs or vines in this habitat are: elderberry (*Sambucus canadensis*), Virginia creeper (*Parthenocissus quinquefolia*), riverbank grape (*Vitis riparia*), poison ivy (*Toxicodendron radicans* ssp. *negundo*), and rough-leaved dogwood (*Cornus drummondii*). The herb layer might include nodding bur marigold (*Bidens cernua*), yellow giant hyssop (*Agastache nepetoides*), bog hemp (*Boehmeria cylindrica*), American bellflower (*Campanula americana*), Gray's sedge (*Carex grayii*), fox sedge (*Carex vulpinoidea*), wood reed (*Cinna arundinacea*), pony grass (*Eragrostis hypnoides*), wild madder (*Galium obtusum*), small-flowered crowfoot (*Ranunculus abortivus*), swamp buttercup (*R. septentrionalis*), wood nettle (*Laportea canadensis*), spotted touch-me-not (*Impatiens capensis*), and stinging nettle (*Urtica dioica*). On the surface of the standing water, duckweeds (*Lemna minor, L. trisulca, Spirodela polyrhiza*) and watermeal (*Wolffia* sp.) normally occur. On the muddy shore are water plantain (*Alisma plantago-aquatica*), duck potato (*Sagittaria latifolia*), sweetflag (*Acorus calamus*), blue flag iris (*Iris shrevei*), nut rushes (*Cyperus esculentus, C. rivularis, C. filiculmis*), bluejoint (*Calamagrostis canadensis*), rice cut grass (*Leersia oryzoides*), seedbox (*Ludwigia alternifolia*), and soft stemmed bulrush (*Scirpus validus*).

FENS OR PEATLANDS

Peatlands occur on most Iowa landforms. On the Southern Iowa Drift Plain, a good example is located near Nichols, Muscatine County, in an ancient channel of the Cedar River. High-quality peat is currently being mined from a portion. In recent years the rare plants bogbean (*Menyanthes trifoliata*) and royal fern (*Osmunda regalis*) were discovered here. This site was the subject of a study by Baker

Floodplain marshes are fairly common on the Southern Iowa Drift Plain but have not been studied in detail. Monroe County.

Nichols Marsh, Muscatine County. This peatland, located in an ancient channel of the Iowa River, contains high quality peat and is the site of a large wetland flora, with some very rare species.

Seeps are common on the Southern Iowa Drift Plain and often emanate on hillsides where a paleosol is at the surface. The resulting troughs run down the hill and are permanently wet, providing an excellent habitat for a wetland flora, such as this large population of blue flag in a seep in Mahaska County.

et al. (1987). A fen discovered in Guthrie County is cited in Roosa et al. (1991).

SEEPS

One of the most common wetland types on this landform are seeps, issuing from a hillside where a buried ancient soil (paleosol) is exposed. Seeps often form long, narrow drainageways downslope. Along these seepages one might find swamp milkweed (*Asclepias incarnata*), New England aster (*Aster nova-angliae*), nodding bur marigold (*Bidens cernua*), spring cress (*Cardamine bulbosa*), spikerushes (*Eleocharis erythropoda, E. obtusa*), cinnamon willowherb (*Epilobium coloratum*), boneset (*Eupatorium perfoliatum*), rushes (*Juncus dudleyi, J. torreyi*), winged loosestrife (*Lythrum alatum*), monkey flower (*Mimulus ringens*), mountain mint (*Pycnanthemum virginianum*), deep green bulrush (*Scirpus atrovirens*), and cattail (*Typha* sp.).

FARM PONDS

The southern Iowa Drift Plain contains a large number of farm ponds. Migrating waterfowl have transported propagules of wetland plants into these ponds and one may expect to find the following wetland plants growing there or in the water-logged soil adjacent to them: cattail (*Typha* sp.), bulrushes (*Scirpus acutus, S. validus, S. atrovirens*), water plantain (*Alisma plantago-aquatica*), duck potato

PHOTO BY DEAN ROOSA

Farm ponds are common on the Southern Iowa Drift Plain and those that have been in existence some time may have a zone of cattails, emergent bulrushes, pondweeds, and floating plants. Unless good soil conservation accompanies these ponds, they eventually become clogged with silt.

(*Sagittaria latifolia*), Illinois pondweed (*Potamogeton illinoensis*), knotty pondweed (*Potamogeton nodosus*), winged loosestrife (*Lythrum alatum*), and great blue lobelia (*Lobelia siphilitica*).

ALLUVIAL PLAINS

Although alluvial plains, also called floodplains, are common along Iowa's larger rivers, the ones that are the most obvious and are of highest ecological significance for wetland plants are those associated with the two border rivers. These alluvial plains are generally level, with meander scars and higher points that are the remnants of terraces. Alluvial plains are the result of rivers carrying large amounts of glacial meltwater in the geological past.

MISSOURI RIVER ALLUVIAL PLAIN

This alluvial plain is the result of a restless river changing course and of massive amounts of meltwater from retreating Wisconsinan-age glaciers, resulting in a table-top flat surface up to 12 miles wide and once a marvel of aquatic activity. Since then, the river has been straightened and diked, the floodplain has been drained and farmed, bringing to its knees a once world-class wetland complex. From remaining oxbow lakes, drainage ditches, and marshes where oxbow lakes have silted in, we get an inkling of what the flora of this landform was like. Some sand dune

PHOTO BY DEAN ROOSA

Although many oxbows along the Missouri River have been drained, some with their associated sandy shores still contain a significant wetland flora.

fields remain, occasionally harboring a sandy pond where we look for wetland treasures. In spite of the past high level of disturbance, a significant wetland flora still remains. The oxbow lakes and the saturated soil along the shore are known to include the following plants as examples, although the flora is much larger: toothcup (*Ammania coccinea*), water plantain (*Alisma plantago-aquatica*), coontail (*Ceratophyllum demersum*), yellow nut grass (*Cyperus esculentus*), dwarf spikerush (*Eleocharis acicularis*), burhead (*Echinodorus cordifolius*), pony grass (*Eragrostis hypnoides*), water star-grass (*Heteranthera dubia*), rushes (*Juncus dudleyi, J. nodosus*), duckweeds (*Lemna minor, L. trisulca, Spirodela polyrhiza*), American lotus (*Nelumbo lutea*), reed grass (*Phragmites australis*), smartweeds (*Polygonum coccineum*), ladies' tresses (*Spiranthes cernua, S. vernalis*), pondweeds (*Potamogeton foliosus, P. pectinatus*), arrowheads (*Sagittaria brevirostra, S. calycina*), willows (*Salix exigua* var. *interior, S. nigra, S. rigida*), bulrushes (*Scirpus acutus, S. americanus, S. fluviatilis*), cattail (*Typha* sp.), and bladderwort (*Utricularia vulgaris*). Several oxbows are in publicly owned areas—examples being Lewis and Clark State Park, Monona County, and De Soto Bend National Wildlife Refuge, Harrison County. Probably much of this vast floodplain was a mix of low prairie, dominated by cordgrass (*Spartina pecti-*

nata), a complex of meander scars, and sand fields complete with blowouts and sandy ponds.

MISSISSIPPI RIVER ALLUVIAL PLAIN

The Mississippi River Alluvial Plain is more complex, consisting of the floodplain of the Mississippi River and of the alluvial plain referred to as the Lake Calvin basin.

LAKE CALVIN BASIN

Formerly thought to be a glacial lake, this landform is now regarded as an alluvial valley where water was impounded for a brief geological time, not sufficient to be considered a glacial lake. For purposes of this book, we will consider the basin separate from the Mississippi River Alluvial Plain landform. Whatever its origin, this region, with its many oxbows, floodplain wetlands, wooded wetlands, shrub carrs, etc., is the most wetland-rich area in the state and one which has not received sufficient attention in the past. Here certain wetlands most closely resemble a swamp, and woody species emerge from standing water. Good examples of this are in Muscatine County along Pike Creek and in portions of Cone Marsh in Muscatine and Louisa counties. Buttonbush (*Cephalanthus occidentalis*) forms the perimeter of wetlands and is found in standing water throughout part of the year. The beautiful halberd-leaved

This site, along Pike Creek in Muscatine County, is flooded for a considerable length of time each year. The emergent shrubby vegetation is largely buttonbush, with rose mallow in slightly drier sites. This could be termed a wooded wetland, shrub carr, or shrub swamp.

rose mallow (*Hibiscus laevis)* is found at the edge of many wetlands often growing in shallow standing water. There are many oxbows with standing or slowly flowing water and some which become dry late in the year.

OXBOWS

Oxbows are filled with standing water and harbor a diverse wetland flora. In the water, emerging from the water and on the saturated banks one may find the following: water plantain (*Alisma plantago-aquatica*), bog hemp (*Boehmeria cylindrica*), nut rush (*Cyperus odoratus*), waterweed (*Elodea nuttallii*), eastern manna grass (*Glyceria septentrionalis*), duckweed (*Lemna minor, Spirodela polyrhiza*), watermeal (*Wolffia* sp.) yellow waterlily (*Nuphar luteum*), pickeral weed (*Pontederia cordata*), pondweed (*Potamogeton nodosus, P. foliosus*), sago (*Potamogeton pectinatus*), yellow water crowfoot (*Ranunculus flabellaris*), softstem bulrush (*Scirpus validus*), bur-reed (*Sparganium americanum, S. eurycarpum*), and duck potato (*Sagittaria latifolia*).

FLOODPLAIN WOODS

It is rare to find a relatively mature alluvial woods; most have been heavily logged or cleared for agricultural purposes. A few good examples exist in the Lake Calvin basin

Possibly the richest region for wetland vegetation is the Lake Calvin basin, especially near Wapello, Louisa County. No detailed study has been done of this broad floodplain of the Iowa River in what was once considered a glacial lake basin.

and on the Mississippi floodplain. There are alluvial woods which are flooded periodically and which are rich in flood-tolerant species. The Big Timber tract of Mark Twain National Wildlife Refuge and east and north of Wapello are excellent places to see the diversity of wetlands representative of this landform. In these sites one may expect to find the following trees: box elder (*Acer negundo*), silver maple (*Acer saccharinum*), sycamore (*Platanus occidentalis*), green ash (*Fraxinus pennsylvanica var. lanceolata*), swamp white oak (*Quercus bicolor*), shingle oak (*Quercus imbricaria*), pin oak (*Quercus palustris*), black willow (*Salix nigra*), river birch (*Betula nigra*), honey locust (*Gleditsia triacanthos*), Kentucky coffee tree (*Gymnocladus dioica*), and American elm (*Ulmus americana*). Shrubs and vines include false indigo (*Amorpha fruticosa*), wahoo (*Euonymus atropurpureus*), buttonbush (*Cephalanthus occidentalis*), rough-leaved dogwood (*Cornus drummondii*), elderberry (*Sambucus americana*), riverbank grape (*Vitis riparia*), winter grape (*Vitis cinerea*), and poison ivy (*Toxicodendron radicans* ssp. *negundo*). The herb layer will often include green dragon (*Arisaema dracontium*), nodding bur marigold (*Bidens cernua*), hop sedge (*Carex lupulina*), bog hemp (*Boehmeria cylindrica*), clearweed (*Pilea pumila*), moneywort (*Lysimachia nummularia*), cleavers (*Galium aparine*), wood nettle (*Laportea canadensis*), and stinging nettle (*Urtica dioica*).

NORTHWEST IOWA PLAINS

The gently rolling landscape of this landform is reminiscent of the Iowan Surface. There is a well-established drainage pattern which has effectively drained the wetlands. Today the wetlands consist of low-lying areas along the streams, fens, a few marshes, and artificial impoundments. This landscape is different because of the low annual rainfall and near lack of trees except along moist drainageways. There is a small area in the extreme northwest corner where ancient bedrock, the Sioux Quartzite, is at the surface. In this area there is an old quarry lake called Jasper Pool which provides habitat for aquatic plants. An important source for information on plants of northwestern Iowa is Carter (1960).

IMPOUNDMENTS

Dams have been erected on some streams for recreational and flood storage purposes. A good example is the lake at Mill Creek State Park, O'Brien County. A sizeable wetland flora is found in and around this artificial lake.

FENS

Fens on the Northwest Iowa Plains are known to occur in Cherokee, O'Brien, and Plymouth counties (Pearson and Leoschke, 1992), but most have been degraded.

PHOTO BY DEAN ROOSA

The Northwest Iowa Plains receive less rainfall than the remainder of the state. Impoundments, such as this one in O'Brien County, are important in the existence of a wetland flora.

43

This quarry, located in Gitchie Manitou State Preserve, has existed since before the turn of the century. It provides habitat for a complex of wetland plants in a dry portion of the state.

JASPER POOL

This is a quarry dating from the 1880s, which furnished quartzite for buildings. It is located in Gitchie Manitou State Preserve in the northwest corner of the state. The pool provides good habitat for floating plants such as duckweeds (*Lemna* sp. *Spirodela polyrhiza*), watermeal (*Wolffia* sp.), duck potato (*Sagittaria* sp.), and water plantain (*Alisma* sp.) grow at the edges. In temporary pools in the quartzite at the edge of the main pool three rare plants occasionally show up. These are hairy water clover (*Marsilia vestita*), water hyssop (*Bacopa rotundifolia*), and mud plantain (*Heteranthera limosa*).

LOESS HILLS

Perhaps the most unusual habitat in Iowa is the wind-deposited material making up a row of hills which parallel the Missouri River in extreme western Iowa. These are the Loess Hills and, due to their exposure, are very dry. No wetlands occur in these hills, although springs occur at the base. A relatively recent botanical source is Novacek, Roosa, and Pusateri (1985).

RARE SPECIES

Some wetland plants are rare in our state because of the history of wetland drainage; others because Iowa is on the edge of their ranges. Some are rare because of their beauty—resulting in their being picked or attempts being made to transplant them into gardens. Many of these plants are designated as "threatened" or "endangered" by the State Department of Natural Resources and thus given additional protection by the Code of Iowa. A list of plants with such designations is available from the Department. Finding some of these rare members of the state's flora adds excitement to wetland visitation. If found, they should be left undisturbed and their location provided to the Natural Areas Inventory of the Department of Natural Resources, Wallace State Office Building, Des Moines, Iowa 50319.

Rare members of the wetland flora include:

Hairy water-clover (*Marsilea vestita)*. Known from a vernal pool in Lyon County.

Cinnamon fern (*Osmunda cinnamomea*). Known from a single site in Muscatine County.

Arrow arum (*Peltandra virginica*). This member of the arum family is known only from two extant sites—one each in Des Moines and Cedar counties in eastern Iowa. It formerly grew in a single site in Greene County.

Eleocharis xyridiformis. This spikerush was recently found in a single site in Fremont County.

Grass pink orchid (*Calopogon tuberosus*). This is the most elusive member of the orchid family, having not been seen in Iowa since the early 1950s in Linn County.

Hall's bulrush (*Scirpus hallii*). Last known record in Iowa was from Louisa County in 1960.

Hooded ladies' tresses (*Spiranthes romanzoffiana*). Known only from fens in Dickinson and Emmet counties.

Large-leaved pondweed. (*Potamogeton amplifolius*). One of our most distinctive pondweeds and one our rarest. Now only known from a lake in Hancock County and a few sites in the lakes region of northwest Iowa.

Mare's tail (*Hippurus vulgaris*). Last seen in Iowa by Dr. Martin Grant in a marsh in Dickinson County in 1948.

Purple fringed orchid (*Platanthera psycodes*). This is one of our most gorgeous wetland flowers. It grows in peatlands in the northeast and east central parts of Iowa. Finding this plant is well worth getting your feet wet.

Torrey's bulrush (*Scirpus torreyi*). Known only from Clinton County but not seen in Iowa for over a hundred years.

Bogbean (*Menyanthes trifoliata*). Fairly common in more northern latitudes, this plant is known from scattered locations in the northern half of the state and in Muscatine County. It grows in shallow standing water, often in peatlands, and blooms in May.

Pink turtlehead (*Chelone obliqua* var. *speciosa*). Currently known from two sites in southeast Iowa.

Spreading goldenrod (*Solidago patula*). Known currently from a single site in a peatland in Muscatine County.

Water marigold (*Bidens beckii*). This member of the aster family is known only from West Lake Okoboji and there from a single site. It formerly was found in Clear Lake.

Water shield (*Brasenia schreberi*). A small-leaved member of the water lily family. It is known only from Hancock and Worth counties in recent years.

Some of these are illustrated and described later in the book.

TERRESTRIAL FLOWERING HERBS

(in order of flowering)

Skunk cabbage: *Symplocarpus foetidus* (L.) Nutt.

Other common names: Collard, meadow cabbage, pole cat weed, pole weed, skunk weed, swamp cabbage.

Symplocarpus: From Greek, meaning "connected fruits", from the way its fruits are arranged.

Foetidus: From Latin, meaning "foul-smelling", characteristic of the plant when any part is crushed.

Arum family: *Araceae*

Skunk Cabbage is found on humus-rich soil in wet woodlands and seeps in the eastern one-third of Iowa, with the southernmost site being in Muscatine County. It is widespread in northeastern United States. Its flowers appear from mid-February into April.

One of our earliest-blooming plants, skunk cabbage often flowers before the snow is gone. Leaves emerge after the spathe, persist into September, then quickly decay. The leaves are heart-shaped at the bases and are massive—achieving a length of 2 feet and nearly as wide. The smooth margins and thick, pale ribs remind one of cabbage leaves. Several leaves, usually six to eight per plant, stand in a tight cluster beside the spathe. The long petioles have deep grooves on the upper side.

The fleshy spathe, a distinctive mottled brown and yellow-green, emerges tightly closed. A slit-like opening widens to give a sea-shell shape perhaps 6 inches high and half as wide. Within the spathe stands a knobby, inch-high spadix covered with bright yellow anthers of the tiny flowers. Flies and other insects, attracted by the fetid odor or the warmth, provide pollination. The spadix enlarges to a spongy mass with individual fruits just beneath the surface. As it decays, the spadix leaves a pile of pebble-like seeds on the soil surface.

The perennial root system consists of a large upright rhizome with numerous rootlets.

As rapid cellular expansion begins in the flowers, accelerated respiration maintains a more-or-less constant temperature in surrounding plant tissues for as long as two weeks—as much as 30 degrees Celsius above ambient air temperature even when air temperatures drop as low as −14 degrees Celsius. By some still-unknown mechanism, respiration rate increases as air temperature decreases. Other members in the same family produce similar heat but only for a few hours and not at such low temperatures.

Roots and young leaves of skunk cabbage served as food for the Iroquois. Drying or thorough cooking decreases the concentration of calcium oxalate. Careful identification is necessary to avoid confusion with the poisonous Indian poke, *Veratrum viride,* which resembles skunk cabbage and may be known by the same common name. The Meskwaki applied rootlets to ease toothache. They also used crushed leaf petioles as a wet dressing for bruises. The Menomini used a tea of the rootlets to stop external bleeding. Winnebago and Dakota used the plant to treat asthma. Some Native Americans inhaled the sharp odor of crushed leaves as a treatment for headache.

Until late in the nineteenth century, pioneers used skunk cabbage to treat respiratory problems, rheumatism, dropsy, ringworm, skin sores, and muscle spasms.

Marsh marigold: *Caltha palustris* L.

Other common names: Bitter flowers, boots, bull flower, capers, cow lily, cowslip, crazy Bet, drum hards, king's cup, meadow boots, soldier's buttons, water goggles, water boots, water gowan.

Caltha: From the old Greek, and later Latin, meaning "chalice" or "cup".

Palustris: From Latin meaning "of the marsh" in reference to where the plant is normally found.

Buttercup family: *Ranunculaceae*

Marsh marigold is found from Labrador and Alaska south to New England, South Carolina, Tennessee, Iowa, and Nebraska. In Iowa, it is found mostly in the northern two-thirds of the state on wet soils of marshes, woodlands, seeps, and stream edges. Blooming time is April and May.

A soft, spongy perennial root system with masses of fine rootlets gives rise to bunches of stout juicy stems, mostly growing erect to 2 feet tall.

The stems are hollow and furrowed giving an angular appearance. Upper parts of the stem are usually branched. The smooth glossy lower leaves have long petioles. They are kidney-shaped to broadly heart-shaped, measuring as much as 8 inches across. Upper leaves are smaller, often with short petioles. The leaves are smooth and dark green with wavy margins but no teeth. The veins of the leaves are conspicuous.

Bright yellow flowers up to 1½ inches across may put on a spectacular display in April and May. The flower has no petals, but five to nine colorful sepals. Each sepal is broadly oval in shape. Together they form a shallow cup surrounding numerous stamens. This cup shape provides the basis for the name of the genus.

In early medicine, the plant was used to treat dropsy, anemia, convulsions, and coughing. A drop of juice was squeezed daily on a wart to cause its disappearance. Indians used the plant to treat colds, diseases of women, and scrofulous sores. Leaves, gathered in the spring, before the flowers bloom, and thoroughly cooked to destroy a toxic alkaloid, were widely used as greens by northern Indians and pioneers. Livestock have been poisoned by eating excessively of the plants when other forage was not available. Flower buds were pickled and considered a delicacy. Blossoms have been used to make wine and were also a source of yellow dye.

In Irish folklore, this species took on extra significance on May Day when witches and fairies were supposed to be particularly active. Bunches of marsh marigold, known locally as mayflower, were hung over doorways to protect fertility of cattle.

The marigold term probably comes from an old Anglo-Saxon term meaning "horse blister". The common name in parts of England is "horses blob", blob being dialect for blister.

The term cowslip is probably from "cow slop" indicating that the plant grows better where the cows have dropped their dung.

Spring cress: *Cardamine bulbosa* (Schreb.) BSP.

Other common names: Bitter cress, bulbous cress.

Cardamine: From the Greek word *kardamon,* used by Dioscorides for some now unknown species of cress.

Bulbosa: Meaning "bulbous", referring to the tuberous base of the plant.

Mustard family: *Brassicaceae (Cruciferae)*

Spring cress is a perennial plant of springs, bottomland woods, Carex swales, and edges of marshes and seeps. It is distributed over most of the eastern United States. In Iowa it is frequent to common in the eastern two-thirds of the state. It blooms in mid-April to early June.

The stem is erect, rarely branched, smooth, and may achieve a height of a foot and a half, generally less. The basal leaves are long-petioled and oval to round. The upper stem leaves are generally sessile and around 2 inches long. The lower stem leaves may have petioles. The lower leaves may be paddle-shaped, the upper are triangular with large teeth. The flowers are white, up to a ½ inch across. The fruits are slender, up to an inch long and narrow toward the end to a conspicuous tip. The perennial rootstock bears tubers.

The white flowers of this species are sufficiently inconspicuous that it is not sought as a popular spring wildflower. Its early blooming period often means it is the only splash of color in the early wetland environment.

The tops make a good salad and the rootstocks may be eaten throughout the year. The rootstock imparts a taste of mild horse-radish. In fact, the bulbous rootstock can be grated and mixed with vinegar and used as a substitute for horseradish. The young stems have this same taste; the older stems are too coarse or strong to be of use as greens.

Another cress, water cress in the genus *Nasturtium,* is a member of this family and is valued for tasty salads. Bitter cress (*Cardamine pensylvanica*), also called our native water cress, is similar to the common water cress which is naturalized from Europe and has similar tastes and uses. Purple cress (*Cardamine douglassii*) blooms even earlier than spring cress. It likes cold, springy sites but also thrives on wet sand.

Other common names: Bog buckbean, buckbean.

Menyanthes: This name was used by Theophrastus and is derived from *menyein,* "disclosing," and *anthos,* "a flower", later applied to this genus.

Trifoliata: Meaning "three leaved" from the arrangement of the leaves.

Buckbean family: *Menyanthaceae* (sometimes placed in the *Gentianaceae*)

Bogbean is a perennial herb with a thick, creeping rhizome. It ranges from Labrador to Alaska, south to Virginia, Ohio, Iowa, and Wyoming, with a single site in Missouri—although the population at this latter site may now be extirpated. In Iowa it is found in shallow water of marshes and fens. It is known by recent records from Allamakee, Buchanan, Cerro Gordo, Dickinson, Franklin, Muscatine, and Wright counties. It is in bloom in May.

The overall height of this species is up to 1½ feet, growing in small colonies. The leaves are long-stalked, with sheathing leaf bases, and divided into three oval to elliptic leaflets which may be 3 inches long.

The flowers are white, sometimes tinged with pink, and occur in a dense cluster at the tip of the naked stalk. Individual blossoms are about ¾ inch broad, funnel-shaped, with five sepals and five petals which are densely covered by hairs along the margin.

Since bogbean is grazed only in late summer when other fodder is in short supply, it is perhaps avoided due to the presence of the glucoside *menyanthin*. The dried and powdered rhizomes have been extensively used to make bread by the Eskimos and natives of northern Eurasia. The rhizome of bogbean has a reputation as an invigorating tonic, and the leaves were used as a substitute for hops in brewing beer.

The Menomini used this plant as a medicinal, though knowledge of the precise use has been lost. The pioneers used it as a purgative, to promote menstruation, and as a tonic. If taken in large doses, it can be used as a vermifuge and emetic.

Water parsnip: *Sium suave* Walt.

Other common names: Wane-migons, water parsley.

Sium: From *sion*, the Greek name of a paludal plant.

Suave: Meaning "fragrant" or "sweet".

Parsley family: *Apiaceae*

Water parsnip is widespread in North America, growing from Newfoundland to British Columbia and south to Florida, Ohio, Indiana, Missouri, Colorado, Utah, Nevada, and California. In Iowa, it is most common in the lakes area of the northwest where it is found at the edges of marshes, in sedge meadows, and in wet prairies. It blooms in July through August.

This robust perennial may achieve a height of 6 feet. The stem is stout, hollow, smooth, and strongly corrugated, arising from a fibrous root system. The leaves are variable—those of the submerged rosette are 2–3 times compound, stem leaves are once-divided and reduced toward the top. When the lower leaves are entirely underwater, they are finely dissected and thread-like. This is particularly true early in the growing season.

The flowers are small, approximately ⅛ inch across, with five short petals. The entire umbel may be 5 inches across and occurs at the tips of branches or in upper leaf axils. The fruit is small with prominent ribs.

This plant may be confused with the deadly water hemlock but has singly compound stem leaves and corrugated stems. While the plant has been suspected of being poisonous, the toxic principle has not been described.

Canadian Indians are reported to have eaten the roots; this may be true since the plant is related to an edible European species, *Sium sisarum,* commonly called "skirret". One of the early names of water parsnip was *Sium cicutaefolium* because it was suspected of being poisonous like water hemlock, *Cicuta maculata.* The seeds of members of the genus were smoked over a fire by the Ojibwa to drive away the evil spirit, Sokenau, who gives them bad luck when they go hunting. While the roots are reported to be edible in late fall, the leaves and stems are poisonous and have reportedly killed cattle. Because of the similarity of this plant to water hemlock, it is suggested it not be eaten. Both are found in similar habitats, which adds to the possibility of mistaken identity.

Water parsnip is a fairly frequent plant in shallow, standing water and one which serious students of wetlands should learn to recognize.

Tall cotton-grass: *Eriophorum angustifolium* Honck.

Other common names: Bog cotton, cotton-grass, hare's tail, tawny cotton-grass.

Eriophorum: name from Greek *erion,* "wool or cotton", and *phoros,* "bearing", from the appearance of the heads of fruits.

Angustifolium: Meaning "narrow-leaved".

Sedge family: *Cyperaceae*

The range of tall cotton-grass is from Newfoundland to Manitoba and south to Massachusetts, Indiana, northern Illinois, northern Iowa, Nebraska, Colorado, and Oregon where its principal habitats are peatlands—bogs and fens. It is also found in Eurasia. In Iowa, it grows in the northeast quarter of the state in fens, bogs, sedge meadows, and wet prairies.

The flowering time of this species is mid-June, with fruits persisting into late summer.

This species grows to about 3 feet tall, with grass-like leaves at the base and up the stem. The leaves are long and narrow, generally less than ¼ inch wide and flat below the middle, triangular-channeled above the middle. The two to three leaves just below the inflorescence are short and are purple at the base. The inflorescence consists of two to ten spikelets on short peduncles and appears as a dense cluster at the tip of the stem. The bristles which subtend the achenes are white to creamy and give the appearance of a ball of cotton on a slender stem.

There are about a dozen species of cotton-grass in the northern hemisphere. Of these, three occur in Iowa. Tall cotton-grass is similar to slender cotton-grass, *Eriophorum gracile,* now known only from the bog at Pilot Knob and a sedge meadow in Dickinson County. The leaves of slender cotton-grass are shorter and not as wide as the present species and have a sheath of the upper leaves longer than the blade. *E. virginicum* was recently discovered in a fen in Buchanan County.

E. callitrix, a close relative of *E. angustifolium,* was used by the Flambeau Ojibwa as a hemostatic (to check bleeding). Some pioneers used it as an astringent because of its tannic properties.

Tall cotton-grass is difficult to grow under cultivation, but a delight to find in the wild.

Giant manna grass: *Glyceria grandis* L. Wats.

Other common names. American manna grass, rattlesnake grass, reed meadow grass, tall meadow grass, water meadow grass, white spear grass.

Glyceria: From the Greek *glyceros* or *glukeros,* meaning "sweet", an allusion to the taste of the grain.

Grandis: Meaning "large", in reference to the size of the plant.

Grass family: *Poaceae (Gramineae)*

Stout, clustered giant manna grass grows from Newfoundland to Alaska and south to Virginia, Tennessee, Iowa, and Oregon. In Iowa, it is found in shallow water along streams and marsh edges in the northern half of the state. It is in anthesis (bloom) in late May or early June, and its seeds are shed in August.

This perennial grass may grow to 5 feet in height with a large, spreading panicle up to a foot wide. The leaves may be ½ inch wide; the panicle nearly a foot long. The sheaths are rough and overlapping. The lemma is purplish and has seven nearly parallel veins. These parallel veins on the lemma, as seen under a hand lens, help separate the manna grasses from other grasses.

There are four species of *Glyceria* in Iowa, and all grow in or near water. *Glyceria borealis* grows sparingly in the lakes area of northwest Iowa; *G. septentrionalis,* a southern species found mainly in southeast Iowa; and *G. striata,* which grows statewide, and is similar to giant manna grass. All are known to be used by waterfowl and provide cover at the edges of marshes. The roots were used by Flambeau Ojibwa as a female remedy. For some unknown reason, they called this plant a fern!

Manna grass in Europe refers to several species of grass that furnish seeds from which flour is made. The name refers to the manna mentioned in the Bible. The flour is used to make a nourishing and good-tasting bread. The seeds are also used to thicken soup, but care is needed to harvest seeds promptly as they fall quickly upon ripening.

In various parts of Europe the seeds of manna grass (a related species) were considered a delicacy for thickening soups and gruels, but the bread was judged inferior to wheat bread. Seeds of manna grass were collected in Poland and sent to Germany and Sweden and sold under the name of Manna Seeds.

All the manna grasses furnish good forage.

Fox sedge: *Carex vulpinoidea* Michx.

Other common names: Vulpine sedge, dog sedge.

Carex: Derived from the Greek keirein, "to cut", in reference to the sharp leaves.

Vulpinoidea: Name derived from its resemblance to *Carex vulpina,* which has an inflorescence like a fox's tail.

Sedge family: *Cyperaceae*

Fox sedge is a widely occurring species, found from Newfoundland to southern British Columbia and south to the southern United States. In Iowa, it is found as a common species throughout the state. It grows at the edges of marshes, in alluvial woods, on wet roadsides, and in fens. Its inflorescence appears in June through August.

This distinctive sedge occurs in clumps in a wide variety of habitats throughout Iowa, and probably can be found in all Iowa counties. Of the more than 100 species of sedges in Iowa, this is one of the most easily recognizable and a good place to start in gaining acquaintance with this group of plants.

It may grow to 3 feet in height, but more commonly around 1 foot high. The inflorescence is a yellowish or dull brown, the perigynia are clustered and numerous flowering stems arise from one clump. The inflorescence may be up to 6 inches in height and is normally erect, occasionally lax and arched. The leaves are stiff and up to ½ inch wide and longer than the flowering stems.

Plants of the genus *Carex* are important as wildlife food. Due to the difficulty of identifying the sedges, information on individual species is scarce. It is known that 15 species of waterfowl feed on *Carex,* that hoofed browsers utilize them, and fur-bearing mammals use them for food or shelter. Fox sedge is a common component of many Iowa wetlands—growing at the edges of marshes, and often in wet roadside ditches.

Of the many species of *Carex,* few seem to have been used much by Native Americans. Of 20 species on which information was collected, only one, the plantain-leaved sedge, was used. It was utilized by medicine men to protect people from rattlesnakes. To cure the person who had been bitten, the medicine man chewed the root and sprayed the expectorant on the wound.

Cattail sedge: *Carex typhina* Michx.

Other common names: Bottomland sedge, gray-green sedge, meadow sedge.

Carex: Derived from the Greek *keirein*, "to cut", referring to the sharp edges of the leaves. Called "shear grass" in some parts of the world.

Typhina: From a fancied resemblance to *Typha*, cattail, possibly more due to the gray-green color of the leaves in resembling the broad-leaf cattail.

Sedge family: *Cyperaceae*

The attractive cattail sedge is found from southwest Quebec to Wisconsin and eastern Iowa and from Maine to Connecticut, Georgia, Louisiana, and Alabama. In Iowa, it is restricted to southeast Iowa, where it is rare. It has a long flowering and fruiting time, beginning in June; seeds being found on the plant well into September. Its favored habitats are wooded floodplains, seepage areas, and edges of marshes, but it will also grow in open calcareous meadows.

Cattail sedge may achieve a height of 3 feet and has gray-green, coarse leaves over a ½ inch wide. It resembles squarrose sedge, *Carex squarrosa*, in morphology and grows in the same habitat. Both grow in southeast Iowa. There may be as many as six spikes which are subcylindric, up to an inch thick and normally only one per stem.

The leaves are rather weak and rough to the touch and often overtop the inflorescence. The male and female flowers are borne separately with the male flowers below. This is a perennial species which grows from a thickened rootstock.

The sedge can grow in partial shade or full sunlight and helps to stabilize the soil where it grows. The achenes are known to serve several species of waterfowl as food. It is known to hybridize with *Carex shortiana* to form *Carex X deamii.*, although this hybrid has not been detected in Iowa.

Because of the attractiveness of this sedge, it often shows up in floral displays and has been marketed as a persistent and interesting plant for gardeners who tend aquatic gardens. This species, squarrose sedge, and Gray's sedge are among our most attractive sedges. A good place to look is on floodplains in southeast Iowa and these three species are a good place to start becoming better acquainted with this large and interesting family.

Lacustrine sedge: *Carex lacustris* Willd.

Other common names: Lake sedge.

Carex: Derived from the Greek *keirein,* "to cut", in reference to the sharp leaves.

Lacustris: Meaning "of lake margins".

Sedge family: *Cyperaceae*

Lacustrine sedge is found from eastern Quebec to southern Manitoba to Nova Scotia and south to Virginia, Ohio, Indiana, Illinois, Iowa, South Dakota, and Idaho. In Iowa, it is frequent in the pothole country of the northern part of the Des Moines Lobe, infrequent to rare elsewhere. It is found in shallow water at the margins of ponds, marshes, and lakes.

This sedge may achieve a height of nearly 4 feet; it is a stout, robust species with stolons and rhizomes. It often forms mon-odominant stands at the edges of marshes. The culms are sharply angled and coarse at the summit, with purplish basal sheaths. The leaf blades are septate-nodulose from margin to midrib. The leaf is broad—up to ¾ inch across and has a conspicuous ligule. The two to four staminate spikes are held aloft on a slender peduncle. The two to four pistillate spikes are large and may achieve a length of 2–3 inches and ¾ inch thick. These are normally more-or-less erect, but the lower may droop.

This species spreads vegetatively as well as by seed. Its size and method of spreading often cause it to out-compete other plants and form a solid stand. It is a hearty perennial and provides stability in many wetland communities.

There are approximately 110 species of *Carex* in Iowa, many of which are difficult to identify. This species with its large size, septate leaves, and large pistillate spikes is a good one to get to know. It is also common in northern and central Iowa.

The copious seeds are easily collected and seem to possess a high rate of germination. These stands of lacustrine sedge are of value to wildlife by offering excellent cover. We have seen muskrats utilize this species for food, especially early when the tissues are soft, and for construction of their houses.

Woolly sedge: *Carex lanuginosa* Michx.

Other common names: Anticost sedge, pale sedge.

Carex: Derived from the Greek *keirein,* "to cut", in reference to the sharp leaves.

Lanuginosa: meaning "woolly", from the appearance during the flowering period.

Sedge family: *Cyperaceae*

Woolly sedge is found across much of North America—from eastern Quebec to British Columbia and south to New England, Virginia, Tennessee, Arkansas, Oklahoma, Arizona, Texas, and southern California. In Iowa, it is found statewide, but is most common in the lakes area of the northern portion of the Des Moines Lobe. It is found most commonly in wet prairies, but also on edges of marshes. In Iowa, it flowers in late May and early June.

This sedge grows in tufts from long horizontal rhizomes and stolons. The culms are quill-like at the base, obtusely angled and smooth. It may achieve a height of over 3 feet. The leaves are light green, slender, smooth, with revolute edges and end in a rather sharp tip.

The male and female heads are borne separately. The one to three staminate flowers are elevated on a scabrous peduncle. The one to three pistillate spikes are distant and 1–2 inches long. The perigynia are plump, ovoid, and about ⅓ inch long, with a well-developed neck and prominent teeth.

The tufted sedge does a good job of soil stabilization and seems to spread rather well vegetatively. It is an important part of the wetland community. The seeds are easy to collect and have a high germination rate.

There are approximately 110 species of *Carex* in Iowa; many are difficult to identify with certainty. Woolly sedge is common, important to the wetland site, and distinctive. Its closest look-alike is *Carex lasiocarpa* var. *americana,* but woolly sedge is much more common.

Tussock sedge: *Carex suberecta* (Olney) Britton

Other common names: Suberect sedge.

Carex: Derived from the Greek *kierein,* "to cut", in reference to the sharp leaves.

Suberecta: Meaning "suberect" in reference to its habit of reclining due to the rather weak culms.

Sedge family: *Cyperaceae*

Tussock sedge is found from southern Ontario to Minnesota and south to West Virginia, Ohio, Indiana, Illinois, and Missouri. In Iowa, it is infrequent in the north central portion, rare in the remainder of the state. It is in flower in late May and in fruit in July. Its Iowa habitats are mudflats and prairie swales.

This sedge may achieve a height of 3 feet. It occurs in clumps and has slender culms topped by three to six heads which may total over an inch in length. These heads are sub-cylindric to nearly ovoid and may become ferruginous or tawny. The leaves are narrow, only about ⅛ inch wide and overtopped by the fruiting heads.

The species is similar to Bicknell's sedge, *C. bicknellii,* a more common taxon and which occupies a slightly drier habitat, and *C. brevior,* but this latter taxon occupies dry habitats.

There are approximately 110 members of this genus in Iowa, each occupying a slightly different habitat and filling a different ecological niche. The tussock sedge is a good soil binder in an unstable habitat. The nutlets of sedges are enclosed in papery sacs and may be loose or tight. In some species the male and female flowers are on separate spikes and some are mixed inconspicuously in the same spike. Pollination is largely by wind.

Beaver, deer, muskrats, bobwhite quail, and waterfowl all have been reported to feed on sedges. The roots and new sprouts are sought out by muskrats, and birds feed on the seed heads. Their primary benefit to humans are as soil anchors and soil builders in lowland habitats.

Other common names: Stout sedge.

Carex: Derived from the Greek *kierein,* "to cut", in reference to the sharp leaves.

Lupuliformis: Derived from its similarity to *Carex lupulina,* or true hop sedge.

Sedge family: *Cyperaceae*

False hop sedge is found from Vermont to Minnesota and south to Connecticut, Virginia, Kentucky, Louisiana, and eastern Texas. In Iowa, it is only known from the south-central and southeast portions of the state. Its habitats are lake margins, pond margins, calcareous wetlands, and wet prairies.

This robust perennial may achieve a height of 3 feet and resembles the more common hop sedge, *Carex lupulina,* but with broader leaves and peduncled staminate spikes. It forms tussocks and has creeping rhizomes. The three to five pistillate spikes are sessile or have short peduncles and may be 1–3 inches long and an inch thick.

An excellent soil binder, the false hop sedge can spread vegetatively as well as by seeds. The large seed heads and height make it easy to collect seeds.

Its apparent scarcity in Iowa may be due to the under-studied nature of this genus, or it may be mistaken for closely related species.

Other common names: Hop-like sedge.

Carex: Derived from Greek *keirein*, "to cut", referring to the sharp leaves. (Called "sheargrass" in some parts of the world.)

Lupulina: Meaning "hop-like".

Sedge family: *Cyperaceae*

Hop sedge is found throughout eastern North America—from Florida to Texas and north to Nova Scotia, Maine, New York, Michigan, Wisconsin, and Minnesota. In Iowa, it is frequently encountered in the eastern third of the state, rare in the northwest part. It is in fruit from late June into October. It is found most often in wet depressions in alluvial woods and occasionally on the edges of marshes.

The most obvious character of hop sedge is the large, cylindrical female spikes—up to 2½ inches long. The spikes approach the size and appearance of those of *Carex grayii,* which is found in the same part of the state and in similar habitats. Hop sedge is a stout, leafy sedge which grows in small or large tussocks and may grow to over 3 feet high.

There are two to six of the female spikes per stem and the perigynia are much inflated, up to ¾ inch long and taper abruptly to a narrow beak which is sharply two-toothed at the tip. The male spike is narrow, separate, and above the female spikes.

Approximately 110 species of *Carex* are found in Iowa and many are difficult to identify. Hop sedge is distinctive, very attractive, and one you should get to know. It is known to be of value as a waterfowl plant, but is probably of minor significance since its prime habitat is not especially good for ducks. However, sedges in general are an important source of food for many species of wildlife—mostly from consuming the seeds.

Little is found for medicinal uses of hop sedge, but other sedges were used. For example, *Carex plantaginea*, a woodland species served as a medicine for the Menomini. It, and also blue-eyed grass, were considered snake charms—when worn, the bearer would be protected from rattlesnakes. If a person was bitten, the medicine man would chew the root and spray the spittle on the wound.

Other common names: Connected sedge, short-tongue sedge, yellow sedge.

Carex: Derived from the Greek *keirein,* "to cut", in reference to the sharp leaves.

Annectans: Meaning "connecting", probably from the close-knit arrangement of the fruiting head.

Xanthocarpa: From *xantho,* "yellow" and *carpus,* "fruit" or "fruited".

Sedge family: *Cyperaceae*

Yellowfruit sedge is found from Maine to Iowa and south to Virginia, Ohio, Indiana, Illinois, Missouri, and Kansas. In Iowa, it occurs in all but the northwest quarter and is rare to infrequent. Its habitats are edges of marshes, sedge meadows, and it is often found in wet sand. It flowers in late May and in fruit in July.

This sedge is similar to fox sedge and some taxonomists place it as a variety. Yellowfruit sedge has fewer and shorter bracts, a less compound head that surpasses the leaves in height. Sedges will hybridize in portions of their ranges, but yellowfruit sedge has shorter awns on the scales and a more restricted habitat tolerance. Fox sedge is far more common and may be found in floodplains and in abundance in seeps on the Southern Iowa Drift Plain. Both may achieve a height of around 3 feet.

The mature culms of yellowfruit sedge are taller than the leaves, with the fruiting head from an inch to around 3 inches long. The mature head becomes yellowish to brown late and the fruits shatter easily.

There are some 500 species of *Carex* in North America and approximately 110 of these have been found in Iowa. Most are associated with wetland habitats. Some act as excellent soil stabilizers at the edges of marshes or other waterways. Some provide excellent cover and many provide food. There are at least 67 species of wildlife that are known to use members of the genus *Carex* in their diets. Many species are difficult to identify, but fox sedge and yellowfruit sedge are fairly common and attractive and can be separated with a little practice. These may be a good place to start in identifying sedges.

PHOTO BY JIM PECK

Squarrose sedge: *Carex squarrosa* L.

Other common names: Lowland sedge, square-top sedge.

Carex: Derived from the Greek *keirein,* "to cut", referring to the sharp leaves. (Called sheargrass in some parts of the world.)

Squarrosa: Meaning "with wide-spreading parts."

Sedge family: *Cyperaceae*

Squarrose sedge is found from Connecticut to southern Ontario, Minnesota, and Nebraska and south to North Carolina, Tennessee, and Arkansas. In Iowa, it is restricted to counties in the southeast corner of the state. It is found in calcareous bottomlands, alluvial woods, and in depressions in alluvial woods. It is in fruit from early June into September.

Squarrose sedge may achieve a height of 3 feet and has an acutely angled stem. The leaves are weak and rough to the touch, often overtop the inflorescence, and are up to about ¼ inch wide. The spikes are up to an inch thick and normally occur as only one per stem. The male and female flowers are borne separately with the male flowers below. The achenes are smooth and up to ⅛ inch long. The perigynia have two spreading teeth which may be reflexed.

One of our most attractive sedges, look for it in sedge meadows along streams and in wooded wetlands in extreme southeast Iowa.

Gray's sedge: *Carex grayii* Carey

Other common names: Great-headed sedge, lowland sedge.

Carex: Derived from the Greek *keirein*, "to cut," due to the sharp leaves.

Grayii: Named for Asa Gray, renowned botanist, 1810–1888.

Sedge family: *Cyperaceae*

The attractive Gray's sedge is found from Quebec to Iowa, and south to western New England, New Jersey, Illinois, and northern Arkansas. In Iowa it is found in roughly the southeast half of the state in depressions in floodplains. It blooms in early June and is found in fruit in July.

This is one of our most distinctive sedges, and one of our most attractive. It is named for Asa Gray, founder of the Gray herbarium at Harvard University and author of the famous *Gray's Manual of Botany*. In fact, it was formerly named *Carex Asa Grayii*.

The perennial grows in clumps in depressions of floodplains and may achieve a height of 3 feet, normally less. The individual plants are leafy, gray-green, with leaves up to ¾ inch wide. The large head consists of 6–30 swollen perigynia (inflated sac which encloses the ovary), which may be 2 inches in diameter. As with all sedges, it has a stem that is triangular in cross-section.

Although this plant does not appear on the lists of plants of economic importance or of value as a food for wildlife, it is a common component of the floodplain environment and well worth a search.

While not considered important as wildlife food, sedges in general are reported to have been used as food by upland game birds and waterfowl, muskrat, deer, moose, beaver, and elk. The roots and sprouts are eaten by muskrats. One species of sedge has small tubers which are relished by wildfowl.

There are approximately 110 species of *Carex* in Iowa; many are confusingly similar. While this species may be mixed up with *Carex lupulina*, it is distinctive and a good place to start in learning the sedges.

Other common names: Beaver poison, Carotte a Moreau, cowbane, musquash root, spotted cowbane, spotted hemlock.

Cicuta: The ancient Latin name for poison hemlock.

Maculata: From Latin, meaning "spotted" or "mottled" because of the purple mottling of the stem.

Parsley family: *Apiaceae (Umbelliferae)*

Water hemlock is found from Quebec and Manitoba south to North Carolina, Tennessee, Missouri, and Texas. In Iowa, it is rare in the western portion, frequent in the remainder of the state. It is found in low, wet prairies, in shallow water of marshes, wet roadside ditches, and along streams and is in bloom in June and early July.

The stoutish stem of the biennial, or short-lived perennial, grows to 7 feet tall. It is erect with slender branches. The lower part is often lined or mottled with purple, as is the stem of poison hemlock. The thickened base of the stem is hollow but has distinct cross sections.

Fleshy tubers cluster finger-like at the base of the stem. Despite resembling small sweet potatoes and having a fragrance like that of parsnips, these roots are poisonous. When cut crosswise, the roots exude an aromatic, yellow oil.

The dark green pinnately compound leaves have fewer and coarser leaflets than poison hemlock. The larger lower leaves are about a foot long and are on long petioles; they are generally tipped with three leaflets. Other units of leaflets along the central petiole may have one or two leaflets. The leaflets are narrow and lance-shaped, not finely cut like those of poison hemlock. Midribs and veins are prominent on the underside. The veins end in the notches of the leaflet margins.

The flat-topped flower heads, 2 to 5 inches across, are made up of smaller heads. Individual flowers are tiny, about $\frac{1}{16}$ inch across, and have a slight fragrance. The oval fruits, which have alternating rounded ribs and dark furrows, are about $\frac{1}{8}$ inch long.

Though very poisonous, water hemlock is less toxic than poison hemlock. Poisoning from poison hemlock seeds is always fatal, but if given soon enough, treatment for poisoning from water hemlock roots is sometimes effective. One of the chief symptoms of poisoning from water hemlock is severe convulsions, whereas that from poison hemlock is respiratory paralysis.

A poisonous resin, cicuta toxin, is concentrated in the elongate tubers at the base of the stem. If ingested, a piece of tuber the size of a pea is sufficient to cause death in humans. If eaten in spring when the toxin is most concentrated, a piece of root the size of a walnut can kill a cow.

A volatile alkaloid, *cicutine,* **can be extracted** from the oil of the root. When properly used, it is helpful in relieving epilepsy, convulsions, and psychoses. Although prescribed for sick and nervous headaches in the past, it is seldom used now. The Klamath Indians prepared a mixture of rotted deer liver, rattlesnake venom, and the juice of water hemlock and used it as a poison on the tips of arrows.

The Cherokee thought water hemlock could be used as an oral contraceptive. Occasionally, the roots were used in an attempt to induce permanent sterility, but this was a dangerous procedure—one that could be fatal.

Angelica: *Angelica atropurpurea* L.

Other common names: Alexanders, archangel, aunt Jerico, belly-ache root, dead nettle, great angelica, masterwort, purple-stem angelica, wild celery.

Angelica: Named from an early legend which tells of an angel revealing the curative powers of this plant to a monk during one of the plagues which periodically swept Europe during the Middle Ages.

Atropurpurea: From Latin meaning "dark purple" referring to the coloring of the stem.

Parsley family: *Apiaceae (Umbelliferae)*

Angelica is widespread in northeastern United States, growing from Labrador to Wisconsin to Newfoundland and south to New England, Delaware, West Virginia, Ohio, Indiana, and Iowa. In Iowa it is only known from six counties in the northeast. Its favored habitat is calcareous fens, but it will grow in other peatlands, seeps, and along streams. Blooming time is late May and early June.

This coarse herb may grow to nearly 10 feet in height, often less. It has a branching stem and is distinguished by its purple color. The stem, although hollow, is sturdy and may achieve a diameter of over an inch. The perennial rootstock is woody and extensive.

The leaves are divided into three parts, each with its own petiole. Each part is further divided into three to five segments. Individual segments are coarsely toothed at the margins with veins running to the points of the teeth. Lower leaves may achieve a width of 2 feet. Petioles of upper leaves have swollen basal sheaths which envelope the stem.

The tiny white or greenish flowers appear in globular, umbrella-like heads. This head may contain as many as 40 branches and reach a diameter of 8 inches. These heads are on stalks arising from the upper leaf axils.

The fruit is a tiny rounded oval, flattened on one side. A thin edge or wing around the oval gives resemblance to a miniature flying saucer.

Leaf stalks of angelica have been eaten like celery, and the flavor is said to be similar. Early settlers boiled parts of the plant in sugar to make candy—just as they had done in Europe with a closely related species. Careful identification is necessary since this plant resembles the deadly water hemlock. The veins of water hemlock run into the notches between the teeth of the leaves, not into the points of the teeth as with angelica.

Roots of angelica, perhaps confused with the poisonous water hemlock, were supposedly used by members of some Canadian Indian tribes to commit suicide. If angelica roots are poisonous, they lose their toxicity when dried because dried roots have been used for emergency food as well as medicinal purposes—to treat colds, rheumatism, fevers, and urinary problems.

Early European medicine included the belief that the plant could cure alcoholism. The Chinook boiled the roots for use as food; Native Americans in California ate the young sprouts as greens. In Arkansas they smoked the leaves with tobacco. The Meskwaki in Iowa boiled the whole plant to make a tea for hayfever. They also used it with a mixture of other plants to prepare a drink to treat a woman with an injured womb.

PHOTO BY DEAN ROOSA

Other common names: Canada windflower, windflower.

Anemone: From the Greek meaning "wind", possibly referring to distribution of the cottony seed by the wind, or because some delicate members of the genus tremble in a light wind. Some botanists believe the word originates from the Semitic word for the mythological Adonis.

Canadensis: Meaning "of Canada".

Buttercup family: *Ranunculaceae*

Canada anemone is found throughout eastern North America. In Iowa it is frequent to common in all parts of the state, occuring in moist calcareous or alluvial soils, in wet swales, and even wet roadside ditches. It does not compete well with taller members of the flora, but thrives in wet, disturbed soils at prairie pothole edges. It is one of the early events of the wetland wildflower world, beginning to bloom in mid to late May and continuing into July.

The plant grows to a height of 2 feet, but is usually shorter. The leaves are deeply five- to seven-parted and have hairy, prominent veins. The basal leaves have long petioles and are found in whorls of three; the upper leaves are paired.

The solitary, showy white flower, up to an inch and a half across, lacks true petals, but petal-like sepals give this hardy perennial a handsome appearance. The flower is on a long stalk, which holds the flower aloft for pollination by bees and flies and aids the distribution of the seeds by the wind.

The seed head is globular and composed of flat achenes.

Reproduction is sometimes by seed but more often vegetatively by the spread of slender, tough rhizomes. Because of this mode of spreading, this species is often found in a monodominant clone.

The Meskwaki made a tea of the roots for the treatment of headache and dizziness—or to refocus crossed eyes, but this latter was likely more psychological than physical.

An ancient myth tells that a new plant sprung up wherever a teardrop fell from Venus, weeping over the loss of her beloved Adonis.

This coarse, hardy perennial is of little economic but considerable aesthetic value and is often grown in wildflower gardens. A closely related species, the Tall Anemone (*Anemone virginiana* L.), is similar, but has a two- or three-parted bract below the flower head and grows in drier habitats.

Tufted loosestrife: *Lysimachia thrysiflora* L.

Other common names: Water loosestrife.

Lysimachia: Named in honor of King Lysimachus of Thrace.

Thrysiflora: Named for the arrangement of the flowers in a thryse, which is a contracted panicle.

Primrose family: *Primulaceae*

Tufted loosestrife ranges from Quebec and St. James Bay to Alaska and south to Ohio, Indiana, northern Illinois, Missouri, Colorado, and California. In Iowa it is found in the northcentral part, in the lakes area of the northwest, and in Louisa and Muscatine counties. It may be more frequent in southeast and southern Iowa than we realize because it is widespread in Missouri. Since it blooms early in the season, it is possibly being overlooked by botanists and naturalists. It is most commonly found in shallow standing water at the edges of marshes. It is in bloom in late May and early June.

The reddish-colored stems arise from creeping rhizomes and may reach a height of over 2 feet. The leaves are lanceolate, up to 8 inches long and 2 inches wide, and arranged alternately along the stem. The lower leaves are smaller, and the lowest are reduced to scales. The stems seldom branch. In the axils of the middle or lower leaves occur spike-like racemes of yellow flowers with black dots. The erect stamens give the flowers a fuzzy appearance. The corolla is deeply five-parted into short linear divisions. The fruit is a few-to-many seeded capsule.

Tufted loosestrife is a normal component of shallow standing water of Iowa marshes, especially on the Des Moines Lobe.

There seem to be few records of its uses as a source of food for wildlife and apparently it was not used by Native Americans.

This is an attractive, distinctive plant; once seen, not forgotten. There are nine species of *Lysimachia* that occur in Iowa; this is one of the most recognizable taxonomically.

Northern leafy green orchid: *Platanthera hyperborea* (L.) R. Br. var. *huronensis* (Nutt.) Luer (formerly *Habenaria hyperborea* var. *huronensis*)

Other common names: Bog candle, leafy orchis, northern leafy green orchid, northern orchis, northern rein orchis.

Platanthera: From Greek, meaning "broad anthers". Until recently this was in the genus *Habenaria*, which derived its name from *habena*, "a thong or rein," in allusion to the shape of the lip in some species.

Hyperborea: Meaning "far northern", from its distribution in extreme northern latitudes.

Huronensis: Meaning "of Lake Huron".

Orchid family: *Orchidaceae*

This orchid enjoys a wide distribution, being found from Greenland to Alaska to Newfoundland to Hudson Bay and south to Pennsylvania, Ohio, Indiana, northern Iowa, and Nebraska. It is found in a variety of habitats, from peaty bogs, moist or dry woods and limestone barrens in the north. In Iowa it is restricted to fens on the Iowan Surface and the western portion of the Des Moines Lobe. There is a turn-of-the-century record of this species being found in Story County. It blooms in May and June.

The plant may achieve a height of around a foot, with rather thick, soft, angled stems, and thick and tuberous rootstocks. The leaves alternate up the stem, the larger ones near the ground being narrowly oblong, about an inch wide, and up to 4 inches long. The upper leaves are progressively smaller and pass gradually into the bracts.

The flowers exist in a cylindrical spike which is generally rather open. The flowers are greenish-white or green, with a short lip about ⅛ inch long, widened toward the base. The petals are lanceolate and incurved under the upper sepal. The spur is about as long as the lip. These flowers have a strong fragrance suggestive of that of Lily-of-the-Valley.

A similar species, the long-bracted green orchis, was used by the Ojibwa as a love charm. It would be secretly put into food as an aphrodisiac, unknown to the target person. Yet another similar orchid, *Platanthera dilitata*, was used by Potawatomi women as a love charm; it was rubbed or painted on the cheek to help secure a good husband.

The majority of peatlands in Iowa have been drained or subjected to heavy grazing by livestock. The continued existence of this species in our state is dependent on those few last sites for this species being protected.

Other common names: Bog yellow cress, yellow cress.

Rorippa: Name probably derived from an old Saxon name *Rorippen* and altered to Roripa or Rorippa.

Palustris: Meaning "of marshes". *Islandica*: Meaning "of Iceland".

Mustard family: *Brassicaceae* (also *Cruciferae*)

Marsh cress is widely distributed across the continent, ranging from Labrador to British Columbia and south to New England, Virginia, Tennessee, Louisiana, Texas, and California. In Iowa, it is infrequent in the west and northwest, common throughout the remainder of the state. It is found in shallow standing water, sedge meadows, edges of marshes, and seeps.

This annual or biennial may be from a few inches in height to nearly 3 feet. The leaves are variable, ranging from merely dentate to pinnate or pinnatifid. The four sepals fall from the plant early; the four petals are yellow and short—only about ⅛ inch long with six stamens. The fruits (siliques) are ellipsoidal or subglobose, ranging from ⅛ inch to ½ inch long and about half as thick. Flowering time is May and early June. The plant arises from a stout taproot.

Some authorities separate several varieties of this plant, based on leaf and silique characters. Others feel there is a continuum of variability in these features that are environmentally induced.

The mustard family is large, with some 70 species in Iowa. Some are difficult to separate and they occupy nearly every habitat except floating on water. Marsh cress, because of its habitat and early flowering time, is easy to identify.

Marsh cress was sometimes used as food for early settlers. The roots were dried and ground and used as a condiment. The early leaves were prepared as greens.

Dark green bulrush: *Scirpus atrovirens* Willd.

Other common names: Gray-head bulrush, green bulrush.

Scirpus: The Latin name of the bulrush.

Atrovirens: Meaning "dark green" from the deep color of the spikelets.

Sedge family: *Cyperaceae*

Dark green bulrush is a tough, long-lived perennial that is found from Quebec to Saskatchewan and south to Georgia, Tennessee, and Missouri. In Iowa, it is found in favorable habitat throughout the state, probably growing in every county. It is found in a wide variety of habitats, from sedge meadows and edges of marshes to fens, wet roadsides ditches, seeps, and borders of streams. It is nearly ubiquitous—we can depend on it being present in nearly every permanently wet depression and is the most common species of the genus in the state.

Dark green bulrush may achieve a height of 5 feet, although normally closer to 3 to 4 feet.

The culms are normally several from a leafy crown, each with four to nine new leaves. The stems are bluntly triangular in cross section. The leaves are up to an inch broad, with small, blunt nodules and with cross-walls between the veins.

The inflorescence is in the form of a panicle, subtended by several bracts, and often has small bulbs develop in the axil of the flower stalk, or the seeds may germinate while in the head. These are a means of vegetative reproduction as they develop roots when the plant bends after maturity and these roots touch the ground. The numerous tiny achenes are subtended by bristles and mature in late June and July. They easily shatter when the plant is shaken and can be blown by the wind.

Some taxonomists separate this species into several varieties. There seems to be sufficient overlap of characters in the Iowa material to render this distinction impractical.

Most species of this genus are probably edible. Native Americans and early settlers harvested the roots, using the older ones for flour and the younger as vegetables or as a sugar source. Members of this genus are one of the most important sources of food for wildlife. The achenes are commonly eaten by ducks and other marsh birds. The stems and underground parts are eaten by muskrats and they furnish excellent cover for nesting birds.

Curly dock: *Rumex crispus* L.

Other common names: Curled dock, old-field dock, sour dock, wavy-leaved dock, yellow dock.

Rumex: The name is taken from the ancient Greek name for this species.

Crispus: Meaning "curled", referring to the margins of the leaves.

Buckwheat family: *Polygonaceae*

Curly dock is found throughout the contiguous United States and southern Canada. It is widespread and common in Iowa. A native of Europe, it has become naturalized in this country. It has wide ecological amplitude; that is, it grows in a variety of habitats—from open pastures and roadsides to the edges of marshes and low prairies, especially where disturbance has been a factor. Its flowering time is May and June, with fruit remaining into September.

This perennial (some sources maintain it is a biennial) may achieve a height of 3 feet, with alternate leaves which grow to 9 inches and have conspicuous wavy margins. These leaves are thick and up to 2 inches broad, widest at the base. The taproot is carrot-like and up to a foot in length. With age this taproot may become a cluster and stores large amounts of energy. Cutting the plant has little effect as it springs from the rootstock promptly.

The flowers are greenish and individually inconspicuous and crowded in a prolonged raceme. There are six sepals and six stamens. Pollination is achieved by wind. Fruits consist of a three-angled nutlet enclosed by three sepals, with a grain-like tubercle at the center of each sepal.

Because it is a native of Europe, there are no medical uses of the plant by Native Americans or early settlers. It came to this country by unknown means and was spread rapidly as an impurity in commercial seeds. European folklore reports the root, collected after the fruits mature, was powdered and used as a relief for pleursy, urinary tract infections, and inflammation of the bowel. This species forms a basal rosette during its first growing year. These may be harvested spring or fall and cooked as greens. These are commonly cooked with other greens and served with bacon or salt pork.

Members of this genus are important as wildlife food. Because this plant grows in a variety of habitats, a high number of wildlife species feed on the seeds. They include Canada geese, marsh birds like the sora, upland gamebirds like the pheasant, songbirds like the bob-o-link and red-winged blackbird, and small mammals like the white-footed mouse.

There are 11 species in this genus in Iowa, and about half are not native to this country. They range in habitat preference from the driest hillside to shallow standing water, with most being found in moist soil.

Other common names: Little white orchid, ducks, squirrel shoes.

Cypripedium: Incorrectly Latinized from ancient Greek words *Cypris,* "Venus", and *pedilon,* "shoe", or "Venus' shoe".

Candidum: From Latin, meaning "white".

Orchid family: *Orchidaceae*

    Small white lady slipper is found from New York to North Dakota and south to New Jersey, Pennsylvania, Kentucky and Missouri. This small orchid is found in wet prairies, edges of potholes, and on fens. It does best in calcareous, wet soils. Its flowering time is late May and early June.

    The stiff, green stems are usually 6 to 18 inches tall. They grow from a perennial rootstock that is coarsely fibrous and fleshy. The three to five basal leaves, shaped as narrow ovals with pointed tips, sheath the stem and stand mostly erect. The leaves are up to 5 inches long and 1½ inches across.

    One, rarely two, slightly fragrant flowers per stem are typical of this lady slipper. The sepals and petals are greenish yellow, often with purple spots. The upper sepal is narrow, about an inch long; the lateral pair of sepals are united nearly to the tip. Larger than the sepals, the lateral petals are narrow and twisted, perhaps 1½ inches long. The lower petal is pouch-like, ½ to 1 inch long, and waxy white, with purple stripes inside the pouch. Narrow, lance-shaped bracts 1 to 2 inches long are at the base of the flower. The fruit is three-angled and consists of a single cell. It contains numerous tiny, spindle-shaped seeds.

Cypripediums are considered sedative, antispasmodic, nerve medicines, with "all species considered equally medicinal". Early practitioners used a teaspoon of the powdered root dissolved in sugar water to treat insomnia. Glandular hairs on the stems and leaves of *Cypripediums* contain a toxic substance that causes a skin reaction in many people, especially in hot weather when they perspire.

    This diminutive orchid seems to be decreasing throughout its range. However, its relatively short blooming period and restricted habitat may cause it to be overlooked. Because of the special growing conditions they require, all lady slippers should be enjoyed but left where they are found unless they are physically threatened or in imminent danger of destruction.

    The Pillage Ojibwa considered the roots of all species of *Cypripedium* to be a good remedy of all kinds. The early settlers used it as a gentle nerve tonic and also as an anti-spasmodic and stimulant.

Reed canary grass: *Phalaris arundinacea* L.

Other common names: Bride's lace, doggers, ladies' lace, lady grass, spires, sword grass.

Phalaris: From Greek meaning "shining", alluding to the shining seeds or possibly to the crest-like seed head.

Arundinacea: Meaning "reed-like".

Grass family: *Poaceae (Gramineae)*

Reed canary grass is widely distributed in North America, growing from Alaska south to the Carolinas, Missouri, Oklahoma, and California as well as in Europe and Asia. In Iowa, it is common throughout the state. It is a plant of broad ecological tolerance, growing in shallow water at the edges of potholes, in grass waterways, in moist depressions, along streams and often in upland open areas. It is in anthesis in late May and early June.

This species is a native, cool-season, sod-forming perennial that grows from 2 to 6 feet in height. Because it is a cool season grass, it starts growth earlier in the spring than warm season grasses and slows its growth during summer months. It may add more growth in the cooler fall season. Clumps may reach 2 feet across, especially where it is growing in shallow water or where it is just becoming established. It spreads both by seed and creeping rootstocks, and will gradually fill in between clumps and form a continuous sod cover.

The leaves may be 8 inches long and an inch wide and are rough on both sides. The papery ligule is prominent and about a quarter-inch long.

The flowers, and later the seed heads, are in tight dense cylindrical clusters that may be 6 inches long. These clusters contain many shiny, dark seeds in whitish papery husks.

This species grows naturally around the northern hemisphere and has been observed in Europe and Asia for many years. It was used in Sweden for planting in wet locations. Although there is a native species, the first seeds for planting in the United States apparently came from Sweden. This grass has probably been planted more than any other for erosion control. However, in some situations it is so aggressive that it has taken over areas where it is not wanted.

A variety of this species is called canary grass, *P. canariensis,* and is raised for seed which is sold in birdseed mixtures. It occasionally grows in the state near bird feeding stations. Ribbon grass, *P. andrundinacea* var. *picta,* has leaves streaked with white and is often planted as an ornamental.

Blue flag iris: *Iris shrevei* Small

Other common names: Blue flag, fleur-de-lis.

Iris: From the Greek for "rainbow". Iris is the name of the rainbow goddess of Greek mythology.

Shrevei: Named for Ralph Shreve.

Iris family: *Iridaceae*

Blue flag iris is found from Quebec to Minnesota and south to North Carolina, Tennessee, Arkansas, and Kansas. In Iowa, it grows throughout the state, but is most common in the north-central portion where marshes are frequent. It grows on wet, marshy soils, on the margins of lakes and streams and is in bloom in late May and June.

Narrow, sword-shaped leaves up to an inch wide and 3 feet long grow erect with a graceful curve. The leaves, with parallel veins, clasp the base of the flowering stalk.

The flower stalk, round in cross section and extending higher than the leaves, is often branched with a showy flower at the top of each branch. The rootstock is a fleshy, horizontal rhizome with fibrous roots. This rhizome contains a toxic substance, iridin, which imparts an unpleasant flavor. Scars from previous leaf growth appear on the rhizome.

The blue-violet flowers resemble the domestic iris, but with segments more slender and smaller. A single plant often has multiple flowers, often with six or more. The down-curving parts shade to lighter colors and show conspicuous veining. The flower appears to have nine petals; in reality, it has three petals, three sepals and three petal-like branches of the style. These branches arch over the pollen-producing stamens to prevent self-pollination. The sepals have a yellow mid-rib which expands to a bright yellow, pubescent patch at the base. The flowers are enclosed in an envelope of two or more papery bracts.

The fruit is a three-lobed oblong capsule which may achieve a length of 3 inches. The seeds are dull and rounded and occur in two rows in each lobe.

Native Americans used this species to treat earache, sore eyes, respiratory problems, and liver ailments. To relieve swelling and pain from sores and bruises, both Indians and settlers pounded the boiled root to pulp and applied it as a dressing. Early pioneer medical practices sometimes used blue flag iris to induce vomiting or to "cleanse the intestines".

The iris root used in perfumes and flavorings comes from the root of *Iris florentina*. The royal emblem (fleur-de-lis) of France represents the iris, but the exact derivation is obscure. One legend tells that King Clovis could be beaten in battle as long as he had three black toads as emblems on his shield. His queen, Clotilde, learned from a holy hermit about the powers of a shield said to be as shining as the sun with irises as emblems. She convinced the king to change his emblems to irises. He did, and was thereafter successful in battle. Some time later, the number of irises was standardized at three to represent the Holy Trinity.

The native wild iris is blue—but sometimes plants with other color flowers are found and appear wild. These have escaped from gardens. The yellow German iris was brought to this country and has been widely used in growing hybrids of many colors.

Other common names: Black cap, blackamoor, bubrush, bugg segg, candlestick, cat-o-nine-tails, flaxtail, great reed mace, marsh beetle, marsh pestle, water torch.

Typha: From *Typhe,* ancient Greek name for the genus, said to mean "bog".

Latifolia: From Latin, meaning "broad leaf".

Angustifolia: From Latin meaning "narrow-leaved".

Glauca: Meaning "glaucous".

Cattail family: *Typhaceae*

Three species of cattails, *Typha latifolia* L., *T. X glauca* Godron, and *T. angustifolia* L., occur in eastern North America. *T. latifolia*, in particular, is found throughout much of Canada and virtually all of the contiguous states. In Iowa, all three are found throughout the state. All are found in shallow standing water, in wet roadside ditches and virtually any habitat where the soil is saturated. They are in bloom in late May into July.

T. latifolia, common cattail, is distinguished by having wide leaves, about an inch wide, a whitish appearance to the leaves and with dark brown male and female spikes contiguous on the flowering stalk. This is a stout-appearing plant which may achieve a height of 7 feet, normally shorter.

T. angustifolia, narrow-leaved cattail, has leaves around a half-inch wide, green in appearance, has slender red-brown spikes which are separated by a space, and is smaller in stature.

T. X glauca, thought to be of hybrid origin, is by far the most common in Iowa marshes. This plant may achieve a height of 12 feet and plants of 10 feet are not uncommon. The picture is complicated by the fact that back-crossing occurs between this species and the parents, forming intermediate plants.

The flowering stalk ends in two flowering spikes, one above the other on the same stalk. The upper has male flowers, the lower, female flowers. After the pollen has been shed, the upper spike dries and disappears, leaving the familiar cigar-like seed head.

Reproduction is by seed and by spreading rhizome. In autumn, a new shoot will form at the end of a lateral rhizome, and new shoots will form on either side of the adult stem, but will not grow until the following spring. Copious amounts of seeds are formed; each is surrounded by hairs and are light enough to be wind-blown. Even wet ditches along new roads or highways will support a stand of cattails shortly after construction ceases.

Few plants have been more widely used as food. Young shoots less than 18 inches in height were eaten raw or cooked. Just before blooming and while still enclosed in its sheath or husk, the top spike was steamed or boiled and served like corn on the cob. Pollen was collected by shaking it into a basket or pot and was then used as a flour—often in combination with other foods such as corn meal or curly dock seeds. Cattails are excellent wildlife cover and are a favorite source of food for muskrats.

Other common names: Smooth monkey flower, swamp monkey flower.

Mimulus: Diminuitive of *mimus,* "a buffoon", from the grinning appearance of the corolla.

Glabratus: From Latin *glaber,* "made nearly glabrous", or "becoming smooth".

Fremontii: Named for its discoverer, John Charles Fremont, 1813–1890, once a Republican candidate for president and enthusiastic collector of plants.

Snapdragon family: *Scrophulariaceae*

Yellow monkey flower is found from Mexico to Ontario, in Michigan, Wisconsin, Minnesota, southern Manitoba, and Montana. In Iowa, it is known from a few northern, eastern, and southwestern counties. It inhabits cold springs, slowly flowing streams, and fens. A long flowering time extends from June into October.

The stems are smooth, suberect to decumbent, usually rooting at the lower nodes, often growing in a dense, tangled mass in cool, running water. The leaves are arranged alternately along the stem and are up to ¾ inch long. Leaf shape varies from suborbicular to slightly cordate to reniform. The margins are smooth, slightly toothed, or undulate. The lower leaves are on relatively long petioles, the upper ones are sessile.

The corolla is yellow, up to 1 inch long. The upper lip is two-lobed and erect; the lower lip is three-lobed and spreading. The calyx is five-toothed and five-angled, with the upper tooth largest.

The flower is on a stalk which originates in the axil of the upper leaves. The capsule is flattened and ovate and contains numerous seeds.

The leaves of yellow monkey flower were used by the Forest Potawatomi for medicinal purposes but the application is not known. Early pioneers used it for its stimulating qualities.

There are about 40 species in the genus and these are found from central and eastern Canada to Wyoming and Texas. Many horticultural varieties have been developed and grow well in aquatic gardens.

A related species, *M. luteus,* with yellow, dark-spotted corollas, is frequently planted in gardens.

Watercress: *Nasturtium officinale* R. Br.

Other common names: Salad plant, true watercress, water salad,

Nasturtium: This name from the Latin *nasus tortus* meaning "a wry or twisted nose", alluding to the effect of the pungent qualities of the plant.

Officinale: Meaning "of the shops" from the long history of this plant being sold for salads.

Mustard family: *Brassicaceae (Cruciferae)*

Although introduced from Europe, this plant has found habitats to its liking, now being found from Nova Scotia to Virginia and west to California and Manitoba. It is also found in Asia, South America, and the West Indies. In Iowa it is common in the northeast, but widely, though sparsely, distributed over much of the remainder of the state. Its favored habitat is cold-water streams and seeps. The authors observed a big population in a spring at the base of the loess hills in extreme western Iowa. It blooms from late May into September.

Watercress is a perennial with creeping or floating stems which form roots at the nodes. The somewhat fleshy leaves are alternately arranged along the stem, compound, with three to nine leaflets, the terminal largest. The stems, succulent and smooth, are weak and easily broken. It grows in a tangled mass of stems and leaves in shallow water. The stems may get to be several feet in length in flowing water.

The cross-shaped flowers, borne at the ends of stems, are white, 1/8 inch across, and with petals twice as long as the sepals. The resulting fruit, spreading or ascending, is nearly an inch long, 1/10 inch broad, on a pedicel about equal to the fruit in length, and has two rows of seeds inside.

This is an excellent plant to have growing along trout streams in northeast Iowa as it harbors many organisms on which the trout feed. The same plant is often for sale at grocery stores. It has long been known as a good salad plant, giving the salad a mild peppery flavor. It normally grows in clear water streams, however, it also grows well in contaminated water. If picked from the wild, you should know the character of the stream where it was collected, or the plants should be well cleaned before being made into a salad. As a potherb, cook and serve like spinach, or it can be added to more bland salad plants.

Young plants may be harvested much of the year and their removal does not harm the population. This plant has long been cultivated in Europe. It is likely that early settlers brought it to this country for cultivation for greens.

Watercress has an elaborate medicinal history, having been used since the Middle Ages to kill internal parasites, to heal and purify internal wounds and, if taken with olive oil, to eliminate poison. More recent historical records include use as a stimulant, stomachic, diaphoretic, alleviative of catarrh and rheumatism, and as a blood-purifier.

The seeds are more potent than the foliage and were also used in early medicine. Seeds boiled in vinegar were applied to dispel goiter. Taken internally, they relieved lassitude and sluggishness.

This species is sometimes included under the names *Rorippa nasturtium-aquaticum* and *Radicula nasturtium-aquaticum*. Although the scientific name of this plant is *Nasturtium*, it is not the same *Nasturtium* of the flower garden.

Other common names: Frog-fruit.

Phyla: Original name for the species.

Lippia: Named for Agostino Lippi, Italian naturalist 1678–1704.

Lanceolata: Meaning "lance-shaped" from the shape of the leaves.

Vervain family: *Verbenaceae*

Fog fruit is found growing in wet habitats from Florida to southern California, and north to Michigan, Iowa, and Nebraska. In Iowa, it is of common occurrence throughout most of the state, but infrequent in the northwest. Its flowering time is June to October.

The plant trails along the ground and can form dense mats. It is a perennial herb from a woody rootstock and often roots where the stem is in contact with the wet soil. The slender, erect peduncles arise from the axils of the leaves, which are arranged oppositely along the prostrate stem.

The leaves are up to 2 inches long, taper towards each end, and are toothed to below the middle of the leaf margin. The solitary, short head has pink, bluish, or white flowers subtended by broad pointed bracts. The fruit is composed of two nutlets.

Fog fruit is of minor importance as a wildlife food plant, but its seeds are known to be of value to ducks. Its major contribution is as a soil anchor, effective because of the extensive rooting system which occurs and the large mats which occur in good habitat.

Some authorities have maintained that plants with variation in leaf-width should be segregated as separate species. However, such variation occurs in plants within the same colony, so this should be considered normal variation within the species.

Other common names: Bald spikerush, red-footed spikerush, red seeded spikerush.

Eleocharis: From the Greek *elos,* "a marsh", and *charis,* "grace", from the marshland habitat of many of the species.

Erythropoda: Literally, "red foot" from *erythro,* "red" and pod from *podo,* meaning "foot", presumably from the reddish rhizomes and stolons.

Sedge family: *Cyperaceae*

This spikerush is found from Quebec to James Bay, west to Manitoba and south to Nova Scotia, New England, Tennessee, Arkansas, and Oklahoma. In Iowa, it is common in the west half and infrequent in the east. It is found in moist sand, in sedge meadows, and edges of marshes. Its flowering time in Iowa is June.

The loosely stoloniferous plant forms small clumps. It is usually short, 6 inches or so, but may achieve a height of 15 inches under ideal conditions. The culms are slender with reddish sheaths. The spikelets are linear to slenderly ovoid, ⅓ to ¾ inch long. Bristles at the base of the achene may be lacking or present with up to four attached. The basal scale is solitary and completely encircles the bases of the fertile scales.

Spikerushes provide food for ducks and geese across northern North America. Geese graze spikerushes in much of their range, eating the nutlets as well as the rhizomes, stolons, and culms. Propagation, often desired for raising food for wildfowl, is achieved by cutting and transplanting the rootstocks.

Some 45 species of spikerushes are found in the contiguous states. There are 15 members of this genus in Iowa, varying from the diminutive needle spikerush (*E. acicularis*), a few inches in height, to *E. macrostachya,* which may achieve a height of over 3 feet. The needle spikerush often forms mats along the edges of streams or marshes and thus acts as a valuable soil binder. Some members of the genus are difficult to identify and possible only with mature fruiting material. The present species is one of the most common and present at the edges of most relatively undisturbed marshes. It is easily identified and a good place to start in learning spikerushes.

Other common names: Swamp candle, swamp loosestrife.

Lysimachia: In honor of King Lysimachus of Thrace.

Ciliata: From the characteristic of this plant having hairs on the margins of the petioles.

Primrose family: *Primulaceae*

Fringed loosestrife is found from Quebec to British Columbia and south to Florida, Texas, and Colorado. In Iowa, it is found in the eastern part, especially on the Paleozoic Plateau and the extreme eastern part of the state. Its favored habitats are wet soil at the edges of marshes, sedge meadows, and edges of alluvial woods, where it receives nearly full sun. It is in bloom from mid-June into August. Some sources state this species is naturalized from Europe.

The plant may achieve a height of 3 feet, normally less, usually unbranched from a slender rhizome. The leaves are arranged opposite on the stem, are ovate to lanceolate, 1 to 3 inches long and on long petioles which bear a fringe of hairs. There are often clusters of small leaves at the bases of the normal-sized leaves.

The flowers are on filiform axillary peduncles and are about an inch across. The five petals are bright yellow, unspotted, toothed on the ends, and with a red blotch at the base of each petal; this may appear as a colored ring at the center of the corolla. The flowers possess some stamens that lack anthers. The capsule is shorter than the calyx. Pollination is by honeybees and bumblebees.

The term "loosestrife" refers to a custom of ancient times of attaching this plant to the wagon-tongue or harness of unruly oxen. They would then supposedly become quiet and gentle.

This is never a dominant or even common plant in the wetlands of Iowa, so it is of limited use to wildlife. There are references to ground squirrels using it as a food plant, but apparently it has no history as a human medicinal plant.

There are nine species of *Lysimachia* native or naturalized in Iowa and most are denizens of wet soils and all have attractive flowers. All add interest to Iowa's wetlands, are attractive, and are well worth the time and effort needed to find them.

Other common names: Bogbell, marsh bluebell, swampbell.

Campanula: Diminutive of the Latin *campana,* "a bell", from the shape of the flower.

Aparinoides: From its similarity to Cleavers, *Galium aparinoides,* in that both have foliage that adheres to other plants, or to clothing.

Bluebell family: *Campanulaceae*

This interesting and seemingly delicate wetland plant ranges from Maine to Minnesota, and south to Georgia, Kentucky, Missouri, Nebraska, and Colorado. In Iowa, it is frequent in the northern part of the Des Moines Lobe, nearly absent elsewhere. Its preferred habitat in Iowa is marshes, sedge meadows, and fens where it is found growing in rather thick vegetation.

Marsh bellflower may reach a length of 3 feet, normally less. The stem is so weak that it is found climbing or leaning on other vegetation. The stem is slender, three-angled, with rough, backward-pointing hairs or bristles on the angles.

The leaves are alternately arranged, lance-shaped and become progressively smaller toward the tips of the branches. The leaves are up to 2 inches long, about a quarter-inch wide and slightly toothed on the edges. The petioles of the leaves are either very short or lacking.

The flowers are small, about ⅓–⅛ inch long, saucer-shaped with five sepals and five petals, solitary on long, naked stalks at the ends of branches. The petals are whitish, or sometimes have a bluish cast. The fruit is a short, ribbed capsule with three partitions.

Some taxonomists prefer to view a second, similar taxon, southern bellflower, *Campanula uliginosa,* as a separate species. In Iowa, the characters of the two species overlap and they grow in the same habitat, so are lumped together.

There are four bellflowers in Iowa—ranging from the tall, blue American bellflower (*Campanula americana*), which grows in woodland edges and roadsides to the harebell (*Campanula rotundifolia*), which grows on limestone bluffs in the northeast part. A fourth species, *Campanula rapunculoides* L., is grown ornamentally and occasionally escapes to grow in disturbed habitats.

Other common names: Goose-grass, seaside arrowgrass, sour grass, truscart.

Triglochin: A name composed of *treis*, "three", and *glochis*, "point", from the three points of the ripe fruit of *T. palustre*.

Maritimum: Meaning "growing by the sea".

Arrow grass family: *Juncaginaceae*

This **herbaceous perennial** is widespread in North America in saline, brackish, or freshwater marshes from Labrador to Alaska and south to Delaware, Pennsylvania, Ohio, Iowa, North Dakota to northern Mexico. In Iowa, it is found most frequently on fens in the northern part of the state, but also in a wet prairie in Boone County. To date it has been found in Boone, Cerro Gordo, Clay, Dickinson, Emmet, Howard, and Palo Alto counties. It blooms in July–August.

Arrow grass may grow to a height of over 3 feet, but normally less. The grass-like leaves are clustered at the base and have membranous sheaths.

Inconspicuous flowers, perfect and numerous, occur in a slender, spike-like terminal raceme. These flowers are composed of three or six small, greenish petals and sepals. The fruit is a cluster of three to six one-seeded capsules separating at maturity.

This is a cyanogenetic plant—one capable of producing hydrocyanic acid, also called prussic acid, a highly poisonous substance. When ingested in quantity, death results from respiratory failure.

Native Americans in Utah, Nevada, Montana, Oregon, and California parched and ground the scale-like seeds for food and roasted them as a substitute for coffee. Seeds were also parched and eaten by the Klamath Indians. These seeds probably contain little, if any, of the hydrocyanic acid that is in the fresh plant.

A second Iowa species, also an inhabitant of fens, is small arrow grass, *T. palustre*. It differs by being smaller, having six carpels, and a fruit longer than wide. It is also considered to have poisonous properties.

Joe Pye weed: *Eupatorium maculatum* L.

Other common names: Spotted Joe Pye weed, King-of-the-meadow, Queen-of-the-meadow, thoroughwort.

Eupatorium: For Mithridates Eupator, 132–63 B.C., who is said to have used a species of this genus in medicine.

Maculatum: Meaning "mottled" from the purple spotting on the stem.

Daisy family: *Asteraceae (Compositae)*

This tall, attractive perennial grows from Newfoundland to British Columbia and south to Pennsylvania, Illinois, Iowa, and New Mexico. In Iowa, it is common on the Paleozoic Plateau and Iowan Surface and progressively less common as one goes west. It blooms in August into September.

Plants may achieve a height of over 6 feet and grow in loose colonies. The leaves are ovate or lanceolate, have toothed margins, and occur in whorls of four or five and may be 8 inches long and taper toward the base and tip. The upper surfaces are rough to the touch. The stem is stout, purple or with purple spots and arises from a fibrous root system.

The flowers are small, rose-colored, and occur in dense, flat-topped clusters at the top of the stem, with 9–22 individual flowers occurring in each head. This cluster may grow to 10 inches long and is at its prime in mid-August.

Worldwide, there are over 500 species in the genus. A similar plant, *E. purpureum* has a rounded top on the inflorescence and fewer flowers per inflorescence. This is a common plant, especially in eastern Iowa in fens, sedge meadows, and marsh edges.

This genus is known to be of value as food for upland game birds and song birds.

Fresh leaves of Joe Pye weed were used by the Potawatomi to make poultices for healing burns. Some tribes used the root as a medicine to clear up afterbirth. Early settlers used both the root and leaves for medicine. The root was considered to have astringent, tonic, stimulant, and diuretic properties. The root and leaves have been used to treat urinary problems, as well as hemeturia, gout, and rheumatism. Among the Menomini, Joe Pye weed and others in the genus were used in treating diseases of the urethra.

Arrow arum: *Peltandra virginica* (L.)

Other common names: Green arrow, tuckahoe, tuckah, taw-ho.

Peltandra: The name from Greek *pelts,* "a small shield" and *aner,* "stamen", referring to the shape of the stamen.

Virginica: Meaning "Virginian" or "of Virginia".

Arum family: *Araceae*

Arrow arum is found from Florida to Texas and north to southern Maine, Quebec, New York, and southern Ontario. In Iowa, it has been recorded only from Cedar, Des Moines, and Greene counties. It is found at borders of ponds, usually in shallow water, in slow-flowing streams where it can occur in large colonies. It is in flower in July.

The plant occurs in loose colonies with the leaves coming from the base of the flower stalk. These leaves are on the ends of long stalks and may reach a height of 3 feet. The glossy leaves are arrowhead-shaped and thus are often confused with the more common arrowleaf, *Sagittaria* sp. The leaves have a prominent mid-vein and, unlike the leaves of *Sagittaria,* have a vein running along the entire leaf just inside the margin.

Arrow arum is in the same family as Jack-in-the-pulpit and green dragon as is evidenced by the inflorescence. It has a spathe and spadix. A separate stalk supports the spadix which is covered by tiny white flowers. The white male flowers are situated above the green female flowers. A leaf-like spathe nearly encloses the spadix, with only a small opening on the side.

The fruits are a globular head of green or blackish berries enclosed in a green leathery case, with the stalk curved downward at maturity. The stalk arises from a stout, tuberous rootstock. In our experience with the seeds, we found that a few sprouted in the refrigerator after several months of refrigeration.

This plant grows well in the sluggish or standing water in oxbows or slow-flowing streams along the Mississippi River. Because of its similarity to arrowleaf, we are probably overlooking it, especially in southeast Iowa.

Seeds of this species are eaten by wood ducks, marsh birds, and in some parts of its range, by muskrats. Roots were gathered by native Americans, who put them in a trench over which they built a great fire. When dug up, they were "consumed with great avidity". The taste was said to be like that of potatoes.

Rafinesque stated the seeds could be used as a substitute for pepper. The seeds lose their peppery taste upon being heated or upon prolonged drying. Other reports mentioned the boiled berries were "considered a great dainty". From the seeds, a "palatable but unsightly" bread can be made. It is blackish-brown and tastes like corncake with a strong flavor of cocoa.

Other common names: American great bulrush, big bulrush, great bulrush, tall bulrush, tule.

Scirpus: Latin for bulrush.

Acutus: Meaning "acute".

Validus: Meaning "stout".

Sedge family: *Cyperaceae*

These two bulrushes are similar and occur in similar habitats. Hard stemmed bulrush is found from Newfoundland to British Columbia and south to New England, New Jersey, Pennsylvania, Ohio, Illinois, Missouri, Oklahoma, Texas, Arizona, and California. Soft stemmed bulrush grows from Newfoundland to Alaska, south to Georgia, Tennessee, Oklahoma, Texas, northern Mexico, and California. In Iowa, both are frequent to common throughout most of the state. They normally grow in shallow water or in saturated soil at the margins of marshes, ponds, or wet roadside ditches. In certain stages of the marsh cycle, either may form a nearly monodominant stand. The inconspicuous flowers are present in late May and early June.

The two species are nearly indistinguishable and some botanists do not separate them. Both are terete and unbranched, and both may reach heights of over 6 feet. They are separated on the basis of the scales of *S. acutus* being longer than the achene, those of *S. validus* about as long as the achene. Also, hard stemmed bulrush usually has a stem smaller in diameter and more firm, with fewer vacuoles. Both have stem leaves reduced to sheaths at the base of the plant. The inflorescence of these two species is a loose terminal umbel.

Members of the genus are normally aquatic and perennial, infrequently annual. There are about 300 species in this highly variable genus which occurs worldwide.

Fruiting stems arise from horizontal, scaly rootstocks which spread below ground or under water to form a dense mat which gives rise to new shoots. Seeds are dull brown or black and may lie in the muck of the marsh bottom for years until proper conditions for germination occur.

These bulrushes provide food and shelter for many marsh dwellers, and an anchor for loose or eroding soil. The tubers of both species are eaten by wildlife and the stems, especially when young, are extensively utilized by muskrats for food. The bruised rootstocks, boiled, or cooked with cornmeal, or dried and made into sweet flour, have been used by Native Americans and settlers as food.

The Forest Potawatomi gathered the bulrush stems for making baskets and mats. The stems were sunk under water and held down with weights until bleached white. After that, they could be colored for various designs in baskets, mats, or even blankets.

The greatest use of these plants, however, was for wigwam mats, generally 2½ feet wide and 5 feet long. The Potawatomi preferred to use the smaller stems because the pith cavity was smaller and the rushes would wear better. The Forest Potawatomi also said the flowers were used as a love medicine—and that they learned this from the Ottawa women.

A third species, *S. heterochaetus,* looks much like the other two and is widespread in Iowa, but is less common. It can be distinguished by the three-cleft style.

Grass of Parnassus: *Parnassia glauca* Raf.

Other common names: Bog-stars.

Parnassia: Named from Mount Parnassus, a mountain in Greece sacred to the Muses and Apollo; the Grass of Parnassus of Dioscorides.

Glauca: Meaning "blue-green" from the color of the foliage.

Saxifrage family: *Saxifragaceae*

Grass of Parnassus grows from Newfoundland to Manitoba and south to Ohio, Indiana, northern Illinois, Iowa, and South Dakota. In Iowa, it grows in fens in the northern half of the state. It is in bloom in late July into October. Although "grass" is in its name, it is not related to the grasses.

This is a perennial which grows to a height of 15 inches. The leaves are coriaceous, smooth, rounded and form a basal rosette. Leaf bases are rounded to subcordate. A sessile stem-leaf grows at or below the middle of the stem.

The single stem is topped by a star-like flower, with five white petals that have conspicuous green stripes. These petals are about ¾ inch long. The five sepals are persistent and united at the base. They are spreading in flower, reflexed in fruit, and with a broad hyaline margin.

There are five stamens (male flower parts) which alternate with the petals. The fruit is an ovoid, terminal capsule with four valves and contains numerous seeds. Reproduction is apparently only by seed.

The species is widespread in North America, with the Iowa sites on the southern margin of its range. Grass of Parnassus is a consistent member of the calcareous fen flora of Iowa, but it also grows in the calcareous soils of wet prairies.

This genus has its species well distributed over the northern hemisphere. Six species are found in the Rocky Mountains, mostly at the higher elevations. The Grass of Parnassus of Dioscorides was thought by early botanists to be *Parnassia palustris*. Finding a parnassia flower while backpacking, mountain climbing, or fen hunting is a treasured experience.

Swamp milkweed: *Asclepias incarnata* L.

Other common names: Rose milkweed, silkweed, water nerve root, white Indian hemp.

Asclepias: From the name of the Greek god of healing and medicine.

Incarnata: From Latin, for "flesh", referring to the flesh-colored flowers.

Milkweed family: *Asclepiadaceae*

Swamp milkweed is found from Quebec to Manitoba and Wyoming and south to New England, South Carolina, Tennessee, Louisiana, Texas, and New Mexico. It is found in moist soil at the edges of prairie potholes, sedge meadows, and marshes. It is in bloom from June through August.

This tall perennial grows to a height of over 5 feet. The glabrous stem is solitary or clustered. A small amount of milky juice exudes from the broken stem. The deep green leaves, 3 to 6 inches long, are lanceolate or obovate and have petioles ¼ to ½ inch long.

The root system has numerous threadlike roots, 6 to 8 inches long, extending from a sturdy crown that has many buds.

The flowers are fragrant, pale pink to rose-purple, rarely whitish and have short hoods. The hoods equal the length of the anthers. Bees and other insects are sometimes caught by their feet as they try to leave the flower. The erect pods are 2 to 4 inches long and contain many plumed seeds.

Milkweeds have a long medicinal history. Native Americans in Canada drank an infusion of ground root to provide temporary sterility. The Meskwaki made a tea of the root and used it "to expel worms in an hour." Some tribes burned off the plumes, then ground the seeds and steeped them in water for use in drawing the poison out of a rattlesnake bite.

This species, along with other milkweeds were sometimes cultivated for food. The Ojibwa used the flowers and buds in soups. The Chippewa cut and stewed the flowers and ate them like preserves. Some American Indians cooked young pods with buffalo meat. The common milkweed (*A. syriaca*) was the source of a sugar. The Sioux collected the flowers in the morning while they were still dew-covered. The flowers were squeezed to get a juice that was boiled until it yielded a palatable brown sugar. The Dakota and Nebraska Indians are reported to have used the immature flower clusters and fruits as a cooked vegetable.

Livestock have been reported as being poisoned from eating the leaves and stems of the common milkweed. Swamp milkweed probably has similar properties. Most livestock avoid it because of the bitter taste.

During World War II, the milky sap was tested as a rubber substitute and the plumes of the seed heads were tried as a replacement of kapok in life preservers. In Europe, the silky fibers of the plumes have been used for making hats and for stuffing pillows.

Other common names: Downhill of life, herb two-pence, two-penny grass, wandering Jenny, wandering Sally.

Lysimachia: Possibly in honor of King Lysimachus of Thrace. More probably from *lysis*, "a release from", and *mache*, "strife" from a story of Lysimachus, being chased by an angry bull, seizing a plant of loosestrife and pacifying the animal by waving the plant before him—an approach we have not tried but do not recommend.

Nummularia: From the original genus name, meaning "coin-like", from the round shape of the leaves.

Loosestrife family: *Primulaceae*

Moneywort, a prostrate, sprawling herb is naturalized from Europe and is now found from Newfoundland to Ontario and south to New England, Georgia, Missouri, and Kansas. In Iowa, it is common in the northeast and becomes increasingly more scarce toward the west. It is in flower in June through August.

The leaves are round, nearly an inch in diameter, have scattered black dots across the surface, and the lower ones often narrow toward the base. The leaves, with short petioles, are arranged oppositely along the trailing stem, which may be 2 feet long or longer. The stem often takes root at the joints where it touches the moist ground.

The flowers are bright yellow, normally dotted, up to an inch wide and occur singly in the axils of the leaves. Some populations seldom flower, but spread by means of a creeping stem and can form large patches. The plant is easily established by division or by cutting and persists where there is sufficient sun and moisture. There are many small seeds per fruit.

This species is an oddity among the loosestrifes in that this species sprawls flat against the surface of the ground while the other loosestrifes are erect. Also, this is a plant of disturbance and is found in wet areas where some past event has modified the environment. This disturbance may be grazing, flooding, or erosion.

Plants can be grown from cuttings and, once established, easily maintain themselves and can become weeds—but are easy to control. It grows well in wet situations, even in sites where it is temporarily submerged. It is a popular plant for hanging baskets and for filler in gardens, but tends to spread into moist areas where it is not wanted. It may be useful as a ground cover in moist, shady areas.

Water plantain: *Alisma plantago-aquatica* L.

Other common names: Devil's-spoons, great thrumwort, mad-dog-weed, mud plantain.

Alisma: An ancient Greek name for the European water plantain.

Plantago-aquatica: A combining form meaning "water plantain".

Water plantain family: *Alismataceae*

Water plantain is a rather common rooted wetland plant in shallow water of marshes, on muddy banks, and water-logged soils of ditches; occasionally in wet fields. It is an abundant plant of Iowa marshes and occurs statewide. It is found widespread over this country and Canada as well as over much of Europe, Africa, and Asia. Flowering time is from June into September.

It is a perennial herb from a shallow rootstock which is partly ensheathed by the expanded bases of the long petioles of the numerous leaves. The leaf blades are ovate-elliptic and may achieve a length of a foot and a width of over 6 inches. Bases of the leaf blades are cordate (heart-shaped).

The leaves are overtopped by a much-branched flowering scape which may reach 3 feet, normally less. The ultimate branches of the scape terminate in whorls of slender pedicels bearing small flowers. Each flower has three sepals, three petals, five or more stamens and several one-ovuled carpels arranged in a ring. Each ovule becomes a flattened achene. A nectar-bearing region is found at the base of the stamens; this attracts bees and flies which aid in pollination. The flower petals are white and the flower is small—usually less than an ⅛ inch wide.

A stout underground corm helps the plant survive the winter and periods of drought; this also may divide and form new plants. However, the plant produces large amounts of seeds which constitute its most important method of reproduction.

Although it is normally an emergent plant, water plantain can withstand long periods of submergence. It sometimes becomes the dominant plant in shallow water on marsh edges.

Apparently water plantain is of limited value as food for marsh wildlife, although several species of ducks have been reported as utilizing it sparingly for food, and the submerged roots have been used for food by early Americans.

A second species, *A. gramineum*, with pink petals, is rare in Iowa and has been reported only on one or two occasions.

Whorled loosestrife: *Lysimachia quadriflora* Sims

Other common names: Four-flowered loosestrife, marsh calm.

Lysimachia: Named in honor of King Lysimachus of Thrace, or, possibly from *lysis,* "a release from" and *mache,* "strife".

Quadriflora: Meaning "four flowered", because often four flowers occur at a node.

Primrose family: *Primulaceae*

This attractive woodland plant is found in calcareous soils from Ontario and Manitoba and south to New York, Virginia, Kentucky, Illinois, and Missouri. In Iowa, it is common in the northcentral and northeast parts, rare as one goes westward. It is found in wet prairies, at the edges of marshes and in alluvial soils, and is in bloom from early July into August.

The stem is four-angled, generally unbranched, and may achieve a height of close to 2 feet. There are often short branches from the upper nodes. The cauline leaves are sessile, linear, somewhat revolute, 2 to 5 inches long and may have cilia near the base. The lower leaves may be spatulate. There is a wide variation in leaf shape in this genus, but the leaves often have glandular dots and some species have ciliate fringes on the basal margin of the leaves and on the petiole.

There is enough variation within this group that some taxonomists separate some, including the present species and place them in the genus *Steironema*. There are a dozen or so species in the northeastern United States.

The flowers are bright yellow, long-pediceled, axillary, and conspicuously pointed petals. There are five petals and five sepals. The fruiting capsule is short and contains five valves.

There are six native species of *Lysimachia* in Iowa, and all are denizens of wetlands. One normally grows in shallow standing water. Another is here from Europe, but has become naturalized. Two others occasionally escape from cultivation and persist in disturbed sites. They are intolerant of disturbance. When you find one, you can be assured you are standing in a high-quality wetland.

The loosestrifes can be beautiful additions to a wildflower garden, particularly in a moist habitat. They often spread by rhizomes, are quite hardy, and thrive in full sun or partial shade.

Winged loosestrife: *Lythrum alatum* Pursh

Other common names: Common loosestrife, marsh loosestrife, wing-angled loosestrife.

Lythrum: From *lytron,* a name used by Dioscorides for purple loosestrife. Also a Greek name for blood—possibly for the color of some of the flowers; some species also had styptic properties.

Alatum: Meaning "winged" from the margined angles of the branches.

Loosestrife family: *Lythraceae*

The range of winged loosestrife is from New York to British Columbia and south to Georgia, Louisiana, and Texas. In Iowa, its preferred habitat is the wet soil on the edges of marshes, but it will grow in wet prairies, sedge meadows, and the edges of lowland woods. It is common in the lakes area of northern Iowa, infrequent to rare elsewhere. It is in bloom from late June to September.

This species may achieve a height of over 3 feet, normally less, but up to 5 feet when under cultivation. It has a square stem and is much-branched. The stem-leaves are elliptic to lanceolate, and rounded at the base. The leaves are arranged oppositely along the stem and those of the infloresence are similar to the stem leaves but much smaller. The sessile leaves are 1½ inches long and less than ½ inch wide. The petals are purple or deep magenta with five to seven petals, less than a ½ inch long and grow singly in the axils of leaves. It is a perennial with a woody rootstock.

Species of *Lysimachia* are called loosestrifes, but their flowers are yellow, rarely white. Loosestrife is a faulty translation of the Greek word *Lysimachia.* Winged loosestrife is a native species and a long-time stable member of the wetland community. Purple loosestrife, *L. salicaria,* on the other hand, is an introduced species and one which is aggressive.

The loosestrife was a favorite flower of Charles Darwin, who studied the complex pollination system of the plant.

Boneset: *Eupatorium perfoliatum* L.

Other common names: Agueweed, crosswort, Indian sage, thoroughwort (originally throughwort).

Eupatorium: From Greek meaning "good father", in honor of Mithridates Eupator (132–63 B.C.) who is said to have used a species of this genus in medical practice.

Perfoliatum: From *per,* "through", and *folium,* "leaf", relating to the arrangement where the leaves are joined at their bases and the stem seems to grow through.

Daisy family: *Asteraceae (Compositae)*

Boneset has a range from southern Canada south to Florida, Alabama, Louisiana, and Texas, where it is found on the edges of marshes, along streams, and in Carex swales. In Iowa, it occurs frequently throughout the state. It is in bloom from June into September.

A coarse, long-lived plant, boneset cannot survive draining its wetland habitat. The stem often branches toward the top of the plant, which may reach a height of 5 feet. The leaves are opposite and joined at their bases so that the stem appears to pass through. The leaves, which may be 8 inches long and 1½ inches wide, are widest at the bases, and taper evenly to the tips. The margins are finely toothed. Veins are prominent on the undersides of the leaves, which are hairy below.

Flowers are in heads, with 10–40 white flowers in each head. Occasionally flowers have a bluish cast. The fruit is five-angled, black or dark brown with light yellow dots, and a crown of hairs which acts as a parachute. These fruits are shed late from the fall into winter.

This species is widespread in eastern North America and was extensively used in medicine. The leaves contain the glucoside *Eupatorin* which was used as a tonic or stimulant, or, in larger doses, as emetic. It was popular among Native Americans, who used it as a tonic in dyspepsia and general debility and as a remedy for influenza and muscular rheumatism. In the southern United States, an ounce in a pint of boiling water was a favorite treatment of dengue or breakbone fever, hence the common name boneset.

Boneset was also used by the Menomini as a tea to dispel a fever. It was also used to treat bronchitis, sore throat and colds. It was raised as a drug plant and used by early doctors. It is said to be a laxative and a stimulant in smaller doses.

There are nearly 30 members of this genus in eastern North America, and many have varieties and forms. In Iowa, there are eight species of *Eupatorium,* several of which are plants of moist habitats. A close relative is Joe Pye weed, *E. maculatum,* which also grows statewide, but is taller, up to over 6 feet, has pink or purple disk flowers, leaves in whorls around the stem, and a purple-spotted stem.

Stinging nettle: *Urtica dioica* L.

Other common names: Burning nettle, dog nettle, wood nettle.

Urtica: From Latin meaning "nettle". Originally, the Latin derivation was from *uro,* meaning "to burn", from the sensation felt upon contact.

Dioica: From Greek meaning "two households", referring to the fact that male and female flower parts are borne separately.

Nettle family: *Urticaceae*

Stinging nettle is widespread in eastern North America. In Iowa, it is found throughout the state in partial shade in rich, moist soil. It has a wide variety of habitats, from roadsides to moist upland woods and moist disturbed sites, but is most at home in partial shade on floodplains and other moist lowlands. It has a long flowering time—from June into September.

This species has an erect, unbranched stem, covered with short bristly hairs. It normally grows to a height of 5 feet, but may reach over 7 feet in rich, shaded habitats. The stem is hollow, fibrous, and squarish in cross section. The closely spaced leaves are opposite, coarsely toothed with conspicuous veins. The leaves are up to 4 inches long, broad at the base and tapered to a pointed tip. The lower leaves may be cordate at the base. The petioles are less than half the length of the leaf. Bristly hairs are also found on the leaf blades of this perennial.

The tiny, green flowers, individually inconspicuous, occur in branched clusters arising from the leaf axils. Most clusters are around half the length of the leaves. Male and female flowers are usually on the same plant.

The stinging nettle is naturalized from Europe where it was cultivated for fiber since the days of early Egyptians. It is related to hemp, which also is grown for production of fibers. In World War I, this plant was grown for fiber which was used for tents, wagon covers, and clothing, and a yellow dye was prepared from the roots. Young shoots, after being boiled, make good ingredients for a salad.

Swamp loosestrife: *Decodon verticillatus* (L.) Ell.

Other common names: Water oleander, water willow.

Decodon: From the Greek *deca*, "ten", and *odous*, "tooth", from the toothed summit of the calyx.

Verticillatus: Meaning "whorled" from the whorled arrangement of the leaves.

Loosestrife family: *Lythraceae*

    This perennial herb, somewhat shrubby, ranges from Florida to Louisiana and north to Maine, New Hampshire, southern Ontario, and Iowa. It is one of the rarest members of the Iowa flora, having been found in Allamakee County on the Paleozoic Plateau recently and in Scott County in 1890.

    The stem is smooth or finely downy and often is corky near the base. It may achieve a height of nearly 6 feet. It nearly always grows at the edges of pools or streams or in shallow standing water. The leaves are opposite or whorled, tapered toward both ends, up to 8 inches long and 2 inches wide.

    The short-stalked flowers are clustered in the axils of the upper leaves. These magenta flowers have five petals which are up to ½ inch long, and 10 stamens, half of which are short. The calyx has five to seven erect teeth, hence its species' name. The flowering time for this species is July into August. The capsule is globose, with three to five locules.

    The arching branches root at the tips as they come in contact with moist soil and these start new plants. The plant spreads rapidly in a favorable habitat.

    This plant is on the northern edge of its range in northern Iowa. Its scarcity may provide a challenge to those interested in the Iowa's native flora to find new sites for this species.

Water horehound: *Lycopus americanus* Muhl.

Other common names: American bugleweed, bugleweed.

Lycopus: From Greek *lycos,* "a wolf", and *pous,* "foot", from the fancied likeness in the leaves.

Americanus: Meaning "American".

Mint family: *Lamiaceae (Labiatae)*

Water horehound occurs widely in North America—from Newfoundland to British Columbia and south to Florida, Alabama, Mississippi, New Mexico, and California. In Iowa, it is rare on the Paleozoic Plateau, frequent to common in the remainder of the state. It is in flower in July and continues into September.

This is a slender, erect, perennial mint, which may achieve a height of 3 feet. The stems are square in cross section and glabrous. Stolons lead from each plant and are important in vegetative reproduction. The lower stem leaves are incised or pinnatifid—the upper ones are lanceolate and sinuate to sharply toothed on the margins and all have petioles.

The petals of the flowers scarcely extend beyond the teeth of the calyx. The calyx teeth have awl-shaped tips. Although this is a mint, it does not have the minty odor.

Water horehound is easily confused with *L. virginicus* which has blunt-triangular calyx lobes, and with *L. asper,* which has sessile lower and median leaves. There are four species of *Lycopus* in Iowa, differing principally by the shape and lobing of the leaves.

The word "bugle" as used in one of the common names, is not the musical instrument but comes from a medieval Latin word which meant a kind of pin that ladies wore in their hair.

Most members of this genus have crisp tubers which are considered edible. *L. uniflorus* and *L. amplectens* are mentioned specifically, but tubers of all members of the genus are considered edible, varying only in flavor. Some are said to possess a muddy flavor, others a radish-like taste. They are better boiled in salted water or pickled. Apparently *L. americanus* lacks tubers.

The horehounds are important and consistent members of the Iowa wetland flora, and common enough that a visit to most marshes or sedge meadows will yield a successful search and you will have one more wetland acquaintance.

Marsh skullcap: *Scutellaria galericulata* L.

Other common names: Common skullcap, European skullcap, hooded skullcap.

Scutellaria: From *scutella,* "a dish", referring to the appendage on the fruiting calyx.

Galericulata: From the Latin *galer,* "a cap", referring to the shield-like crest or cap on the calyx.

Mint family: *Lamiaceae (Labiatae)*

Marsh skullcap is widespread in North America, occurring from Newfoundland to Alaska and south to New England, Delaware, West Virginia, Ohio, Indiana, Missouri, New Mexico, and California. It is also found in Europe and Asia. In Iowa, this rhizomatous herb is common in the lakes area of the northwest, infrequent to rare elsewhere. It inhabits the edges of lakes, sedge meadows, and wet prairies, blooms from late June into August.

This perennial has slender creeping rhizomes and underground thickened stolons. The stem is erect, normally unbranched, reaching a height of 3 feet, normally less. The angles of the square stem have recurved hairs. The stem is often procumbent and may root at the nodes. The leaves are minutely pubescent, up to 5 inches long and with stout petioles.

The corolla is blue-violet with a whitish throat which contains hairs. Flowers are solitary and arise from the axils of leaves and may achieve an overall length of an inch. Two flowers are formed per node in the upper axils. These petals arch and are composed of an upper lip and conspicuous protruding lower lip. The calyx is two-lipped, has a shield-like crest on the upper side, is strigose and covered with sessile glands.

Six species of skullcaps exist in Iowa, with the present species and mad dog skullcap, *S. lateriflora,* the most common. The others occur in prairies or dry woodlands. Mad dog skullcap was used by early pioneers to treat chorea, fits, convulsions, delirium tremens, and other nervous ills. It was said to have tonic and antispasmodic properties and was listed by herbalists. Marsh skullcap was used to prepare a decoction for use as a heart remedy.

Water smartweed: *Polygonum amphibium* L.

Other common names: Ground willow, heart's-ease, redshanks, showy smartweed, water dock, water persicaria.

Polygonum: The name from *poly*, "many", and *gonu*, "knee" or "joint", from the thickened joints of the plants.

Amphibium: Meaning "amphibious" from its occurrence in shallow water or on wet ground.

Buckwheat family: *Polygonaceae*

Water smartweed is found from Newfoundland to Alaska and south to Iowa, Nebraska, Ohio, and Colorado. In Iowa, it occurs at the edges of marshes, in shallow standing water, and wet roadside ditches. It is common in central Iowa and the lakes area of the northwest part of the Des Moines Lobe, less common in the remainder of the state. It is in bloom in July through September.

The species may occur with leaves floating in standing water, or sprawling on muddy banks. The plant can reach a height of over 2 feet, with oblong leaves up to 4 inches long, and petioles up to 4 inches. The leaves are narrowed at the base. The sheaths at the leaf bases are longer than the distance between the joints, so the stem is nearly hidden.

The inflorescence is pink or red, held erect on the stem, and the head of flowers may be 2 inches long. When found in extensive beds, it adds to the beauty of the marsh. Flowers are in compact, erect, flame-shaped clusters at the tips of stems. The calyx is rose-red and a large stand of this species has a pinkish cast from a distance.

Water smartweed provides food and shelter for a variety of invertebrates and the roots serve as an efficient soil anchor. Plants of this species may form a large pure stand. Seeds are important as a food for waterfowl, with at least 15 species benefitting. Often smartweed undergoes great growth when the water level is lowered in late summer for waterfowl management. Reproduction is by seed or rootstock.

Smartweed is a highly variable species and forms various varieties and ecological forms throughout its range in North America and Europe.

The Meskwaki have used it as an emetic for poisons. For the Flambeau Ojibwa, it was a source of tea for treatment of stomach aches. They also dried the flowers for use as an ingredient in hunting medicine to attract deer. The Forest Potawatomi used it to treat stomach disorders. Early pioneers used the root as a blood purifier. This and other smartweeds have been used in Appalachia as diuretics and in Europe as a hemostatic drug to control internal bleeding.

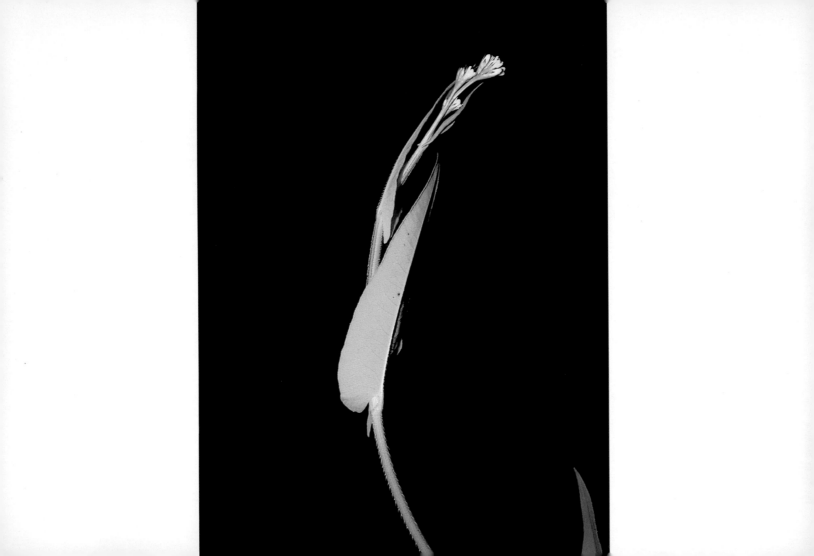

Tear thumb: *Polygonum sagittatum* L.

Other common names: Arrow-leaved tear thumb, arrow-vine, scratch-grass, tear-grass.

Polygonum: From *poly,* "many", and *gonu,* "knee", or "joint" from the thickened nodes.

Sagitattum: From *sagittate,* meaning "arrow-shaped".

Buckwheat family: *Polygonaceae*

Tear thumb is found from Florida to Texas and north to Newfoundland, Quebec, and Ontario. In Iowa, it is common in the northeast quarter, infrequent in the remainder of the state. It is in bloom in late June to September.

This weak, loosely branching plant is supported by other vegetation. It has a four-angled stem which often branches. These angles are equipped with sharp, backward-pointing barbs. The leaves are oblong to lanceolate, sagittate, 1 to 4 inches long and up to an inch wide.

The flowers are pinkish or white and occur in heads. The achene is sharply three-sided, shiny, and about 1/10 inch long.

Its habitat is sedge meadows or on the edges of marshes in full sun. The sharp barbs and arrowhead-shaped leaves make it easily recognizable. One is immediately aware of its presence when walking through a population of tear thumb. This is a plant which requires effort to like.

Tear thumb provides effective cover for a variety of wildlife because the barbs, late in the year, discourage predators and humans from visiting. It often occurs in pure stands, especially in wet sandy areas.

White vervain: *Verbena urticifolia* L.

Other common names: Nettle-leaved vervain.

Verbena: The Latin name for a sacred herb, but the relationship to this species is now obscure.

Urticifolia: Meaning "with leaves like Urtica", because of the resemblance of the leaves with those of stinging nettle.

Vervain family: *Verbenaceae*

White vervain is found from Quebec and Maine to southern Ontario and South Dakota and south to northern Florida, Alabama, Louisiana, and Texas. In Iowa, it is frequent to common throughout the state. Iowa habitats are stream banks, alluvial woods, and moist depressions, but white vervain also may be found in moist disturbed areas. It is in flower in June and the fruits ripen in September.

The erect, perennial herb may reach a height of 5 feet and often branches from near the base. The stems are square in cross section and minutely hairy. The leaves are opposite, rounded at the base and decurrent, oblong to lanceolate, acuminate, up to 7 inches long and coarsely serrate, often doubly so. The veins on the lower surface of the leaves are adorned with stiff hairs. The leaves bear a resemblance to those of stinging nettle, hence one of its common names. The flowers are about 1/10 inch across and occur in numerous interrupted spikes.

There is a substantial underground system which helps this species withstand unfavorable conditions, but it is not adapted to withstand drought or frequent burning. It spreads principally by seed.

The flowers are normally white but occasionally may be a pale blue.

There are about 30 species in this genus in North America. Among them, some are sufficiently attractive to be grown as ornamentals; others are serious weedy pests. The dead stalks persist upright throughout the winter and thus provide food for some birds.

In Iowa, there are six species of vervains, plus a number of hybrids. They range from prostrate, creeping weeds and marsh dwellers to those which persist best in dry, overgrazed pastures. The white vervain is known to hybridize with *V. hastata*. White vervain is easily recognized by its interrupted spikes and white flowers.

Purple loosestrife: *Lythrum salicaria* L.

Other common names: Bouquet violet, long purples, red sally, spiked loosestrife.

Lythrum: From *Lytron,* a name used by Dioscorides for this species.

Salicaria: An old generic name meaning "like a willow".

Loosestrife family: *Lythraceae*

Purple loosestrife is found from Newfoundland and Quebec to Minnesota and south to Virginia, Ohio, Indiana, and Missouri. It is found in scattered locations throughout Iowa and is becoming more widespread and common each year. It inhabits moist banks of wetlands, shallow or deep marshes, river banks, wet roadsides and seems to do best where disturbance has occurred. It is in bloom from June into September.

This stout, perennial herb possesses a squarish stem with opposite or occasionally whorled leaves with cordate bases. The leaf margins are smooth, the leaves without petioles and may clasp the stem. The plant may achieve a height of over 6 feet.

The flowers are an attractive magenta and occur in a dense spike which may be a foot in length. Individual flowers have four to six petals. Darwin studied the flowers of this species and found among the individual plants three forms of flowers, based on the length of the style and the stamens. This prevents self-pollination and made more likely a good seed-set from the activities of bees.

This species has been known from northeastern United States and eastern Canada since the early 1800s. It did not become a troublesome weed until the 1930s, when it became aggressive in floodplain pastures of the St. Lawrence River in Quebec. It has since spread to the glaciated areas of eastern and northern United States. Purple loosestrife has the ability to become established in a wetland, and out-compete native species. It forms large quantities of seeds and occupies a wide array of habitats and thus has the potential of upsetting any balance in the wetland.

In Iowa, it has been known from Little Storm Lake, Buena Vista County, for many years. Now it is spreading to surrounding wetlands, dredge ditches, and streams. It has been documented as occurring in perhaps 10 counties, although no systematic search has been made. The loosestrife often spreads from a homeowner's garden where it has long been planted as an attractive addition and as a "bee plant" for honey producers.

Although plants of this genus are not known for their medicinal value, purple loosestrife was mentioned by Dioscorides in the first century, when he recommended it for stanching the flow of blood, as an astringent, and as a treatment for dysentery. It has no appreciable value as a wildlife plant, but those species it replaces often are utilized by many species of wildlife.

Sweet flag: *Acorus calamus* L.

Other common names: Beewort, bitter pepper root, calamus, flagroot, myrtle grass, myrtle root, pine root, sea sedge, sweet case, sweet cinnamon, sweet grass, sweet myrtle, sweet sedge, sweet rush.

Acorus: An ancient name, of Latin origin, for an aromatic plant.

Calamus: An ancient name for a reed.

Arum family: *Araceae*

Sweet flag is found from Prince Edward Island west to Montana and Oregon and south to Florida and Texas. It is found throughout our state, but is most common in the northcentral and rare in the western and extreme northeast parts. It grows in marshes, edges of ponds, and in hillside seeps or wet roadsides. It is nearly restricted to water-logged soils, but is occasionally found in soils only slightly wet. Flowers from May through July.

This species grows erect and reed-like to as much as 6 feet, but 2 to 4 feet is more common. The long narrow leaves are sword-shaped, usually less than an inch wide. Each leaf has a stiff midrib. The leaves tend to grow in pairs, one sheathing the other at the base. The aromatic perennial rootstock is long and branching with coarse secondary roots.

Inconspicuous flowers are borne on a small club-like spadix which extends upward at an angle from the erect flowering stem. This flowering stalk (scape) is triangular in cross section. Above the spadix the scape becomes more leafy—a modified spathe. The flower-bearing spadix is usually 2 to 3 inches long, and less than a half-inch in diameter. The pattern of tiny greenish yellow diamond shapes is made by the numerous flowers.

The fruit is in the form of small berries. Few seeds are produced by the plant, and few of those produce new plants. New plants arise mostly from the spreading root system.

The Meskwaki used the aromatic roots as a physic. They also combined it with other "medicines" as a treatment for burns. The Menomini considered the root to be a cure for stomach cramps. A tea of the root was used to treat coughs and tuberculosis. Pioneers used it to treat colic, dyspepsia, and typhoid fever. Some chewed pieces of the dried root to clear the throat. Candied root was a popular pioneer confection. The root was boiled continuously for a day or more. It was then cut into small pieces before boiling again for a few minutes in a thick maple or sugar syrup.

The inner parts of tender young shoots of sweet flag have been used to make a tasty spring salad. Reports indicate that the early Pennsylvania Dutch used the root to flavor pickles. Powdered sweet flag roots have been used to make sachets and in production of perfume.

Calamus, a town in eastern Iowa, was named for the great numbers of calamus, or sweet flag, plants once found in that locality before soils were drained for farming.

This is the only species of this genus found growing naturally in the United States. An Asiatic species with yellow and green striped leaves is sometimes used in landscape plantings.

Yellow nut grass: *Cyperus esculentus* L.

Other common names: Amande de terre, chufa, flatsedge, galingale, ground almond, nut grass, nut rush, sweet rush.

Cyperus: From *Cypeiros*, the ancient Greek name.

Esculentus: Meaning "eatable" or "edible".

Sedge family: *Cyperaceae*

Yellow nut grass is a plant of ditches, pond margins, and soil that stays saturated for long periods of time. It is widespread in North America, growing from Florida and Mexico north to Canada and is also found in tropical America, Europe, and Asia. It is frequently encountered in Iowa, particularly in the lakes area and in the southern part of the state. Its inconspicuous flowers appear in summer and persist into autumn.

This perennial plant may achieve a height of nearly 3 feet, usually less. The stem is acutely angled and triangular in cross section. The stem leaves are narrow and short. The three to ten bracts at the base of the flower cluster are wider and usually considerably longer than the flower cluster.

The flower cluster is a broadly cylindrical to nearly round, yellowish to golden brown umbel, composed of several strongly flattened spikelets. Fruits are small nutlets, less than ⅒ inch in length, triangular-shaped, and yellowish.

Yellow nut grass has slender, underground stolons which terminate in rounded tubers ⅕ to ⅖ inches in diameter. These are often separated from the parent plant, each growing into a new plant. This is the main mode of reproduction of this species. It may invade low, wet cultivated fields and become a nuisance.

Both seeds and tubers are sought by wildlife. The tubers are important to waterfowl in mudflats that are covered by water in late fall and winter. This is a most important waterfowl food in the central flyway and can be cultivated for this purpose. The tubers are gathered and planted just below the surface of the ground in an area that will remain flooded until early summer. They are palatable for humans and can be taken raw, boiled, candied, dried, ground into flour, as a beverage, and as a coffee substitute. A variety of this species has been introduced into the United States to be cultivated as a source of tubers. This is a large genus, mainly tropical, and many species are difficult to separate.

This species has been used for food in North Africa, Egypt, and Ethiopia for more than a 1,000 years and is found in Egyptian tombs more that 2,000 years old. It has been cultivated in the southern states in this country, but the cultivated strain does not grow well in the northern states. It has been reported as having been grown in all of Germany and also Hungary in the eighteenth century as a substitute for coffee.

Pendant bulrush: *Scirpus pendulus* Muhl. (Formerly *S. lineatus*)

Other common names: Nodding bulrush, reddish bulrush, slender bulrush.

Scirpus: From the Latin name for the bulrush.

Pendulus: Meaning "nodding" from the habit of the plant.

Sedge family: *Cyperaceae*

This slender bulrush is found from Maine to Iowa and south to Virginia, Alabama, Mississippi, Arkansas, Oklahoma, and eastern Texas. In Iowa, it is frequently encountered in the north-central and southeast portions of the state, rare in the northeast and apparently does not occur in the western part. It can inhabit a variety of habitats but is by far most common in wet roadside ditches. It begins to flower in June and sets seeds in July. In August the seedhead shatters and the plant becomes inconspicuous. At the time of early development, the spikelets are light brown and become reddish as they mature—hence the origin of one of its common names.

The culms of pendant bulrush are strongly ascending and may reach a height of over 5 feet, but normally closer to 3 feet. It has a terminal and usually one or two axillary umbels. These often droop and the culm bends toward the ground. The leaves are pale green, firm, and up to ⅓ inch wide. There are five to ten leaves with long internodes. The umbel is pale brown with pale green keels on the scales. The achene is long-beaked, obscurely three-angled, and brown or purple-brown. The plants grow singly from a slender rhizome, but in a loose colony that may number in the hundreds.

This is one of our most attractive bulrushes, but one which blends into the landscape and is easily missed. Once you "develop an eye for it", you will be able to spot it in the ditches with ease.

The bulrush forms copious amounts of seeds and, when in proper habitat, these seeds have been an important source of food for waterfowl. Some species of *Scirpus* are hard to separate from closely related species. The pendent bulrush is easily identified and a good place to start in identifying bulrushes. An added bonus—since it grows frequently in roadside ditches, you won't have far to walk or drive to find it.

Bog twayblade: *Liparis loeselii* (L.) L. C. Rich.

Other common names: Fen orchid, Green twayblade, Loesel's bog orchid, Loesel's twayblade, Yellow twayblade.

Liparis: Named from the Greek *liparos*, "fat" or "shining" from the smooth and lustrous leaves.

Loeselii: Named for Richard Loesel, 1607–1655.

Orchid family: *Orchidaceae*

Bog twayblade is widespread in North America, found from the Gaspé Peninsula to Saskatchewan and south to New England, Ohio, Indiana, Missouri, and North Dakota. In Iowa, it is one of our rare plants, found mainly in fens in northern and northeastern Iowa, with one record from Guthrie County. Though widespread, it shows a narrow ecological tolerance. For example, it is known from a single site in Missouri even though similar habitats have been searched without success. It is apparently hanging on there as a glacial relict. In Iowa, habitats that are seemingly suitable are not uncommon, but most do not have the species. Perhaps the seeds have not managed to find suitable substrate at these sites. This species flowers in late June and July.

Bog twayblade is easy to pick out on the landscape, with its yellow, strongly keeled pair of leaves. These leaves are variable in length, from around 2½ to over 5 inches. The flowering scape, which arises from between the leaves may achieve a height of 12 inches, but is normally much shorter. Those in full sun seem to be smaller than those that grow in shade. As few as two or as many as 25 flowers may occur on the stalk, each about ⅓ inch wide, yellowish green on ascending pedicels with a concave lip about as long as the flower is wide.

The purple twayblade (*Liparis liliifolia*), the other twayblade in Iowa, is a woodland species and is much more common.

The orchid family is large and represented in Iowa by 31 species in 12 genera and include some of our rarest plants. Most are showy and beautiful; those most showy have been at risk of being collected or dug for much of this century. Many orchids require special fungi in the soil to persist. For this reason, transplanting them almost always fails.

Seedbox: *Ludwigia alternifolia* L.

Other common names: Bushy seedbox, false loosestrife, rattle-box, smooth seedbox.

Ludwigia: Named in honor of Christian Gottlieb Ludwig, professor of botany at Leipzig in the late 1700s.

Alternifolia: This word refers to the arrangement of leaves along the stem.

Evening primrose family: *Onagraceae*

Seedbox is found from east Texas northeast to Massachusetts, New York, southern Ontario, Michigan, Illinois, Iowa, and Kansas. In Iowa, which is near the western edge of the species' range, it is of infrequent occurrence in the southeast and south-central parts of the state. Its habitat ranges from the edges of marshes to moist sand, but the plant is occasionally found in wet roadside ditches and in seepage areas. It is an erect perennial, although it often is prostrate and forms roots at the nodes. Its blooming period is late June into August.

Seedbox may achieve a height of nearly 3 feet, usually less. The leaves, arranged alternately along the stem, are lanceolate, 1 to 3 inches long, and normally less than ½ inch wide. The petiole of the leaf is less then ¼ inch long. The flowers, on short stalks, have yellow petals which are up to about ⅓ inch long, and about equal to the calyx-lobes. The flowers are about ¾ inch broad.

The capsule is four-sided but may appear sub-globose to nearly cube-like and rounded at the base, about ¼ inch across, and wing-angled. Inside are numerous tiny seeds which become detached and rattle inside when the capsule is shaken—hence one of the common names. There is an opening—a pore or slit—in the top of the capsule for dispersal of the seeds.

There are four species of *Ludwigia* in Iowa; all are denizens of marshes and grow in shallow standing water or on mud banks. One, the water primrose, *L. peploides,* also known as *Jussiaea repens,* is extremely rare, being known only from Fremont, Louisa, and Lucas counties. It grows in water and has large yellow flowers. Water purslane, *L. palustris,* is a rare plant and only found in the eastern portion of Iowa. False loosestrife, *L. polycarpa,* is found throughout Iowa, except in the west-central part.

Cardinal flower: *Lobelia cardinalis* L.

Other common names: Red lobelia.

Lobelia: In honor of the sixteenth-century Flemish herbalist Matthias de l'Obel.

Cardinalis: From Latin meaning "of a cardinal", for the brilliant color of the flower and shape of the flower which bears some resemblance to the cardinal's miter or cap.

Bluebell family: *Campanulaceae* (Sometimes placed in the *Lobeliaceae*)

Cardinal flower is found from New Brunswick to Quebec and south to Michigan, Wisconsin, Minnesota, Florida, and Texas. In Iowa, it is found mainly in the eastern half of the state. Its habitat is principally moist alluvial woodlands; in bloom from late July through September.

This species has an erect, leafy stem, usually without branches, and grows to around 4 feet high. Numerous lance-shaped leaves are arranged alternately along the smooth stem. These leaves grow to 6 inches long on the lower stem, seldom more than 2 inches on the upper stem. They are usually three or four times longer than wide. Lower leaves have short petioles; upper leaves are sessile. A basal rosette of leaves is typical. The leaves are dark green with finely toothed margins. The plant parts contain a milky juice which is considered poisonous—or at least toxic to some degree.

The coarsely fibrous perennial root system is extensive. It develops slender offshoots from which new plants arise.

Showy flowers add a flash of brilliant crimson to moist woodlands and wooded wetlands in late summer and early autumn. Cardinal flower is one of the most striking of all flowers found in Iowa's wetlands. Numerous flowers crowd the top of the stem to form a dense terminal spike. Lower flowers may appear on short stalks in the axils of upper leaves. Individual flowers, about an inch long have two lips divided nearly to the base. The upper lip has two pointed lobes which flare upward. The lower lip has three pointed lobes which curve downward. A bundle of five long stamens protrude from the center of the flower. A "beard" or brush at the end of the stamens is a glistening white—a striking feature when the flower is given close examination. The split lower lip with descending lobes provides an unstable landing pad for the larger bees so the smaller species are more important for pollination. Hummingbirds also assist in pollination.

This species was used in early medicine, probably more or less interchangeable with other species in the genus. Early reports tell of use to treat syphilis and internal parasites. The juice of the plant is poisonous—similar to nicotine.

The Meskwaki crushed the entire plant for a ceremonial "tobacco". It was not for smoking, but to throw to the winds to ward off an approaching storm. It was also scattered over a grave as a final ceremonial rite. The roots were also used in preparation of a love charm.

Barnyard grass: *Echinochloa crusgalli* (L.) Beauv.

Other common names: Barn grass, cockspur grass, common wild millet, loose panic grass, water grass, wild millet.

Echinochloa: The name is derived from Greek *echinos*, "sea urchin", and *chloa*, "grass", referring to the bristling awns.

Crusgalli: Meaning "cockspur".

Grass family: *Poaceae (Gramineae)*

Barnyard grass has been introduced from the old world and has become a nearly cosmopolitan weed. It grows in a variety of moist, usually disturbed habitats, from roadsides and edges of cultivated fields to edges of marshes and prairie potholes. In Iowa, it undoubtedly occurs in every county. Its flowering time is July and August.

This grass may grow to 5 feet in height with leaves up to 18 inches long and an inch wide. The stems are erect or reclining at the base. The leaves have open sheaths, with a ligule at the junction of the leaf and stem. It often forms dense stands in wet ditches and these stands become obvious in late summer.

The inflorescence consists of single-flowered spikelets, with the entire inflorescence covered with hairs which have swollen bases, and are terminated by a long bristle. The inflorescence may achieve a length of 10 inches with lower branches more widely separated than the upper ones. The inflorescence has a purplish cast, making it distinctive.

The large seeds of this and related species are important food for ducks and other wild birds. These species are often used by marsh managers for sowing, along with seeds of smartweeds (*Polygonum* sp.) in mudflats which can later be flooded. This provides migrating waterfowl with the best of all possible worlds. Native Americans in Utah ground the seeds into flour for making bread or mush.

There are two additional species of barnyard grass in Iowa: *E. muricata,* also widespread in the state, and *E. walteri,* which grows occasionally in the southeast part. All have been introduced and all are of value as wildlife food plants.

Seeds of barnyard grass are commonly found as impurities in commercial seeds. It was thus planted along with the crop seed and greatly increased its range. This grass is commonly considered to be a weedy species by most of the stockmen of the Great Plains.

Acuminate rush: *Juncus acuminatus* Michx.
Dudley's rush: *Juncus dudleyi* Wieg. (Shown in photo)

Other common names for the acuminate rush: Autumn rush, sharptip rush, tapertip rush.

Other common names for Dudley's rush: Alkaline rush, yellow rush.

Juncus: The classic name for the genus.

Acuminatus: Named for the characteristic of the sepals to taper toward the tip.

Dudleyi: Named for its discoverer, William Dudley, botanist, 1849-1911.

Rush family: *Juncaceae*

Acuminate rush is found throughout Iowa, but is most frequent in the southeast part and becomes rare in the western portion of the state. Its range includes much of the continental United States except for southern California, Florida, and the arid parts of the west. Its preferred habitat is moist or wet sandy prairies and sandy vernal pools. This perennial has a very long flowering time, beginning in June and extending into late August.

Dudley's rush is frequent to common throughout most of the state. Its range is much like the preceding species but includes more of the northwest. Its preferred habitats are wet prairies, shorelines, and wet sand.

Rushes are grass-like tufted herbs, normally perennial and grow in wet, often sandy soil. They are survivors, being able to withstand prolonged periods of inundation and a considerable amount of disturbance.

The cylindrical leaves have auriculate bases, are hollow, and are septate (bear conspicuous cross partitions). The stem is smooth, erect, up to 3 feet in height and bears one to three leaves. The stems are cespitose from inconspicuous root stocks.

The inflorescence of the acuminate rush consists of an open panicle with 5–50 hemispherical heads, each with eight or more flowers. At maturity, the capsules are narrowly ovoid, pale brown, about ⅛ inch long and contain numerous tiny seeds.

The inflorescence of Dudley's rush has the solitary flowers clustered at the tips of erect branches.

When young, rushes provide food for a variety of wildlife which feed on the tubers. In sufficient quantity, rushes act as soil-binders. They seldom grow in dense stands, but usually occur as scattered individuals or small populations throughout the site.

There are 14 species of *Juncus* in Iowa, ranging from those of mesic woodlands to those which require shallow water or saturated soils. They reproduce by seed or can spread vegetatively from the roots. Once established, rushes often expand and become an integral part of the wetland.

Wood nettle: *Laportea canadensis* (L.) Wedd.

Other common names: Lowland nettle.

Laportea: Named for Francois L. de Laporte, Count of Castelnau.

Canadensis: Meaning "of Canada".

Nettle family: *Urticaceae*

Wood nettle is common throughout the eastern and midwestern United States on moist, wooded, floodplains. It is frequent to common throughout Iowa, likely occurring in every county. Its inconspicuous, greenish flowers appear in mid-summer through September. Plants may achieve a height of 3 feet and grow well in the shade of trees along streams.

The leaves, alternately arranged along the stem, are ovate, coarsely serrate, slender-tipped, 3 to 6 inches long and have long petioles with axillary stipules. The stem, when broken, exudes a watery sap. The plant is a perennial and often forms large colonies by vegetative reproduction.

The female flowers occur in loose, elongate, spreading branched cymes from the upper axils. Male flowers are in cymes in the axils of lower leaves.

The plant is covered with stinging hairs which are hollow with a jagged point and a bulb at the base. The fine tip can penetrate the skin and inject a bit of formic acid through the action similar to that of a hypodermic needle. This acid causes intense itching of short duration. The sting can be lessened by rubbing it with the juice of jewelweed. The sting of wood nettle is more intense than that of stinging nettle.

The nettle family is large and primarily of tropical occurrence. Most have stinging hairs, some produce a strong substance which can be dangerous—very different from the nuisance itching we feel from the members which grow in Iowa.

Relatives of wood nettle have furnished useful products. The stinging nettle, *Urtica dioica,* has been grown for fiber for tents and clothing. A yellow dye could be obtained from its roots. Stinging nettle has also been used as food because the preparation destroys the stinging quality. The plants were boiled in a kettle, as in the preparation of spinach, then used as greens. Some say it is superior to spinach in taste.

The Pillager Ojibwa used the root of wood nettle for its diuretic qualities and considered it a good medicine for urinary ailments. It was thought to be a diuretic, an astringent, and a tonic was derived from the roots and leaves. Seeds and flowers were given with wine as treatment for the ague. Ammonia has been distilled in notable amounts from this species.

Torrey's rush: *Juncus torreyi* Cov.

Other common names: Big-head rush, pond rush.

Juncus: The classical name for the genus.

Torreyi: Named for John Torrey, botanist who lived 1796–1873.

Rush family: *Juncaceae*

Torrey's rush occurs from New York to Washington and Saskatchewan and south to Maryland, Virginia, Alabama, Texas, and California. In Iowa, it is frequent in the western half, infrequent in the eastern half of the state. It grows best in wet, sandy soil.

Rushes are grass-like tufted herbs, normally perennial, and usually grow in wet soil. This species may achieve a height of over 3 feet, normally less than 2 feet. It has an erect, smooth, unbranched stem. The leaves are elongated, terete (round in cross section), and hollow. They are also auricled, about ⅒ inch thick, and diverge abruptly from the stem.

The flowers are borne in spherical, terminal heads which are about ½ inch in diameter, with up to 20 heads per stem, each with 30–80 flowers. There are three sepals, three petals, and six stamens. The inflorescence is overtopped by an involucral leaf. The flowering time is long—extending from July into October.

The fruit is an elongate capsule as long or longer than the sepals and petals. There are numerous small seeds in the capsule. Reproduction is by seed or it can spread vegetatively. The stem arises from tubers on a slender, creeping, horizontal rootstock. This species, along with two close relatives, *Juncus acuminatus* and *Juncus nodosus,* are found with inflorescences changed into horn-like galls, a result of insect activity.

In sufficient quantity, this species acts as a soil binder. Its tubers are eaten by muskrats and the foliage provides cover for marsh wildlife.

There are 14 species of *Juncus* in Iowa, ranging from those in upland woods to those which grow in shallow water. Torrey's rush is one of the most common in Iowa and in the United States.

Mint: *Mentha arvensis* L.

Other common names: Marsh perfume, sweet mint.

Mentha: Minthe of Theophrastus, from a nymph of that name said to have been changed by Proserpine into mint.

Arvensis: Meaning "of cultivated ground", or "of fields".

Mint family: *Lamiaceae (Labiatae)*

Mint is a widespread species—growing from Labrador to Washington and south to New England, Virginia, Kentucky, Nebraska, and California. It is circumboreal and originally naturalized from Europe. In Iowa, it is rare in the northwest, but frequent to common elsewhere. It is found at the edges of marshes, in sedge meadows, and occasionally in shallow water. It is in flower in July and August.

This herbaceous perennial may achieve a height of 3 feet, generally less, in a variety of wet habitats. The leaves are opposite, on short stalks, with wedge-shaped bases and pointed tips. The margins are toothed to below the middle of the pubescent leaves.

The flowers occur in dense, globose clusters in the axils of the upper leaves. Individual flowers are small, up to ¼ inch long, with four pink to pale purple petals. The fruit is a cluster of four brown nutlets which form large clusters that persist on the stem into winter.

The foliage emits a strong mint fragrance when crushed and is obvious when one walks through a wetland habitat where this species grows.

Another plant in the genus, spearmint, *M. spicata,* has been collected a few times in the state from near dwellings where it escaped from a planting. Mint may be confused with horehound, *Lycopus americanus,* but the latter has white flowers and no fragrance to the crushed leaves.

The Potawatomi used the leaves as well as the tops of this plant to make a tea for curing or treating fevers. For the early settlers, the entire plant was used for its antispasmodic and antirheumatic properties as well as its bitter, pungent taste.

Blue vervain: *Verbena hastata* L.

Other common name: Simpler's joy.

Verbena: The Latin name for a sacred herb; the relationship to this species is now obscure.

Hastata: Meaning "halberd-shaped", because the material from which the species was described had basal leaves of this shape.

Vervain family: *Verbenaceae*

Blue vervain is a coarse perennial, found throughout the continental United States—from Nova Scotia to British Columbia and south to Florida, Tennessee, Missouri, Texas, and California. In Iowa, it is a common member of the flora throughout the state. Its favored habitats are edges of marshes, wet prairies, and along streams. It begins blooming in July and continues into September.

The erect plant grows in small colonies and up to 4 feet in height. The leaves are up to 6 inches long, stalked, tapering to the tip and with a rough surface. The stem branches above so there are up to a dozen or so flower spikes per plant.

The flowers are small and blue in upright cylindrical spikes. The leaves are opposite, lanceolate, and coarsely toothed. The stem is four-sided and somewhat rough to the touch.

The calyx is five-toothed, with one tooth generally shorter. The flower tube is tubular, often curved, with the outer edge divided into five sections. The flowers are sessile. The fruit is divided into four nutlets, each $\frac{1}{10}$ inch long.

Native Americans gathered the seeds of this species and those of a related species, hoary vervain *(Verbena stricta),* which they roasted and ground into a flour or meal. The Omaha prepared a tea from these two species' leaves. American Indians in California gathered seeds of blue vervain for use as meal.

Vervains in general are coarse, persistent plants that some people have classed as weeds. They have an extensive underground system which protects them from severe trampling and this also makes them effective as soil binders in eroded fields.

The seeds persist throughout the winter and serve as a source of nutrients for wildlife. Another vervain, the nettle-leaved vervain, *Verbena urticifolia,* is also found in wetland habitats; it has small white flowers and leaves which resemble those of nettles. These plants are often grown in flower gardens; they are reasonably easy to grow, do not require a great amount of care, and are tolerant of droughts.

Ditch stonecrop: *Penthorum sedoides* L.

Other common names: Virginia stonecrop.

Penthorum: The name from Greek *pente,* "five", and *horos,* "a mark", from the five-parted arrangement of the flowers.

Sedoides: Meaning "like Sedum", a plant in the *Crassulaceae* family where some taxonomists place ditch stonecrop. The flowers of the two taxa are similar.

Saxifrage family: *Saxifragaceae* (sometimes in its own family, *Penthoraceae*)

Ditch stonecrop is found from Ontario to Minnesota and south to Florida and Texas. There are three species of the genus occurring in eastern North America, Japan, and China. In Iowa, it is infrequent in the northwest portion of the state, common in the remainder. Its favored habitat is a variety of low, wet soils in marshes, shores of lakes and ponds, wet prairies and alluvium. It blooms in late summer and into October.

This is a perennial, stoloniferous plant which may achieve a height of 3 feet, but seldom more than 2 feet. The stems are often curved at the base and root at the nodes. The leaves are arranged alternately along the stem, are lanceolate, finely toothed, taper toward the base and the tip, and are about 4 inches long by 1½ inches wide.

The flowers are small and yellow, but the petals are normally absent. These flowers are crowded along the upper sides of branches at the top of the plant. The flowers have five yellowish-green sepals. The flowering structure gives the plant a flat-topped appearance.

The fruit is a cluster of five small pods united at their bases and consists of a five-angled, five-horned and five-locular capsule which contains many seeds. The capsule is small—about ⅛ inch across. The fruits turn reddish as they mature.

The Meskwaki used the seeds of this plant to make a cough syrup. Stonecrop was highly valued by the eclectic practitioners who used it for treating catarrh.

White turtlehead: *Chelone glabra* L.

Other common names: Balmony, bitter herb, codhead, fish mouth, shellflower, snakehead, snake mouth, turtlebloom, turtlehead.

Chelone: From Greek for "tortoise" since the flower resembles the head of a tortoise.

Glabra: From Latin meaning "smooth", referring to the lack of hairs or other texture on the leaves and stems.

Snapdragon family: *Scrophulariaceae*

White turtlehead is found throughout the state, but most frequently in the east and southeast along streams, in fens or seeps, and in bottomland woodlands. It is in bloom in August and September.

A single smooth squarish stem arises from a creeping perennial rootstock and grows to 3 feet tall. Short lateral branches may appear toward the top of the stem.

Smooth dark green leaves from 2 to 6½ inches long and on short winged petioles are paired opposite along the stem and branches. The leaves are long and narrow, with pointed tips. Veining is prominent and margins are sharply toothed. The shape of the leaves may be variable with this species. The leaves may also be slightly hairy, but this also varies.

The flowers, as the common name indicates, are shaped somewhat like the head of a turtle with its mouth open. The upper lip is broad and arching. The lower lip is three-lobed with the outer lobes larger than the middle one. This lower lip has a white to pale yellow beard. The color of the corolla is whitish to yellow-green, sometimes tinged with pink. The flowers are usually 1 inch to 1½ inches long.

The blooms usually crowd along a dense terminal spike. At times, a few additional flowers may occur in the axils of the upper leaves. Close examination shows five stamens (male flower parts) one of which is smaller than the other four and is sterile. When a bumblebee enters the flower and disappears inside after nectar, its movements and the resulting vibration of the flower give the appearance that the bee is being chewed up by the turtlehead blossom.

The fruit is an oval capsule about ½ inch long. Each of its two cells contains many small winged seeds.

This plant provided a favorite tonic and laxative for Native Americans despite its bitter taste. Pioneers used leaves of turtlehead as a tonic and as a treatment for jaundice, constipation, and internal parasites. Leaves were also made into an ointment to relieve itching and inflammations.

Varieties of this species are often available from dealers in wildflower seeds and plants.

Pink turtlehead, *C. obliqua,* is a much less common species with rose-purple flowers and now known from two sites in Iowa.

Sundew: *Drosera rotundifolia* L.

Other common names: Dailey dew, dew plant, eye bright, lust-wort, red rot, rossolis, round-leaved sundew, youthwort.

Drosera: from the Greek *droseros*, meaning "dewey", from the drops of clear glutinous fluid exuded from the glands on the leaves.

Rotundifolia: meaning "round-leaved" from the spherical nature of the leaves.

Sundew family: *Droseraceae*

Sundew is a perennial found in North America in peaty or moist acid soils from Greenland and Labrador to Alaska and south to Newfoundland, northern Florida, Illinois, Iowa, Montana, and California. About 90 species are scattered over the world. In Iowa, it is known only from the *Sphagnum* mat at Pilot Knob State Preserve. It blooms from July through August.

Leaves, in a rosette nearly flat on ground, are expanded at the terminal end to a round blade which bears on the upper surface sticky-tipped reddish hairs. These hairs secrete dew-like drops of a sticky fluid that traps and digests minute animal life. This is a method by which a bog plant obtains nitrogen.

The leaves wither in autumn, and a small winter bud-rosette is formed. The rosette unfolds its leaves and begins early growth the following spring.

The flowers are small, up to ⅛ inch long, and borne along a slender erect stem that may be 10 inches high and may bear as many as 25 flowers. Petals are white, and numerous seeds are found in a three-parted capsule.

The sticky hairs on the leaves trap and digest small insects. Adaptations such as this are necessary for bog plants to compensate for the lack of nitrogen in their habitats.

This interesting so-called predator plant has leaves that are richer in vitamin C than any other known plant.

Sundew is a classic plant, due to Darwin's studies and later reporting in his *Insectivorous Plants*. This plant and its habitat, probably in Iowa since the end of the Pleistocene, somehow escaped detection until 1954 when Grant and Thorne studied and described the bog at Pilot Knob.

Prairie cord grass: *Spartina pectinata* Link

Other common names: Cord grass, freshwater cord grass, marsh grass, slough grass, tall marsh grass, rip gut.

Spartina: From Greek *spartine,* "a cord", probably referring to the strong, tough leaves.

Pectinata: From Latin, meaning "comb-like", from the toothed edge of the leaf blades.

Grass family: *Poaceae (Gramineae)*

Prairie cord grass is widespread—from Newfoundland to Alberta and Washington and south to New England, North Carolina, Indiana, Illinois, Missouri, Texas, and New Mexico. In Iowa, it is frequent to common throughout the state, growing in low places, like wet prairies, along dredge ditches, wet roadside ditches, and other sunny, wet areas. It flowers from July into September.

This tall, warm-season perennial forms a dense sod in wet areas on the prairie, often crowding out all other species. Firm, airy stems, which are about ¼ inch thick at the base, grow 4 to 10 feet tall. It begins growth in April and is 2–3 feet high by June, standing well above big bluestem and switchgrass at that time. In favorable sites, it may reach 10 feet when mature.

The root system includes heavy, woody, multibranched, creeping rhizomes. The coarse rhizomes often form a dense mat close to the surface of wet soils but also may penetrate the soil to as deep as 10 feet. They are usually brown to purplish. Most propagation is by rhizome because viable seeds are seldom produced.

The light-green leaf blades, ranging from 12 to 30 inches long, and ¼ to over ½ inch wide, taper gradually to a whip-like point. They are flat when freshly cut but roll up when dry. A distinctive feature of the blade is its margin, which is so sharply toothed that it looks as if the leaf had spines. The margins are so sharp that the blades must be handled carefully to avoid being cut.

The flowers, as in all grasses, are inconspicuous because they lack showy petals. They exist as flattened spikelets in two rows along the rachis.

Prairie cord grass was often used by American Indians and pioneers because the blades were coarse and tough—ideal for thatched roofs before they added a final layer of sod. The sod provided a heavy material for sod-house construction. Pioneers covered haystacks and corncribs with cord grass because of its ability to shed water. One report from Minnesota indicates settlers used cord grass for fuel when wood was in short supply. A handful was twisted, doubled over and tied. An hour was needed to prepare fuel for a day.

Because of its coarse stems and rough-edged leaves, cord grass is not readily eaten by livestock—except in early spring. In hay, the stems and leaves intertwine, making it difficult to handle from the stack, often necessitating the use of a hay knife.

Prairie cord grass provides protection for wildlife, and muskrats eat the roots. Related species along the gulf coast furnish food for geese. It is suspected, probably without merit, as a cause of hay fever.

The mats of coarse, woody, thick, branching rhizomes that form the upper few inches of soil beneath stands of cord grass are good for soil conservation. So it is sometimes cultivated around ponds and artificial lakes.

River bulrush: *Scirpus fluviatilis* (Torr.) Gray

Other common names: River clubrush, three square.

Scirpus: The Latin name of the bulrush.

Fluviatilis: Meaning "of rivers".

Sedge family: *Cyperaceae*

River bulrush is found across southern Canada, south to New England, Delaware, Virginia, Pennsylvania, Ohio, Indiana, and west to California. In Iowa, it is found statewide, but is most common in the pothole region of the Des Moines Lobe. Dense colonies, often entirely vegetative, occur at the edges of marshes, in shallow water of stream backwaters, wet roadside ditches, and waterlogged soil along streams. It is in flower from July into September.

The stems of this coarse perennial are sharply triangular and may reach a height of 6 feet. The leaves are flat, pale-green and up to ¾ inch wide. The leaves continue up the stem to the inflorescence; the upper leaves and involucral bract exceed the compound umbel. The rays of the umbel number from 5 to 12, each terminating in several brown spikelets, ¾ inch to 1½ inches long. The seed is a brownish triangular achene which has six barbed bristles attached at the base.

River bulrush has a tough, brown, underground rhizome with thickened corm-like enlargements up to 2 inches long. It spreads principally by growth of rhizomes because the seeds are notoriously difficult to germinate.

The seeds are eaten by waterfowl and may provide the major source of food for ducks at times. The plant, particularly when young, is a favorite food of muskrats, which also use it in construction of their houses. It also provides cover for a variety of wetland animals.

This is a common and important wetland plant in the midwest. It varies widely from year to year in the number of culms which produce inflorescences and seeds, but is easily recognized by the sharply triangular leafy stem and robust habit. The sharp edges of the plant can cut through skin. It is closest in appearance to *S. paludosus,* which is shorter, has a flattened achene, and grows in calcareous habitats.

This and several other bulrushes have enlargements along the rootstock. These dried enlargements have been used by Native Americans for a variety of food uses. They are reputed to be thirst quenchers. When dried and ground, they can be a base for making bread. The roots, when boiled, provide a sweet syrup.

This is one of those plants that wetland enthusiasts must learn to recognize.

Wool-grass: *Scirpus cyperinus* (L.) Kunth

Other common names: Woolly bulrush, woolly sedge.

Scirpus: The Latin name of the bulrush.

Cyperinus: Meaning "like Cyperus".

Sedge family: *Cyperaceae*

The range of wool-grass is from Newfoundland to Saskatchewan south to North Carolina and Florida and west to Texas and Oklahoma. In Iowa, it is found commonly in sandy areas in the northeast and infrequently or rarely in the southern half of the state. It is most abundant on the Iowan Surface, where it often forms monodominant stands. The flowering time is July into September.

The overall height of the bluntly triangular stem is 5 feet and usually grows in a clump which has a fibrous root system. The stem leaves are up to 16 inches long, ¼ inch wide, with three to five leaves just below the inflorescence. The stem is sheathed except at the summit. The plant occurs in dense tussocks with many curving basal leaves.

The inconspicuous flowers are in the axils of the overlapping scales of the brownish spikelets, which occur in clusters at the ends of drooping branches. The entire flower cluster may be as much as a foot long. The fruit is a seed-like nutlet with long bristles attached at the base. These bristles give the spikelets a woolly appearance, hence the common name.

Wool-grass and other members of the genus serve to anchor soil and provide considerable habitat for wildlife. Some have been boiled and cooked with cornmeal or dried to make into a sweet flour.

The Forest Potawatomi used the soft, fruiting, wool-like tops as stuffing for making pillows.

There are some 150 species in this genus worldwide; 14 of these have been known to occur in Iowa, although four are extremely rare and one has not been seen in the state since 1878. Wool-grass is one of the most attractive of the bulrushes.

Jewelweed: *Impatiens capensis* Meerb.

Other common names: Balsam, celandine, impatience, kicking colt, orange snapweed, quick-in-the-hand, silver slipper, snapdragon, solentine, speckled jewels, touch-me-not, weather cock, yellow snapweed.

Impatiens: From Latin, for impatient, from the sudden bursting of the capsules when touched.

Capensis: From "of the Cape", wrongly thought by its author to have been introduced into European gardens from the Cape of Good Hope.

Touch-me-not family: *Balsaminaceae*

Jewelweed is found throughout the state in damp woodlands, alluvial woods, along streams, and in wooded edges of marshes. It is in bloom from July into early October.

These annual plants may grow to a height of around 5 feet. The branched stems are weak and watery. The color of the stem and foliage is pale green with a translucent appearance. The stem nodes are enlarged and the leaves are pale bluish green. The leaves, arranged alternately along the stem, are oval to egg-shaped and have coarsely toothed margins. They may achieve a length of 3½ inches, with a petiole about equal to the blade in length. Dew often accumulates in glistening droplets on the leaves, giving rise to the common name jewelweed.

The flowers are orange with dots of reddish brown. These flowers are up to 1¼ inch long, singly or in loose clusters. The flower has a curious shape—like a funnel partially closed at the larger end. The smaller end is a curved spur holding nectar. Bees may disappear into the flower as they search for nectar. A slender flower stalk curves from the leaf axil and attaches to the center of the funnel, suspending the flower like a pendant.

The fruit, a slender capsule perhaps an inch long, shrinks in drying. As it splits, seeds are scattered in all directions as if propelled by a small explosion. Often the splitting occurs when the fruit is touched or pinched. The seeds taste delicious—like butternuts—but may be hard to catch.

The Potawatomi applied the juice of the jewelweed to relieve the itch of poison ivy. Pioneers learned of this remedy and used it extensively. A pulp of leaves and stems provided treatment for other skin problems among the Omahas and others. The Blackfoot included roots in similar preparations. In pioneer folk medicine, the leaves were sometimes made into a general tonic. Fresh juice squeezed from the plant was rubbed on an aching forehead to ease the pain.

Even today, juice of the jewelweed is used to relieve the burning sensation of touching stinging nettle or wood nettle. This is handy since these plants often grow in the same habitat.

A second species, pale jewelweed (*Impatiens pallida*), similar except with yellow flowers, is found throughout the state and grows in slightly drier habitats.

Brook lobelia: *Lobelia kalmii* L.

Other common names: Kalm's lobelia.

Lobelia: Named in honor of the sixteenth-century Flemish herbalist Matthias de l'Obel.

Kalmii: Named for its discoverer, Pehr Kalm, 1715-1779.

Bluebell family: *Campanulaceae* (some taxonomists place it in the *Lobeliaceae*)

Brook lobelia is found from Newfoundland south to Nova Scotia, Maine, Ohio, Illinois, Iowa, South Dakota, and Colorado. The species is widespread in Canada and in the northern states; the southern margin of its range is in northern Iowa, where it is restricted to calcareous fens. It is in bloom from July into September.

This perennial herb grows to a height of 15 inches, normally less. The basal leaves are spatulate to ovate, petioled, and pubescent. Stem leaves are linear or lanceolate. The stem may be single or diffusely branched.

The inflorescence is a loose raceme, often one-sided. The irregular flower has a tube that is split on the upper side. It is two-lipped, the upper lip with two erect lobes, the lower with three spreading lobes. The corolla is blue with a white "eye" on the upper portion of the lower lip. The corolla is short—up to ¾ inch long. Two of the anthers are bearded at the top. The fruit is a two-locular, many-seeded capsule which opens at the top.

Brook lobelia is similar to *L. nuttallii*, an eastern counterpart of wet sand.

Some members of this genus are poisonous, and in the early days caused poisoning of cattle, sheep, goats, and people. These species possess a variety of poisonous alkaloids, 14 of which are found in Indian tobacco, *Lobelia inflata*. It is probable that brook lobelia has a similar array. These are pyridine alkaloids which are not much different from nicotine.

Tall coneflower: *Rudbeckia laciniata* L.

Other common names: Floodplain coneflower, floodplain sunflower, goldenglow, slashed-leaf coneflower.

Rudbeckia: Named for Olaf and Olaf (father and son) Rudbeck, predecessors of Linnaeus at Uppsala.

Laciniata: Meaning "slashed" or "torn", from the dissected character of the leaves.

Daisy family: *Asteraceae (Compositae)*

Tall coneflower is found throughout a considerable portion of North America—from western Quebec to Montana and south to Nova Scotia, New England, Florida, Texas, and Arizona. In Iowa, it is frequent to common throughout the state. Its habitat is rich, moist, shaded areas, such as floodplains. Its blooming time in Iowa is mid-August and September.

This is a coarse perennial which may achieve a height of over 6 feet in ideal growing conditions, but normally less. The stem is glabrous, unbranched and often glaucous. The leaves are alternately arranged along the stem, scabrous and the lower ones with petioles. The leaves are pinnate, with five to seven cut or three-lobed leaflets.

The flowering heads are showy and on long stalks. The outer petals are yellow and up to 2 inches long. These petals are reflexed, giving the shape of a cone, hence the common name. The achenes are flattened and ⅕ inch long.

There are four species in this genus in Iowa, including such familiar prairie species as black-eyed Susan, *R. hirta,* and fragrant coneflower, *R. subtomentosa.* Tall coneflower is characteristic of floodplains, where it is common but never forms a dominant cover.

A variety, *R. laciniata* var. *hortensia,* has been developed from native species for flower gardens. This variety has an increased number of ligules, resulting in double heads. It occasionally is found escaped from cultivation and persisting in the wild.

Tall coneflower is suspected of poisoning in swine where circumstantial evidence connected the species to convulsions resulting in death. However, feeding experiments with swine and sheep resulted in slight symptoms or none.

Often plants characteristic of floodplains have small or nonshowy flowers. Examples are wood nettles, stinging nettles, bedstraws, etc. Tall coneflower is a marvelous exception and provides a splash of color in late summer.

Sneezeweed: *Helenium autumnale* L.

Other common names: Staggerwort, swamp sunflower.

Helenium: From the Greek name for the plant, said by Linnaeus to be named after Helena (Helen of Troy), wife of King Menelaus of Sparta.

Autumnale: Meaning "of autumn" because of the time of its blooming period.

Sunflower family: *Asteraceae (Compositae)*

This lovely and interesting plant occurs from New England to Minnesota and south to New Jersey, North Carolina, Kentucky, and Missouri. It is frequent to common throughout Iowa where it is found in marshes, moist prairies, fens, and sedge meadows.

Sneezeweed may achieve a height of over 6 feet, normally closer to 4 feet. The stem is angled or winged and branches toward the top and is smooth or only slightly hairy. The leaves are alternate, coarsely dentate, may achieve a length of over six inches, a width of two inches, and have a petiole which bears wings which continue down the stem.

The flowers, yellow, and up to 2 inches wide, occur in conspicuous terminal heads on long peduncles. There are from 10 to 20 ray flowers, each with three conspicuous teeth at the outer end. The disc flowers are darker yellow and form spherical heads when mature. Flowering time is from August into October, with fruits becoming mature in late September and persisting into November.

This perennial grows from a fibrous, shallow root and can tolerate disturbance. It is thus sometimes found in heavily grazed wet pastures.

Powdered flower heads were used by Native Americans and early pioneers to induce sneezing. Leaves, stem, and roots all produce an acrid substance, but is most concentrated in the mature flowerheads. Sheep, cattle, and horses have all been poisoned by feeding on large quantities of flower heads. Symptoms are accelerated pulse, labored breathing, staggering (hence one common name), and extreme sensitiveness to noise or touch. If untreated, the condition can become fatal. Cows grazing on this plant may produce a bitter tasting milk.

A second species in this genus, Bitterweed (*Helenium amarum*) has been reported from Johnson County. There are 24 species in the genus, all from North America or Central America.

Sneezeweed is a common plant in Iowa, probably growing in every county. It is easily recognized, colorful, and a good one to add to your list. It would make a nice addition to your wildflower garden.

Pink turtlehead: *Chelone obliqua* L. var. *speciosa* Pennell and Wherry

Other common names: Red turtlehead, rose turtlehead, shell-flower, snakehead, turtlebloom, turtlehead.

Chelone: From Greek work for "tortoise" since the flower resembles the head of a tortoise.

Obliqua: Meaning "oblique", referring to the angle at which the lower lip of the corolla protrudes. *Speciosa* means "showy", because of the intense color of the petals.

Snapdragon family: *Scrophulariaceae*

Pink turtlehead is found in roughly the same habitat as white turtlehead, but perhaps slightly drier sites. It is of restricted distribution in the United States, growing from Indiana to southern Minnesota and south to Arkansas. In Iowa it is known to occur almost exclusively in the counties along the Mississippi River. It has been reported only twice in the last 30 years.

The plant is usually found in swampy wetlands and will grow well in shade or sun as long as the soil is rich. It also grows well from seed. Like the white turtlehead, it blooms late in the season, in late August and September.

Iowa plants may grow to over 6 feet in height. The leaves are opposite, thin, lanceolate, sharply serrate, about 5 inches long and over an inch wide. They have short petioles and are sharply pointed.

The bright pink flowers, up to 1½ inches long, are clustered at the tip of the stem. These resemble the head of a turtle, hence its common names. The upper lip is shallowly two-lobed and arched, the lower is three-lobed and with a pale yellow beard.

Each flower has a sterile stamen that is white and less than half as long as the fertile ones. Pollination is the result of visits by bees, particularly bumblebees. These are strong enough to force their way into the blossom in search of nectar and thus carry pollen from nearby plants. The fruit is an oval capsule about a half-inch long. Each of its two cells contains numerous small, winged seeds.

This is one of the state's rarest flowering plants and is listed as "endangered". Visits to marshes and oxbows in late summer and fall may be more exciting for plant lovers knowing this rare plant may be waiting to be discovered. The white turtlehead has been used medicinally by Native Americans and pioneers. It seems likely this species had similar uses, despite the lack of references in literature.

Red-rooted cyperus: *Cyperus erythrorhizos* Muhl.

Other common names: Flatsedge, galingale, sweetrush, umbrella sedge.

Cyperus: From *Cypeiros*, the ancient Greek name.

Erythrorhizos: From *erythros*, "red", and *rhiz*, "roots or root-like organs".

Sedge family: *Cyperaceae*

Red-rooted cyperus occurs in moist, often sandy soil from Massachusetts to Washington and south to California and Florida. In Iowa, it is infrequent to rare in the north, frequent in the southern half of the state, probably due to the presence of more sand in the southern portions. It is in flower in late summer, August to October.

This annual plant may attain a height of nearly 3 feet in good growing conditions or only a few inches along rivers where inundation frequently occurs. The stem leaves are about one-half inch wide and often purplish near the base. Up to eight bracts subtend and often greatly exceed the inflorescence.

This species is 6–36 flowered, with overlapping reddish-brown scales. The inflorescence is a compound umbel. The achenes are three-sided, small, and whitish or pearly colored.

The root system is fibrous and the individual roots are red, hence its common and scientific names.

The group to which red-rooted cyperus belongs is important as a source of wildlife food. Sometimes this and related species grow in great abundance on mud flats and the seedheads generally grow low enough for most waterfowl to eat.

There are 11 species of *Cyperus* in Iowa. They range from inhabitants of dry sand to those that grow in saturated soils or shallow water. This species is easily confused with *Cyperus odoratus.*

Red-rooted cyperus is a member of a large and important plant family, which includes all the bulrushes, beaked rushes, nut rushes, spikerushes, and members of the genus *Carex*. There are over 160 members of this family in Iowa and it is known for its taxonomic difficulty.

Blue lobelia: *Lobelia siphilitica* L.

Other common names: Blue cardinal flower, great blue lobelia.

Lobelia: Named in honor of a sixteenth-century Flemish herbalist Matthias de l'Obel.

Siphilitica: So named because it was once thought a cure for syphilis.

Bluebell family: *Campanulaceae;* sometimes placed in the *Lobeliaceae*

Blue lobelia is found from Maine and western New England to Minnesota, South Dakota and south to Virginia, Mississippi, Alabama, and Kansas. In Iowa, it is infrequent in the northwest, frequent to common in the remainder of the state. It is in bloom from early August into September.

The plant produces a single erect leafy stem rising to 5 feet from a basal rosette of long narrow-oval leaves. Alternate leaves crowded along the coarse stem are of similar shape but are pointed at the tip. They have toothed margins and tiny stiff hairs on the upper side. The size varies from 2 to 6 inches long with the smaller leaves toward the top. Lower leaves have short petioles; the upper leaves are without petioles. The perennial root system is coarsely fibrous and white.

Light blue flowers up to an inch long grow form the axils of the upper leaves. The upper lip of the flower has two erect and slightly diverging lobes that are divided to their base. Through this slit emerges a curved column consisting of the stamens joined in a ring around the style. Close examination shows that two of the stamens are tipped with anthers that are tufted or hairy. These unique characters are typical of the genus. The lower lip has three spreading lobes and is striped with white. Flowers and small leaves crowd together on the upper stem to appear almost as a flower spike.

Some American Indians believed this plant to be a secret cure for syphilis. The "secret" was purchased from the Indians and taken to Europe where it failed to perform to expectations. The Indians did not disclose that they used it in combination with mayapple roots plus bark of wild cherry and afterward dusted open sores with powdered bark of New Jersey tea. There seems little reason for the Indian treatment to have affected a cure, either.

Other American Indians used blue lobelia as a love potion by secretly placing finely ground root powder in the food of an arguing couple. The flowers were used to produce an inhalant for catarrh.

Lobelia inflata, a closely related species sometimes called Indian tobacco, is still used in parts of Appalachia to treat respiratory troubles. It also yields lobeline sulfate which is used in anti-smoking products. While Indians were said to have chewed and smoked this plant as a tobacco substitute, this seems unlikely because of the poisonous nature of the plant. It seems more logical that its use was as a ceremonial "tobacco" alone or in combination with other plants.

The lobelias have been considered a cure for most diseases of pioneers at one time or another.

Reed grass: *Phragmites australis* (Cav.) Trin. ex Strudel

Other common names: Bennels, common reed grass, Dutch reed, pole-reed, wild broom-corn.

Phragmites: From Greek, meaning generally "growing in hedges" or "fence-like", apparently from the hedge-like appearance as it grows along ditches.

Australis: From Latin meaning "southern" or "southerly".

Grass family: *Poaceae (Gramineae)*

Reed grass is found growing in marshes and along the banks of streams and lakeshores, often in extensive colonies. It grows worldwide; in North America it is widely distributed, occurring across southern Canada south to California, Louisiana, and Florida. It is usually found growing amid or near cattails. Flowering begins in late August.

The stout, leafy stems of this species grow erect to as much as 16 feet tall. It seldom produces viable seed but spreads from an extensive network of stout, creeping rhizomes or from stolons that may extend as far as 30 feet from the point of origin.

The leaf blades tend to be wide, as much as 2 inches across, but taper to a point. Their length usually 6 inches to 2 feet. Leaf sheaths overlap each other because they are longer than the internodes.

The large seed heads, usually 6–16 inches long, are tawny or sometimes purple. Most of the branches of the seed head tend to be ascending and are shorter toward the top of the seedstalk, creating a triangular seed head. Hairs on the branches of the seed stalk are longer than the individual flowers, giving the entire seed head a fuzzy appearance.

The stems of reed grass were sometimes used as shafts for arrows. The leaves were woven into mats and screens. Fibers from reed grass were used to make ropes and nets. In the southwest, this species, along with a related exotic species, *Arundo donax*, has been used for lattices in the construction of abode huts.

Apparently some Native Americans used the grains as food. When cooked, the rootstock served as a starchy vegetable.

When punctured, the stem exudes a pasty substance called honeydew that hardens into a gum. This was collected and eaten as candy. The punctured stems were also collected, the sugar shaken off and dissolved in water to make a sweet drink. American Indians of the Mojave desert collected, dried, and ground the stalks into a flour. Because of its high sugar content, this flour swelled and turned brown when placed near a fire. This was then eaten like taffy. The Yuma Indians made pipes from the internodes of the stem.

The underground root system of a patch of common reed is so interlocked and strong that other species are crowded out. However, this quality makes it valuable in flood and erosion control.

Obedient plant: *Physostegia parviflora* Nutt.

Other common names: False dragonhead, Lion's heart, Small-flowered false dragonhead.

Physostegia: From the Greek *physa*, "a bladder", and *stege,* "a covering", referring to the inflated calyx. An earlier generic name was *Dracocephalum,* which means "dragon head".

Parviflora: Meaning "small flowered".

Mint family: *Lamiaceae (Labiatae)*

Obedient plant is a stoloniferous perennial which is found from Wisconsin to British Columbia and south to Indiana, Illinois, Kansas, and Colorado. In Iowa, it is frequently encountered in the northeast half of the state, infrequently in the remainder. Its habitats are streamsides, edges of marshes, and other open wet areas. It is in bloom from late July into September.

This species grows to a height of over 3 feet. The leaves are elliptic to lanceolate and taper toward the base. They are about ¾ inch wide, up to 5 inches long, and arranged oppositely along the stem.

The flowers are rose-colored, less than ¾ inch long, and occur in a spike up to 6 inches long. They occur close together in vertical rows along the spike. Their shape resembles a snapdragon, resulting in the common name false dragonhead. It is more funnel-shaped, with a gaping mouth. The upper lip is arching and hood-like. The lower lip is three-lobed, with the middle lobe having additional shallow notches.

If the flowers in a row are pushed to the side, they tend to remain in that position for a considerable time. This unusual characteristic gives rise to the common name obedient plant.

The calyx encloses the four-celled ovary which is less than ½ inch long. It remains open at the tip with its five lobes flaring outward slightly. The smooth brown nutlets are three-sided ovals with surfaces somewhat channeled.

Because of its beauty, this, and other members of the genus, have been selected for cultivated gardens. The Meskwaki made a tea of its leaves.

This species is just uncommon enough to be interesting, just frequent enough to ensure success, and sufficiently attractive to make the search worthwhile.

False dragonhead: *Physosostegia virginiana* (L.) Bentham (Also referred to as *Dracocephalum virginianum* L.)

Other common names: Lion's heart, large-flowered false dragonhead, obedient plant.

Physostegia: From the Greek *physa*, "a bladder", and *stege*, "a covering", referring to the inflated calyx. An earlier generic name was *Dracocephalum*, which means "dragon head".

Virginiana. Meaning "of Virginia".

Mint family: *Lamiaceae (Labiatae)*

False dragonhead is a perennial which is found from Vermont to Ohio, Illinois, and Oklahoma and south to South Carolina, Alabama, and Texas. In Iowa, it is infrequently encountered in most of the state. Its habitats are streamsides, edges of marshes, and floodplain woods. It is in bloom from mid-August into September.

This species grows to a height of around 4 feet. The principal leaves, firm and subcoriaceous, are elliptic to lanceolate. The uppermost leaves are similar in shape but much reduced in size. The stem leaves are about ¾ inch wide, up to 5 inches long, rather sharply toothed and arranged oppositely along the stem.

The flowers are rose-colored, 1 to 1½ inches long and occur in a spike. They occur close together in vertical rows along the spike. Their shape resembles a snapdragon, resulting in the common name false dragonhead. It is more funnel-shaped, with a gaping mouth. The upper lip is arching and hood-like. The lower lip is three-lobed, with the middle lobe having additional shallow notches. There are four stamens ascending under the upper lip of the corolla. Secondary spikes sometimes occur in the axils of the upper leaves.

The calyx, up to nearly ½ inch long, encloses the four-celled ovary which is less than ½ inch long. It remains open at the tip with its five lobes flaring outward slightly. The smooth brown nutlets are three-sided ovals.

Because of its beauty, this, and other members of the genus, have been selected for cultivated gardens. The Meskwaki made a tea of its leaves.

This species grows in nearly the same habitat as cardinal flower, blooms at nearly the same time and occasionally will be found growing in close proximity. When this happens, you have found two spectacular flowers of the floodplain woods—an event you will not soon forget.

Burhead: *Echinodorus cordifolius* (L.) Griesb.

Other common names: Upright burhead.

Echinodorus: From Greek *echinos*, "hedgehog", and Greek *doros*, "leather sack", because the clustered sharp-beaked achenes resemble a rolled-up hedgehog, and the wall of the ovary is sack-like.

Cordifolius: From Latin *cordis*, "heart", and *folium*, "leaf", because some of the leaves have heart-shaped bases.

Water-plantain family: *Alismataceae* (originally *Alismaceae*)

Burhead ranges from northwest Florida to Texas and Mexico and north to Virginia, southern Indiana, Illinois, eastern Kansas, southwest Iowa, Nebraska, and California. Its habitats are shallow water of ponds, in mud banks of streams and dredge ditches. In Iowa, it is infrequently encountered in the southwest part, absent elsewhere. It grows at the borders of backwaters of the Missouri River, in dredge ditches and borrow pits, and seems to do particularly well in sandy substrates. Its flowering time is June into August, with fruits persisting into fall.

The leaves are long-petioled with flattened, obtuse blades, like arrowhead and water plantain, the other common members of the family. Leaf blades are up to 8 inches long and with cordate (heart-shaped) bases. The leaves are overtopped by a flowering scape which may be erect, arching, or creeping and which bears many whorls of flowers. The white-petaled flowers are up to ¾ inch broad. Total height of the plant may be up to 3 feet, but often individual plants, stranded on a dry site, may be diminutive and reach a height of 2–3 inches. The flowering scape, if it arches sufficiently to touch wet soil, occasionally will form a new plant and take root at a node.

This species is an annual or short-lived perennial and has a shallow, fibrous root-system which is easily dislodged. Roots sometimes bear cylindrical tubers along their length.

Burhead is widespread in the southern United States, and western Iowa is the northern extension of its range. There are at least two other related species to be found in the midwest and south which are used in tropical fish aquariums as submerged aquatic plants—adding to the beauty of the tanks. Trade names used are "poor man's lace plant" and "dwarf cellophane plant".

Water willow: *Justicia americana* (L.) Vahl

Other common names: American dianthera, American water willow.

Justicia: Named for James Justice, Scottish horticulturalist and botanist of the eighteenth century. The genus of which this plant belongs was originally named *Dianthera* by Linnaeus.

Americana: Meaning "of the Americas".

Acanthus family: *Acanthaceae*

Water willow is found from Georgia to Texas and north to southwest Quebec, Vermont, New York, Wisconsin, Iowa, and Kansas. In Iowa, which is near the western edge of its range, it is a rare plant, having been found in the southeast, in Des Moines and Henry counties in recent years; old records mention it in Jefferson and Lee counties. Finding new sites should be a challenge for Iowa naturalists.

This perennial herb may achieve a height of approximately 3 feet. The stem is smooth, erect and normally does not branch. Leaves are smooth and arranged oppositely along the stem and are 3 to 6 inches long and ¼ to 1 inch wide. The lower nodes of the plant are often swollen and commonly form adventitious roots. The plant arises from buried rhizomes and often forms a large colony.

The flowers are in a spike-like axillary head ⅓–1½ inches long. Flowers are pale purple or white with purple markings with a wide spreading lower lip. They are situated on a 1¾–6-inch stalk. Its flowering time is from June into August.

This species is more common south of Iowa and is frequent along streams in the Ozarks. It belongs to a large family more typically found in the tropics. In Iowa, the family is represented by water willow and two dry land species of wild petunia (*Ruellia* sp.)

When the plant forms large colonies, it provides good habitat for a variety of wildlife. It is a hardy plant and tends to spread after becoming established. These factors may indicate it is being overlooked in southeast Iowa.

Monkey flower: *Mimulus ringens* L.

Other common names: Gape plant.

Mimulus: Diminuitive of *mimus,* "a buffoon", from the allusion of the grinning face of the corolla.

Ringens: Meaning "gaping".

Snapdragon family: *Scrophulariaceae*

This herbaceous perennial is found from Nova Scotia to Virginia and west to Manitoba and Texas. In Iowa, it is common throughout the state in alluvial woods, edges of marshes, in seeps, and in wet roadside ditches. It is in bloom in late July through September.

The four-angled, four-winged stem may achieve a height of 3 feet. The stem arises from a shallow, horizontal rhizome which gives rise to runners which root at intervals. The leaves are opposite, clasping at the base, up to 4 inches long and 1 inch wide, with a long point.

The flowers are borne in the axils of the uppermost leaves on slender petioles that may be 2 inches long. The corolla is blue and erect, with a two-lobed erect or reflexed upper lip and a spreading, three-lobed lower lip.

The common name is in reference to the assumed resemblance of the corolla to the face of a monkey, but this is not obvious to all that see it. There are about 40 species in the genus, three of which occur in Iowa. The winged monkey flower, *M. alatus,* is rare in the southcentral and southeast and has wings on the angles of the stem and petioled leaves. Yellow monkey flower, *M. glabratus,* is found in cold streams of fens or seeps.

This species has been cultivated to a small extent. Several horticultural varieties have been developed, including *M. lutens,* with yellow, dark-spotted corolla.

Native Americans and pioneers sometimes used species of this genus for greens.

Umbrella sedge: *Cyperus rivularis* Kunth

Other common names: Galingale, river sedge, shining cypress, stream-side sedge.

Cyperus: From *Cypeiros,* the ancient Greek name for the genus.

Rivularis: Meaning "of streams".

Sedge family: *Cyperaceae*

This small, annual sedge is found from Georgia to Mexico and north to Maine, southwest Quebec, southern Ontario, Wisconsin, Minnesota, and Nebraska. In Iowa, it is rare to infrequent throughout the state. It grows in a variety of wet habitats—from muddy stream edges and wet sand to peaty substrates. It flowers and sets fruit in late summer and early fall.

Umbrella sedge may grow to 15 inches in height, normally less, and in poor growing conditions, may be an inch or so high. The culms are slender and the plant normally tufted, but occasionally solitary. It has leaves at the base which are up to 6 inches long and ¼ inch wide. It has three widely spreading involucral leaves, the longest exceeding the umbel. The umbel has two to five rays which may reach a length of 3 inches. The spikelets are reddish-brown or green with a purple-brown margin, with 6–32 occurring on each spike. The style is two-cleft. The root system is tufted and shallow.

This species is easily confused with *C. diandrus,* which has the style cleft nearly to the base. It may also be confused with *C. aristatus,* which has a three-cleft style.

These are among our most attractive sedges but usually bloom so late that many botanists and naturalists miss seeing them.

There are 11 species of *Cyperus* in Iowa, ranging from those which grow in the driest, sandiest places to those which grow on the saturated soils of riverbanks and marsh edges. The inconspicuous nature of this species is reflected in the lack of reference to its value to wildlife or use by early Americans.

Meadow beauty: *Rhexia virginica* L.

Other common names: Deer grass, handsome Harry.

Rhexia: A name used by Pliny for an unknown plant.

Virginica: Meaning "of Virginia".

Melastoma family: *Melastomataceae*

Meadow beauty ranges from Nova Scotia to New York, west and south to Georgia, Louisiana, and Oklahoma. There are about 15 species in North America, most of which are in the southeast. In Iowa, this species is known only from moist sandy sites in Cedar, Clinton, and Muscatine counties. It is in bloom in mid-July through August.

This erect perennial, which ranges from a few inches to nearly 3 feet, arises from a tuber, normally is unbranched, and with four wing-angles on the stem. The leaves are oval, rounded at the base, sessile, and have toothed margins. These are arranged opposite on the stem. The flower petals are crimson and occur in terminal cymes. The seeds are small and textured.

Because of its beauty, it is a favorite with gardeners, but must be planted in open, wet areas and grows best where the soil is sandy or peaty. The Maryland meadow beauty is found from Long Island south and is more hairy. The stems are not angled and the leaves are more spreading.

Some sources state this species makes a pleasant salad, the leaves having a sweetish, slightly acid taste while the tubers have a pleasant nutty quality. Some say it is too beautiful and too local to recommend for general use as a food.

This is one species for which you have to get off the beaten path. When you find one, you often find dozens more. Looking and finding can be a late summer treat.

Mountain mint: *Pycnanthemum virginianum* (L.) Dur. and Jackson

Other common names: Basil, mountain thyme, pennyroyal, prairie hyssop.

Pycnanthemum: From the Greek *pycnos*, "dense", and *anthemon*, "a flower" from the compact flower head.

Virginianum: Meaning "of Virginia".

Mint family: *Lamiaceae (Labiatae)*

Mountain mint is found in a variety of habitats, ranging from mesic to wet prairies, sedge meadows, edges of marshes and on fens. It is widely distributed in North America, from Maine to North Dakota and south to Virginia, Tennessee, Missouri, and Kansas. There are about 17 species in this genus which are native to North America. In Iowa, it is common in the eastern two-thirds of the state, infrequent to rare elsewhere. Its blooming period is from July through September.

This stout, erect perennial tends to be multibranched toward the top. As is typical with the mints, the stem is four-angled and covered with a whitish bloom. The sides are smooth, but the angles have a covering of hairs. It may achieve a height of 3 feet, normally less.

Mountain mint and other members of the genus are fragrant when crushed. The opposite leaves are narrow and lance-shaped, rounded at the base and pointed at the tip. The margins and upper surfaces are smooth and the underside may be hairy. The main leaves are as long as 2 inches and less then ½ inch wide. Short, leafy branches often arise from the axils of the upper leaves.

This plant has tiny flowers with a lower lip with three rounded lobes and an upper lip that may have a slight notch at the tip. The upper lip is white; the lower lip is often spotted with purple. The flowers are arranged in numerous, dense, head-like clusters that are about ¼ inch across. The clusters arise from axils of the upper leaves and the stem tip. Only a few are in bloom at one time. The seeds are tiny, with a smooth or slightly rough surface.

The Meskwaki used mountain mint as an unspecified medicine and for baiting mink traps. The Potawatomi considered it one of the best tonics for a rundown condition. A tea made from the leaves was preferred, but roots were also used.

Early settlers once used a mountain mint poultice on dog bites as a rabies preventative. A tea brewed from the leaves served as a general tonic, as a treatment for mild indigestion and for the chills and fever of ague. The leaves have been used as a seasoning for cooking. The common name is not accurate as most are found in lowlands, not in the mountains. It has inaccurately been called basil.

Three species of mountain mint, all similar, occur in Iowa. Hairy mountain mint, *Pycnanthemum pilosum* has villose stem angles; slender mountain mint, *Pycnanthemum tenuifolium* has longer calyx teeth. All are similar in their utilization for medicinal purposes.

Other common names: Clown's woundwort, common wound-wort, marsh woundwort, woundwort.

Stachys: Derived from Greek meaning "an ear of wheat", referring to the terminal raceme.

Palustris: Meaning "of marshes".

Mint family: *Lamiaceae (Labiatae)*

Hedge nettle ranges from British Columbia south to Arizona and east to James Bay, Quebec, Wisconsin, Illinois, and Iowa. There are several varieties of this species, all similar; some taxonomists prefer to separate them, but the Iowa material seems to have enough overlap of characters to make such separation impractical. In Iowa, this species is found frequently throughout the state in suitable habitats: edges of marshes, sedge meadows, low prairies, drainageways and occasionally in wet roadside ditches. It is in flower in July and August.

This species has the typical square stem of mint, which is hairy. The stem is normally unbranched and about 2 feet tall. The leaves are opposite, without petioles, and taper abruptly toward the base. The leaves are pubescent beneath and hairy on the top surface and have distinctly toothed edges.

The dark brown ovary is deeply four-lobed and oval-shaped. Reproduction is by seeds or by horizontal rootstocks which bear subterranean stolons which terminate in tubers. The plant can spread rapidly and form dense colonies.

Early settlers used parts of this plant as a nauseant, an expectorant, an antihysteric, and a vulnerary, which is a substance that promotes healing. The Chippewa used it as a colic medicine. Medicinally, this species is thought to be the most important of the nearly 200 species in the genus. The tubers have been boiled, dried, or made into bread for human consumption. Several varieties of this species are naturalized in this country from Europe. An Asiatic species has been cultivated and the tubers sold as Chinese artichokes.

Marsh hedge nettle, *Stachys tenuifolia,* another wet prairie or pothole-edge species, is similar and quite common. Its lower leaves are stalked and the spike has spacing between the individual flowers. A leaf tea made from this species was alleged to cure the common cold.

Hedge nettles can occasionally be troublesome weeds in wet cropground because they thrive in disturbed ground and because of their method of spreading.

American germander: *Teucrium canadense* L.

Other common names: Germander, wood sage.

Teucrium: From Teucrion, a name used by Dioscorides for a related plant. Or, possibly for Teucer, the first king of Troy.

Canadense: Meaning "of Canada".

Mint family: *Lamiaceae (Labiatae)*

This mint is found from New England to Minnesota and Nebraska and south to Georgia, Alabama, Mississippi, and Texas. In Iowa, it is frequent to common throughout the state. Its habitats are alluvial woods, marshes, and wet prairies. It is in bloom from July into September.

This is an erect, usually unbranched plant that may grow 4 feet tall, usually less. It is a rhizomatous perennial with four-sided pubescent stems. The leaves are ovate to oblong, up to 5 inches long, toothed, rounded at the base, with opposite arrangement on the stem and on short petioles.

The inflorescence is a crowded raceme that may range from 3–10 inches in length. The corolla is pink-purple, ¾ inch long, cleft on the upper side, therefore appearing as a single five-lobed lower lip and as though the upper lip is missing. This is a helpful character in identifying plants in this genus, as it is found in no other mint.

The stamens are arched over the corolla. The calyx is two-lipped, with the upper three lobes wider and more blunt than the lower two. This species spreads by underground rhizomes and may form a large, monotypic population.

There are two varieties of this species in Iowa, but the differences are slight and the habitats much the same. About 300 species in this genus occur in temperate and tropic regions of each hemisphere. Several kinds of germander grow in Europe.

This easily grown plant is often found in rock gardens. It is aromatic, but not to the degree of many other mints.

Rose mallow: *Hibiscus laevis* All.

Other common names: Halberd-leaved mallow, mallow rose, swamp mallow, water mallow.

Hibiscus: Old Greek and Latin name for a kind of large mallow.

Laevis: Meaning "smooth".

Mallow family: *Malvaceae*

Rose mallow is found from Minnesota and Nebraska east to Pennsylvania and Ohio and south to Florida and Texas. In Iowa, it is found mostly in the southern half of the state in wooded bottomlands where soils are continuously wet, often growing at the edges of floodplain wetlands in shallow standing water. It blooms in August and September.

Clusters of smooth, soft pithy stems grow to 7 feet, but normally less. The leaves are arranged alternately along the stem with petioles sometimes longer than the leaf. Leaves may be as much as 6 inches long. Their shapes vary from that of an elongated triangle to having three to five lobes. Three-lobed leaves are common with two short but sharp basal lobes and a longer center lobe, also sharp. This shape resembles that of the halberd, a hand weapon of ancient times. Leaf margins have coarse teeth that are shallow and somewhat rounded.

The flowers are among the most spectacular of our wetland flora because of their size and coloring. They have five oval petals, each sometimes more than 3 inches long. The petals are pink to flesh-colored with a reddish-purple blotch at the base. Thus, the flower appears to have a much darker center. From this dark center protrudes a long style surrounded by a cylinder of delicate stamens. Each flower has its own short slender stalk arising from the axil of an upper leaf. Surrounding the base of each flower are several green linear bracts up to ¾ inch long. The flowers tend to open briefly about mid-morning and provide a spectacular sight.

An inch-long pointed-oval seed capsule with five cells tends to remain on the plant into the winter. Each cell contains several seeds covered with silky hairs—showing the relationship of this plant to the cotton plant.

No food or medicinal uses of rose mallow could be found. Seeds are eaten by waterfowl and sometimes by quail. Some mallows are locally known as shoeblack plants because the petals were once used as a polishing cloth to put a mirror polish on shoes.

The mallow family includes such well-known plants as cotton, hollyhock, okra, rose of sharon, and several species of hibiscus flowers.

Other common names: Flower of gold, yellow top, yellow-weed (names also include several other species of goldenrods).

Solidago: Named for the Latin *solidus,* "whole", in reference to its reputed vulnerary (wound-healing) properties.

Riddellii: Named for its discoverer, John Leonard Riddell, 1807–1865.

Sunflower family: *Asteraceae (Compositae)*

This attractive goldenrod is found in wet prairies and on fens from southern Ontario to Minnesota, Indiana, Ohio, and Missouri. In Iowa, it is most frequent in the northcentral part and in the lakes region of the northwest, and rare in the northeast quarter. An 1895 record exists from Muscatine County. It is in bloom in late August or early September into November.

Riddell's goldenrod grows from less than 1 foot to over 3 feet high, depending on the habitat. The plant is smooth, stout, and leafy. The leaves are linear or lanceolate, longitudinally folded, generally recurved, sickle-shaped, and from 4 inches to over 1 foot in length. They are three-nerved and glabrous. The lower leaves are longer and more persistent than the upper.

The inflorescence is a dense corymb that is pubescent, flat-topped, and with 20-30 yellow flowers per head.

Reproduction is apparently only by seed and the plants occur singly, scattered across suitable habitat.

In some parts of its range, it may be confused with *S. ohioensis,* a plant of similar habitat, but which has not yet been found in Iowa.

The goldenrods are notoriously difficult to identify, but Riddell's goldenrod is a happy exception. It is attractive, distinctive, and scarce enough that once seen, is not forgotten.

There are about 125 species in this genus. Hybridization occurs, making identification of individual species difficult. Goldenrods are often blamed for causing hay fever, but this is exaggerated. Pollination is mostly by wind, so some pollen grains may be carried by the wind, but not nearly to the extent as with the ragweeds.

Both American Indians and pioneers used goldenrods for treating burns, intestinal disorders, and lung problems. The leaves of some species were used to prepare a tea. They were also used to treat fevers, bee stings, and diseases of women. The Meskwaki also burned the plant to produce a smoke inhalant to treat a person who had fainted. In their early medicine, some tribes cooked goldenrods with bone of an animal that had died about the same time a baby was born—then washed the baby in the liquid to ensure the ability to talk and laugh.

Ladies' tresses: *Spiranthes cernua* (L.) Rich.

Other common names: Common ladies' tresses, drooping ladies' tresses, nodding ladies' tresses, screw auger, spike orchid, wild tuberose.

Spiranthes: From the Greek *speira*, "a coil", or "a spiral", from the spirally twisted flower spike.

Cernua: From Latin, meaning "nodding".

Orchid family: *Orchidaceae*

This small orchid is found from Nova Scotia to southwest Quebec and southern Ontario to Michigan, Wisconsin, Minnesota, and South Dakota, south to Texas and Florida. In Iowa it is found statewide, except perhaps the northwest counties. It blooms from mid-August through September.

The stout, erect stem of ladies' tresses grows to 2 feet in height and may be covered with fine hairs toward the top. The perennial root system has thick, fleshy branches that only descend a few inches into the soil.

Pale green, grass-like basal leaves are 2–12 inches long and about ½ inch or less in width. The basal leaves normally wither by the time the flowers appear. Stem-leaves, which are nearly without blades, provide alternate sheathing along the stem.

Three spirals of flowers form a dense spike 2–6 inches long and ½–1 inch across. Each flower, on its own short stalk, is less than ½ inch long. The delicate flowers are ivory white. A "hood" is formed by three petal-like sepals that arch upward. The fiddle-shaped "lip" is about ⅜ inch long and bends downward. Unlike many orchid species, these flowers have no spur. The flowers spread outward from the flowerstalk and often droop slightly.

Since they begin blooming from the bottom of the spike, it takes a few weeks before those at the top are in bloom. Flowers are sometimes fragrant, reminding one of the lily-of-the-valley scent or that of vanilla. This is reasonable, since vanilla is obtained from another orchid species.

The fruit, an oval capsule about ¼ inch long, is borne more or less erect. Each seed has two or more embryos.

The Meskwaki called the plant *soa num*, meaning "tail of a rattlesnake", but did not use the plant as medicine. The Ojibwa used the root of the slender ladies' tresses, *S. gracilis*, as an ingredient in a hunting charm to bring game within range of the bow and arrow.

Ladies' tresses is our most common orchid and occurs in a variety of habitats nearly statewide. Looking for it can provide some late-season botanical fun.

Stick-tight: *Bidens cernua* L.

Other common names: Beggar-lice, beggar-ticks, boot-jacks, bur-marigold, pitchforks, sticktights, tick-seed.

Bidens: From Latin *bidens,* "two-toothed" from the sharp awns or teeth on the achene.

Cernua: From Latin meaning "nodding", from the heads which are strongly nodding when in fruit.

Daisy family: *Asteraceae (Compositae)*

Stick-tight is found from Quebec to British Columbia and south to North Carolina, Tennessee, Iowa, Idaho, Wyoming and California. It also occurs in Europe. In Iowa, it grows in open mudflats, edges of marshes, wet roadsides, and streambanks and probably grows in every county in the state. It blooms in late August until frost.

This annual with a soft stem may achieve a height of 5 feet, but normally much less. Larger plants often have decumbent rooting bases. Late season plants in unfavorable habitats may grow to a height of only a few inches. Some authors consider these small plants dwarf forms. The stem is normally hairy and often branches freely. The leaves are oblong to lance-shaped, and oppositely arranged on the stem.

The bright yellow flowers are numerous, each consisting of many-flowered erect heads, which become nodding with age.

The fruits are achenes, usually four-sided, and crowned with two hispid awns. These awns have backward-pointing barbs which attach to nearly any material which brushes against them to be dropped at a distant point. This is an effective method of dispersal and every field biologist, hunter, and nature enthusiast spends much time removing these stick-tights or boot-jacks from clothing. This plant can easily fall from favor.

While the seeds of stick-tight are occasionally eaten by wood duck, pheasant, quail, and a few species of songbirds, it is of minor value as a wildlife food. Although the species appears only sparsely in the annals of plants with medicinal value, it is sometimes listed as a plant which may cause mechanical injury to animals. Such injury is caused by the sharp barbs.

Stick-tight is a normal component of Iowa's marshes, especially when marshes are drawn-down for waterfowl management purposes. During this time the exposed mud-banks provide proper conditions for germination of the seeds in the seedbank. The result is often a near dominance by this species.

Early settlers used this plant as an expectorant and emmenogogue (to promote menstrual discharge), and as a cure for the croup. Modern flower-gardeners occasionally grow it as a garden annual.

Fringed gentian: *Gentianopsis crinita* (Froel.) Ma (Formerly *Gentiana crinita*)

Other common names: Small fringed gentian.

Gentianopsis: From Gentius, King of Illyria, who, according to Pliny, discovered the medicinal uses of the plant.

Crinita: From Latin *crinitus* "provided with a covering of hair", in reference to the bearded fringe of the petals.

Gentian family: *Gentianaceae*

This beautiful plant is found in a variety of moist habitats ranging from sedge meadows, wet woods, and fens from Maine to southern Manitoba and south to Georgia, Ohio, Indiana, and northern Iowa. In Iowa, it is found in most counties in the northeast quarter of the state and in Clay, Dickinson, Emmet, and Palo Alto counties in northwest Iowa. It blooms in mid-August through late September. The favored habitat for this species in Iowa is on wet peatlands, often called "fens", in full sunlight.

The stem is simple or branched, with from one to many flowers. The lower leaves are spatulate, but the middle and upper ones are ovate or lanceolate and are rounded or cordate at the bases. The bases of the upper leaves clasp the stem.

The corolla is deeply four-lobed, 1½–2½ inches long, and violet-blue. The petals are conspicuously fringed with slender teeth which may be ¼ inch long. The calyx is unequally four-cleft with individual sections as long as the tube of the corolla. The flower is spreading during sunny days and apparently closes at night.

The small, numerous, papilose seeds often are blown from the plants to new sites and the plants disappear from the original site. Reproduction is by seed alone, and, since the plants in Iowa are annuals, the persistence of the species on a site is uncertain.

Because ants like the taste, or crave the nutrition of the nectar of the flowers, the plant has developed a system to protect itself—some authorities believe the fringe on the petals provides a measure of this protection.

The roots were used in the distant past as a tonic, emetic, and cathartic, according to Pliny, the Roman naturalist.

Fringed gentian blooms in late summer and autumn in remote habitats, and so many naturalists have not seen this species in its natural habitat. Those botanists and naturalists with late-season wanderlust may be rewarded by viewing one of Iowa's really spectacular wildflowers.

Closed gentian: *Gentiana andrewsii* Griseb.

Other common names: Barrel gentian, blind gentian, bottle gentian, cloistered heart.

Gentiana: Named for the ancient King Gentius of Illyria who supposedly discovered the medical properties of some gentians. The gentian he knew, however, was of another genus.

Andrewsii: Honoring Henry C. Andrews, English botanical artist and engraver of the early nineteenth century.

Gentian family: *Gentianaceae*

Closed gentian is found from Quebec, Ontario, Manitoba, and Saskatchewan, and south to Georgia and Arkansas. In Iowa, it is of frequent occurrence on the Iowan Surface and in the central portion, infrequent or rare in the remainder of the state. Its habitat is rich, damp soils of low prairies, and moist woodland edges. It is in bloom from late August to frost.

The stout, erect, leafy stems, usually without branches, grow to 20 inches tall. The perennial root system is long and coarse. The leaves are long-oval to lance-shaped, pointed at the tip and narrowing toward the base with parallel veining. Margins tend to be smooth, sometimes irregular with a tiny fringe. The leaves are opposite along the stem and without petioles, or essentially so. The upper leaves are larger than lower ones and those toward the top may be 4 inches or longer. Uppermost leaves tend to form a whorl of four to six at the base of the main flowerhead. In late summer a bronze tinge may develop at the leaf tip and along the nearby margin.

The unusual bottle or club-shaped flowers, 2 inches long, vary from an intense bright blue or purple to lighter shades and rarely to white. They are closely set, without individual flower stalks, in the axils of upper leaves. Usually, only the uppermost cluster has more than just one or two "bottles." The petals remain essentially closed, joined by a whitish membrane, even when in full bloom. They appear more as a bud about to open. Closed gentian is one of the last of the flowers to bloom in the autumn—sometimes just before the first hard frost of the season. Authorities disagree about whether or not closed gentian is self-fertilized. Only strong and persistent bees, such as the bumble bee, can force entry. The fruit is a dry upright capsule containing many extremely small seeds.

Both Meskwaki and Potawatomi used the closed gentian to treat snakebite. Women of some tribes ate a piece of closed gentian for caked (congealed) breasts. The Catawaba boiled roots in water and used the resulting liquid to treat backache.

Pioneers ate the root of this species to promote appetite. They also used a tea brewed from the plant to aid digestion—especially following malaria and infectious diseases. Still later, some Appalachian mountain men carried, or wore around their necks, a piece of the rhizome of a closely related species, *G. villosa* L. in the belief that it increased their physical powers.

In Switzerland, a potent alcoholic beverage called Gentiane is fermented from the roots of a related species (*G. lutea* L.). The poorer people of Sweden used *G. campestre* L. in place of hops to brew their ale.

The roots of the yellow gentian were collected and used by the Forest Potawatomi for making a tea used as an alterative. The pioneers also used it medicinally as a stomachic and bitter tonic.

This is another example of a late-season treasure awaiting a visit from one of Iowa's naturalists.

FERNS, FERN ALLIES, AND LOWER VASCULAR PLANTS

(in alphabetical order, by common name)

Adder's-tongue fern: *Ophioglossum vulgatum* L.

Other common names: Adder's spear, adder's fern, serpent's tongue, snake's tongue.

Ophioglossum: From the Greek *ophis,* "a serpent", and *glossa,* "tongue", from the fancied resemblance of the fertile stalk to the tongue of a serpent.

Vulgatum: Meaning "common".

Adder's tongue family: *Ophioglossaceae*

Adder's-tongue fern is found from southern Quebec south to New England, Delaware, Virginia, Ohio, Indiana, Illinois, Nebraska, and Arizona. In Iowa, it is found in sandy sedge meadows and peaty depressions in the eastern third of the state. It becomes fertile in late June.

One of our most elusive plants, because the fern is small, grows in the shade of taller plants and is quite unfern-like in appearance. The leaves, or fronds, normally are around 4 inches long and less than an inch wide. The single leaf is attached about half way up the smooth, delicate, fleshy stalk. The leaves are undivided, tongue-shaped and resemble leaves of a plantain more than it does other ferns. The leaves are slightly coriaceous, simple, and have reticulate veining. The fleshy stalk bears a fertile spike that arises from near the base of the leaf. This somewhat resembles the tongue of a snake, hence the common name. The fertile portion bears spores in two rows which appear like rows of beads. The spores are released and the plant withers by mid-summer.

This is one of the most primitive ferns. Its interesting life cycle includes an underground gametophyte with no chlorophyll which forms an association with a fungus for nourishment. These gametophytes may exist in the ground for eight years.

While only one representative of this genus occurs in Iowa, there are 54 species worldwide. As recently as 1975 it was known from only one Iowa county. After its habitat requirements were determined and a "search image" was formed, it has been documented in additional counties from central, eastern, and northeastern counties, but mainly along the Cedar River in moist sandy soil. Finding the first plant in an area is a challenge. Once this is done, finding others becomes somewhat easier. This is one of those wetland plants that does not require getting wet feet during the search. It may grow in large patches in moist, peaty areas.

Adder's-tongue fern is also found in similar habitats in Europe. It can be cultivated in partial shade in moist peat. The name adder's tongue is also applied to another completely different plant. The trout lily is called adder's tongue or dog tooth violet.

Cinnamon fern: *Osmunda cinnamomea* L.

Other common names: Buckhorn, fiddlehead.

Osmunda: This was derived from the name for Osmunder, the Saxon equivalent of the God Thor.

Cinnamomea: Meaning "cinnamon colored", from the tufts of brown "wool" at the base of the pinnae.

Flowering fern family: *Osmundaceae*

This large and beautiful fern grows from Newfoundland to Minnesota and south to New England and the Gulf states. It is found in wet woods, edges of marshes, and on wet cliffs. In Iowa, it is restricted to moist sandy seeps in the southeast.

The fronds may reach a length of 5 feet. These are dimorphic—that is, of two forms. The sterile fronds are green and oblong-lanceolate and the pinnae are lanceolate. The fertile fronds that bear the spores are shorter, twice pinnate, soon turn cinnamon brown, release the spores and wither. The plant arises from a shallow underground rhizome.

This beauty has two close relatives: the royal fern (*Osmunda regalis*), which has fertile pinnae at the tip of the frond; and the interrupted fern (*Osmunda claytoniana*), which has fertile pinnae mixed in with normal sterile pinnae. These are the most gorgeous ferns in Iowa. The interrupted fern is common in eastern Iowa and infrequent in central Iowa. The royal fern is rare—known only from perhaps as few as six counties in Iowa. The cinnamon fern, one of our rarest plants, is currently known from a single site. It may well be lurking in remote corners and offers a challenge to Iowa's natural historians.

In parts of the country where this fern is more common, it is often transplanted for landscaping purposes and will thrive, especially in peaty or sandy soil and in partial shade.

Common horsetail: *Equisetum arvense* L.

Other common names: Field horsetail, horsetail fern, meadow pine, scouring rush.

Equisetum: From *equus*, "horse", and *seta*, "hair" or "tail".

Arvense: Latin meaning "pertaining to fields", from the habitat where common horsetail is often found.

Horsetail family: *Equisetaceae*

Common horsetail ranges widely across North America, from Greenland to Alaska and Newfoundland, south to Alabama, and west to Nebraska and California. In Iowa, it is of common occurrence throughout the state. It also occurs in Europe and Asia. Common horsetail thrives in a variety of disturbed moist areas, such as roadsides, field edges, edges of marshes and sedge meadows.

First to appear are the flesh-colored fertile stems which are short and terminate in a cone-like spike about an inch long from which spores are released. These appear in April, before the green, branched sterile stems. They last for a short time, then turn dark brown and release the spores. The sterile plant, by far the most commonly seen, may achieve a height of 2 feet and has whorls of slender green branches arising from the joints.

The stems arise from a horizontal underground stem and the sterile plants may become very dense as they spread vegetatively. The stems are rough to the touch due to silica deposited in the surface. This roughness makes the plant generally unpalatable and animals tend to avoid it in pastures.

The plant is known to be poisonous to livestock, especially when fed in dried hay. The substance *eqisetin*, an alkaloidal nerve poison, has been shown to be present in some species of horsetails. The symptoms are loss of weight followed by loss of muscular control resulting in staggering and swaying, eventually losing the power to stand.

This species acts as a good soil anchor because of the branching, underground parts and may become a problem in moist cultivated fields, but is usually controlled by cultivation.

Horsetail is a common plant in Iowa, occurring in every county and it probably grows within walking distance of your home. Common horsetail is a good place to start learning this family. They are an ancient group of plants, and much larger relatives were abundant during the Carboniferous times when coal was formed.

Crested wood fern: *Dryopteris cristata* (L.) Gray

Other common names: Crested fern, crested shield fern, narrow swamp fern, shield fern, wood fern.

Dryopteris: From Greek *drys,* "oak", and *pteris,* "fern", because some members of the genus are called oak ferns.

Cristata: Meaning "crested".

True fern family: *Polypodiaceae* (Some taxonomists place it in the *Aspleniaceae.*)

The crested wood fern ranges from Newfoundland to Alberta and south to Tennessee, Nebraska, and Idaho. It is also found in Europe. It is found in several habitats in Iowa—from fens to *Sphagnum* bogs, Carex swales, and seeps. It is a rare plant in Iowa and found sparingly in the eastern half of the state.

This fern may achieve a height of over 3 feet, but normally less, and a width of about 5 inches. The fertile fronds are longer than those which are sterile. The lower part of the stem is green and has many dull-brown scales. It is practically an evergreen fern and grows in clumps from a horizontal rootstock.

The leaflets are broadly triangular, the lowest ones about an inch long but become longer and less triangular as they approach the upper part of the stem. The leaflets are held generally horizontal rather than in a plane parallel to the frond. The sterile fronds remain green throughout the winter.

This is a very handsome plant and one well worth the search.

Marsh fern: *Thelypteris palustris* Schott

Other common names: Meadow fern, quill fern, snuffbox fern, swamp fern, wood fern.

Thelypteris: Greek *thesus,* "female", and *pteris,* "fern".

Palustris: Meaning "of marshes", from its habitat.

Fern family: *Aspleniaceae*

One of our most common ferns, marsh fern is found in marshes, wet sandy slopes, fens, and seeps and is most common in the northern half of Iowa. In North America, it grows from Newfoundland to Manitoba and south to Georgia, Tennessee, and Oklahoma. Nearly identical taxa occur worldwide.

Marsh fern arises from a slender, blackish, forking rhizome. The annual fronds may grow to nearly 1½ feet in length and are of two types—sterile and fertile. The sterile fronds are very thin and shorter than those that are fertile. The sterile fronds are thicker, firmer, and with narrower segments with revolute margins. The sterile fronds develop earlier and the pinnae are cut into rather blunt sections.

This delicate, thin green fern produces leaves throughout the summer. The young fronds uncoil as they mature and the plant can form a dense, dominant layer in favorable sites. The species normally grows in full sun and is sensitive to the first frost in fall. It usually grows in areas where acidity is low, but also is found on *Sphagnum* bogs, where the acidity is high. It seems to need a continuous water supply to survive and will not prosper in any environment where the soils dries out periodically.

No reference to its uses for food or medicine could be found.

Meadow spikemoss: *Selaginella eclipes* Buck. (Formerly *S. apoda* L. Fern)

Other common names: Meadow moss, wetland spikemoss.

Selaginella: Diminuitive of *Selago*, an ancient name of a *Lycopodium* from which this genus has been separated.

Eclipes: Probably from the Greek *ecleipo*, "to be deficient", alluding to the sessile and inconspicuous spike.

Spikemoss family: *Selaginellaceae*

Meadow spikemoss is found from Florida to Texas and north to Maine, Ontario, Michigan, Wisconsin, and Missouri. In Iowa, it is one of our rarest plants, being found in Muscatine and Worth counties. However, because its inconspicuous nature makes it difficult to find, it may lurk in undiscovered sites—a challenge for naturalists. Its favored Iowa habitat is moist sand.

This is a weak, slender, freely-branching prostrate plant that forms pale green mats. The leaves are dimorphic, four-ranked with two rows oblong to oval, and two rows smaller and appressed. This characteristic is visible in the photograph.

It sprawls along the ground and is quite difficult to find if other vegetation is present. Spikemoss does not compete well with taller vegetation that provides shade. It has long been known from a sandy, moist, pastured area in Muscatine County, but once grazing stopped, grasses may have provided too much shade or out-competed the spikemoss. Recent searches failed to locate it.

Another species, rock spikemoss, *Selaginella rupestris*, is much more common in Iowa and grows in dry sand and dry sandstone. Both species have two kinds of spores—microspores generally in the axils of the upper leaves and macrospores, generally in the axils of the lower leaves. The name *Selaginella apoda* has long been used for meadow spikemoss and many manuals still use this name.

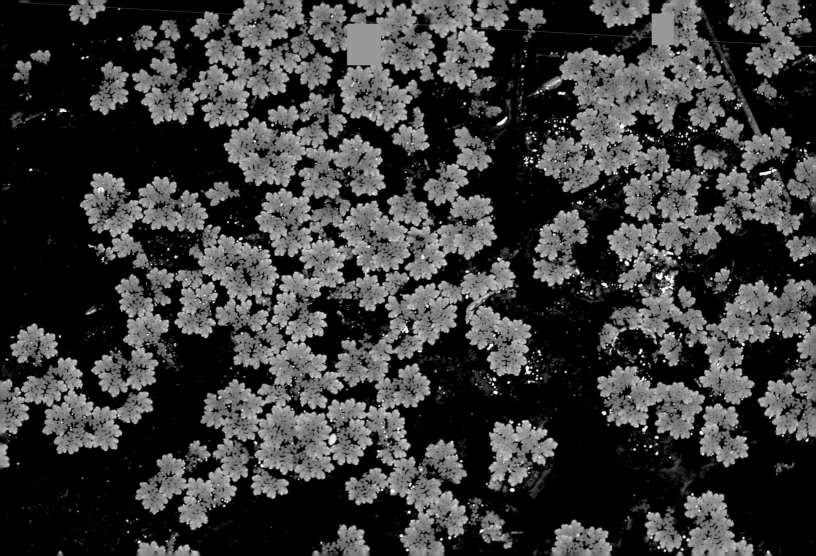

Mosquito fern: *Azolla mexicana* Presl.

Other common names: Water fern.

Azolla: An unexplained derivation, proposed by Lamarck in 1783.

Mexicana: The name originally given to this taxon believing it was from Mexico.

Mosquito fern family: *Azollaceae*

This diminuitive plant is found from Wisconsin, Illinois, and Missouri, throughout western United States and south to Bolivia. In Iowa, it is restricted to quiet, often sandy, ponds in counties along the Mississippi River and in Johnson and Linn counties. Also, there is an old record from Fremont County.

This is a small floating fern, moss-like with numerous small, reddish leaves. It becomes obvious on the surface of sandy ponds from August until frost. Sometimes the plant becomes so dominant on the surface of a pond that it imparts to the water a reddish cast. When well-established, mosquito fern forms such dense masses on the surface that it reputedly smothers mosquito larvae. The species produces relatively large female spores and minute male ones.

This fern is not native to Iowa, but was introduced from the south and does fairly well in the southern part of Iowa. It is not winter hardy in the northern portion of the state.

Royal fern: *Osmunda regalis* L.

Other common names: Bog onion, flowering fern, herb Christopher, king fern, male fern.

Osmunda: Name for Osmunder, the saxon equivalent of the god Thor.

Regalis: Meaning "royal".

Flowering fern family: *Osmundaceae*

The royal fern is an exceptionally beautiful fern. In Iowa, its beauty is exceeded only by its scarcity—presently known from four sites in the eastern portion. Its range includes southern Canada, much of eastern Unites States, and south to Mexico. Its favorite Iowa habitat is wet sand or peat where it may occur in dense stands. The fertile fronds are conspicuous from early June through July.

The fronds are twice-pinnate and achieve a length of 5 feet. They are pale green with entire margins. The frond is naked for about half its length, greenish or reddish, and arises from a stout, creeping rhizome. The fertile portion is clustered in a dense mass at the tip of the frond. This cluster is green when young and turns brown as the spores mature. At a glance, the young clusters may remind one of blossoms, resulting in the common name "flowering fern". The frond has five to seven pairs of nearly opposite, oblong, ascending pinnae, the lower pair slightly shorter than the others.

In Iowa, royal fern occurs most frequently on wet sands; this habitat is not unusual in eastern Iowa along the Cedar, Wapsipinicon, and Mississippi rivers. It is a bit of a mystery why this beautiful plant is so rare. Normally the species requires a slightly acid environment. Its frequent failure as an ornamental plant probably stems from improper soil condition.

Few uses of this plant by pioneers or American Indians could be found. It is known that a mucilage from the stem was used in treating coughs and diarrhea. The Menomini secured a medicine from the roots, but its application has been lost.

A material called *osmundine* is obtained from the root masses of the interrupted fern (*Osmunda claytoniana*) and cinnamon fern (*Osmunda cinnamomea*) and used in growing orchids. A similar substance obtained from the royal fern was tried, but found to be "too sour".

This fern, along with its relatives interrupted fern and cinnamon fern, are perhaps the most gorgeous of the Iowa ferns.

Sensitive fern: *Onoclea sensibilis* L.

Other common names: Bead fern.

Onoclea: This was the name used by Dioscorides for another plant, later confused with this species.

Sensibilis: Meaning "sensitive" because of its sensitivity to frost.

Fern family: *Aspleniaceae*

Sensitive fern is found in wooded swamps and moist woodlands from Newfoundland to Manitoba and south to Florida and Texas. In Iowa, it is found in moist woodlands, on the edges of marshes, and in fens in most of the counties in the eastern two-thirds of the state. Fertile fronds appear in mid-summer and produce spores in late summer.

This fern may achieve a height of 3 feet, usually closer to 1 foot and occurs as solitary fronds, but may form a dense stand in a variety of moist habitats. The broadly triangular sterile fronds are long-stalked and the blade is deeply divided. These sterile fronds are rather "un-fern like" in appearance. The margins are wavy and each frond may possess as many as 16 pairs of wide segments. The very different fertile fronds are at first green but turn brown in late summer and consist of hard spikes of berry-like structures which contain the spores. These fertile fronds persist throughout the year and are often visible the following year. When disturbed, the somewhat ragged fertile fronds will often shake out the remaining spores that have over-wintered inside.

This species is very sensitive to cold and will wilt and turn brown at the first frost, hence its common name. This must not be a disadvantage as this fern is very successful and occupies a variety of habitats in Iowa, often forming a nearly monodominant stand.

The Pillager Ojibwa made a tea from the powdered dry root to give relief to the patient with sore breasts and to stimulate the flow of milk.

Spinulose wood fern: *Dryopteris carthusiana* (Vill.) Fuchs. (Formerly known as *D. spinulosa* [O. F. Muell.] Watt)

Other common names: Fancy fern, florist's fern, wood fern, spinulose oak fern.

Dryopteris: From the Greek *drys*, "oak", and *pteris,* "fern", because some members of this genus are called oak ferns.

Carthusiana: Name based on the village Carthusium in the Dauphine region of France where it was first collected by Villers.

True fern family: *Polypodiaceae*

The Spinulose wood fern is found from Labrador to Alberta and south to Virginia, Ohio, Illinois, and Missouri. It is also found in Europe and Asia. In Iowa, it is common in the northeast, infrequent in the southeast, and rare in the central portion. It inhabits a variety of habitats—from moist woods to swamps and occasionally in mesic woods. In Iowa, it is found in moist humus in wet woods.

This is a fairly small fern, reaching a height of around 2 feet, and is a pale green. The fronds grow from a horizontal rhizome which grows on the surface of the soil, usually under a covering of leaves. This rhizome is covered with old stipe bases and is terminated by a crown of several fronds. The lowest pinnae are deltoid-ovate, the others progressively narrower. The pinnules are oblong, pinnately cleft, and the ultimate segments are mucronate—this is where the common name "spinulose" arises.

This is a highly variable species across its range and consists of a series of freely intergrading varieties.

Members of this genus are beautiful and popular with florists. This leads to their being cut and sold in the ornamental trade. They are easily transplanted and used in landscaping in suitable habitats.

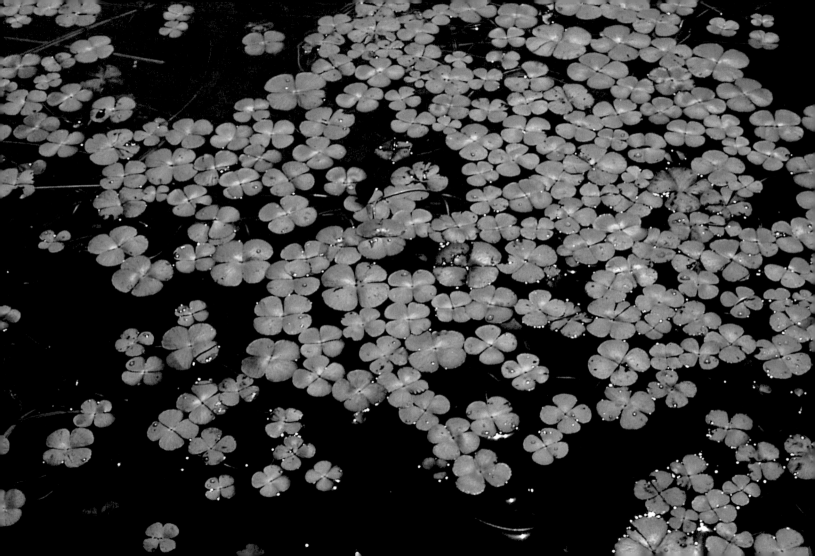

Water clover: *Marsilea quadrifolia* L.

Other common names: European marsilea, pepperwort, water shamrock.

Marsilea: Named for Luigi Fernando, Conte Marsigli, Italian naturalist.

Quadrifolia: So named because the leaf is divided into four equal parts.

Marsilea family: *Marsileaceae*

Water clover is found growing in shallow standing water. In Iowa, it is known only from an impounded lake in Nine Eagles State Park, Decatur County. It is native to Europe, cultivated in this country, and has persisted in water bodies where it may have been discarded. Apparently it was introduced into Connecticut in 1862 and has become established, mainly in the northeastern states. It is a long-lived perennial.

This aquatic fern grows from roots embedded in the bottom of a lake or pond with leaves floating on the surface. The leaves are four-parted like a shamrock. The leaflets are equal, wedge-shaped, petal-like with rounded edges—like a four-leaf clover, or the leaves of *Oxalis*. The leaves are about an inch across.

Fruiting bodies, actually large spores, appear in late summer and persist through the winter, appearing like peppercorns borne on short branches near the bases of the fronds. These may dry for years only to come to life when proper conditions return. It can grow very dense and in some areas become a nuisance. Water clover is a very attractive plant, however, and rare enough in Iowa to be interesting. To the uninitiated, it has no resemblance to a fern.

This species has been sold in commerce in the eastern United States. In some instances it has been discarded in favorable habitats where it has become a nuisance. It reproduces from small sections of the runners, which makes it difficult to eradicate. Its ability to grow on the mud at the edges of ponds makes it an attractive cover plant.

A related species, *Marsilea vestita*, is also known from a single location in Iowa—on the Sioux Quartzite in the extreme northwest corner. It is a native species, however.

Water horsetail: *Equisetum fluviatile* L.

Other common names: Pipes, paddock-pipes, swamp-horsetail, tad-pipe, toad-pipe.

Equisetum: From *equus*, "horse", and *seta*, "tail".

Fluviatile: Meaning "of a river".

Horsetail family: *Equisetaceae*

Water horsetail may be found from Newfoundland to Alaska and south to Iowa, Nebraska, Wyoming, and Oregon. In Iowa, it is found sparingly mainly in the northeast half of the state in shallow standing water, fens, seeps, and marshes. It becomes fertile in May through August.

The smoothest and most hollow of the horsetails, it may grow to nearly 6 feet, normally 3-4 feet, with whorls of ascending or spreading branches. Spores form in a strobilus borne on the tip of the main stem. Reproduction by spores means this species has the capability of colonizing a new habitat quickly. This is one of the oldest living plants.

The perennial grows from branched, widely creeping rhizomes. Because of this rhizomatous system, this species, as well as other horsetails, are good soil binders. The extensive spreading rhizomes allow this species to become the dominant, often the only, plant where it occurs. This underground mass of rhizomes may account for 80 percent of the fresh-weight biomass of water horsetail.

Horsetail has a low amount of silica in its cell walls and is used for food and material for houses by muskrats in northern parts of its range. An alkaloid nerve poison, which may be dangerous to livestock, has been found in this species. Symptoms include unthriftiness and weight loss, followed by loss of control of muscles, which causes the animal to stagger and sway.

Other species of *Equisetum* have been used by Native Americans to cure kidney troubles and were used by women to clear up the system after childbirth. It has also been used in South America as a urethral and intestinal astringent.

The Pillager Ojibwa fed *E. arvense* to their domesticated ducks and to their ponies to give them a glossy coat. An infusion of this plant has been used as a wash for infected wounds and ulcers. Different species of the genus were used by early settlers as a scouring material for pots and pans.

This species hybridizes the *Equisetum arvense* to form *Equisetum X littorale,* one of our rarest plants.

Woodland horsetail: *Equisetum sylvaticum* L.

Other common names: (for *Equisetums* in general) Bottlebrush, cat's tail, horsetail rush, jointgrass, snakegrass, snakepipe, snakeweed, toadpipe, wood rush.

Equisetum: From Latin *equus*, "horse" and *seta*, "bristle".

Sylvaticum: From Latin *sylva*, meaning "wood", "forest", or "woodland".

Horsetail family: *Equisetaceae*

This attractive horsetail is found from Greenland and Labrador to Alaska and south to Michigan, Wisconsin, and Iowa. Its habitats are wooded swamps, wet meadows, and around springs. In Iowa, its preferred habitat is sandy seeps and it is currently known only from Bremer, Buchanan, Fayette, Howard, Iowa, and Linn counties.

It is a fairly common plant in the eastern United States; in Iowa, it is sufficiently rare to be placed on the state's endangered species list.

At first, the woodland horsetail's fertile stems are flesh-colored, narrow, with small abortive branches and capped with a strobilus (cone where spores are borne). After the cone disappears, the plant becomes green, and resembles the sterile stems except shorter and somewhat flat-topped. The sterile stems achieve a height of 18 inches and occur as solitary plants. The branches occur in whorls, achieving a length of around 3 inches and are branched. The strobilus, about an inch long, becomes ripe and sheds spores in May and June, then withers and drops off. The rootstock is slender and branches deep in the soil.

This is our prettiest horsetail. The lacy, delicate, emerald green branches form the upper two-thirds of the stem in horizontal whorls. These spread outward and droop downward.

Young shoots of some *Equisetum* species have been used as far back as ancient Rome. Meadow horsetail (*E. pratense*) forms spherical tubers which were eaten by some American Indians in Minnesota. Woodland horsetail forms large ovate tubers, but no reference to their edibility exists. Western tribes made a tea of certain horsetails for treatment of kidney ailments and dropsy. In Washington, some species of horsetails were boiled to prepare a shampoo for treatment of lice and mites.

The Menomini made a tea from the stems to cure dropsy. They also pulverized the plant and used it as a poultice to stop the flow of blood. It is known that plants of this genus contain thiaminase and aconitic acid, which is suspected of poisoning grazing animals. Anyone eating any part of this plant would be at risk of being poisoned. Experiments have not definitely identified the poisonous principle and more research is needed.

Our *Equisetum* species are what remain of an ancient genus. Fossils of species, which grew as much as 90 feet tall and 1 foot in diameter, have been found in coal beds.

TREES, SHRUBS, AND VINES

(in alphabetical order, by common name)

Black ash: *Fraxinus nigra* Marsh.

Other common names: Bottomland ash, swamp ash.

Fraxinus: From the classical Latin name.

Nigra: Meaning "black".

Olive family: *Oleaceae*

This handsome tree is found from Newfoundland to Manitoba and south to Virginia, Ohio, Iowa, and North Dakota. In Iowa, it ranges from absent in the western part to frequent on the Paleozoic Plateau. It is a tree of alluvial bottoms and moist wooded slopes. In other parts of its range it may be found in swamps, sometimes dominating the hardwood swamps in the south.

Black ash may achieve a height of 100 feet, with a trunk diameter of 2 feet. It has opposite, compound leaves, each with 7–11 leaflets that may become 6 inches long by 1½ inches wide. These are stalkless and have rounded bases. The buds are black, hence the common name, and the leaf scars are circular.

The root system is shallow and the tree is easily uprooted by wind. It seems to have a high tolerance for insect damage and diseases.

The flowers of this species are purplish, small, and occur in May. The fruit is a flat, winged samara, 1½ inches long, with the wing enveloping the seed. Presence of this wing aids in dispersal by the wind. There may be as many as 3,000 low viability seeds per pound.

The wood has some value for interior finish, cabinet work, and for making barrel hoops and baskets.

There are five native species of ash in Iowa. The blue ash (*Fraxinus quadrangulata*) is very rare in the extreme southeast. The white ash (*Fraxinus americana*) is common over much of the state and is a tree of upland woods. The red ash (*Fraxinus pennsylvanica*) is a tree of alluvial or moist woods. The green ash (*Fraxinus pennsylvanica* var. *lanceolata*) is the most common and is found at the edges of moist woods. The black ash can be separated from the others by the presence of black buds and the lack of petioles on the leaflets.

Black willow: *Salix nigra* Marsh.

Other common names: Black osier, river willow.

Salix: This is the classical name for the willows, or taken from *salis* which means "near water".

Nigra: Meaning "black", from the dark brown to blackish bark.

Willow family: *Salicaceae*

Black willow ranges from New Brunswick to North Dakota and south to New England, North Carolina, Alabama, and Tennessee. In Iowa, it is of frequent to common occurrence statewide. Its favored habitats are along streams and edges of lakes, but it will grow in floodplains, seeps, and ravines. This tree is often multi-stemmed. It is in flower during April into June. The bark of the tree is heavily ridged and dark brown to black.

This willow grows to a height of over 100 feet. The leaves are alternate, short-stalked, often becoming falcate (scythe-shaped), and up to 4 inches long. Male and female flowers are in a terminal catkin on leafy shoots in a tight cluster and appear as the leaves begin to expand. When the fruits are ripe, they split open to release the down-covered seeds which are dispersed to the surrounding landscape by wind. This species matures at 50–60 years and may live to be over 70 years old.

The greatest value of this tree is probably as a soil anchor in erodible areas. However, the reddish-brown wood of this tree is used for making charcoal, boxes, crates, excelsior, and baskets. In certain parts of the country, this species is used as an ornamental. There are 18 species of willows in Iowa, ranging from low-growing forms a few feet tall to the black willow and crack willow which become tree-size. Some grow in broad environmental conditions; others are restricted to wet peatlands; some are common and probably grow in every county; others are known from only a few locations.

Willows have been used since the time of Christ for their pain-relieving and fever-reducing qualities. Early settlers used the bark to make a bitter tonic, an astringent, and a treatment for intermittent fever. Fresh bark contains *salicin*, which probably decomposes to salicylic acid in the human body. Aspirin gets its effect from a chemically related salicylic acid.

The Menomini used the roots as a spasmodic and for colic and diarrhea. The Meskwaki used the roots to prepare a tea as an enema for flux. The leaves have been used as a poultice to stop bleeding. A preparation from black willow leaves has been considered an aphrodisiac by some North American Indians.

Buds and twigs are of great wildlife food value for grouse and ptarmigan. Rabbits, elk, moose, and deer eat the twigs, foliage, and bark. The pliable twigs of several species have been used in basket making.

Bog birch: *Betula pumila* L. var. *glandulifera* Regel

Other common names: Low birch, swamp birch, dwarf birch, tag alder.

Betula: The ancient Latin name for the genus.

Pumila: Latin for "dwarf" or "short".

Birch family: *Betulaceae*

Bog birch has a range which extends from Quebec to British Columbia and south to New York, Indiana, Iowa, North Dakota, and Montana. This shrub is on the southern edge of its range in northeastern Iowa, where it is found on fens and calcareous wetlands, primarily on the Iowan Erosional Surface. It is in flower in May and June.

The shrub may reach 10 feet, usually less, and often has multiple stems from the same root system. The stems may be prostrate and matted. The short-petioled leaves are pale green or whitish below, obovate or orbicular, and coarsely dentate. The fruit is a nearly orbicular samara. The fruiting ament (catkin) is erect and cone-like, up to 1 inch long and ½ inch thick.

There are at least three varieties of bog birch; the one that occurs in Iowa is widespread and distinguished from the others by the presence of glands on the lower leaf surfaces and twigs. In Iowa, this shrub is known only from peat deposits in Black Hawk, Chickasaw, Howard, and Mitchell counties.

The Flambeau Ojibwa made the ribs of their baskets from the twigs of bog birch when they used sweet grass as the weaving material.

Buttonbush: *Cephalanthus occidentalis* L.

Other common names: Common buttonbush, globeflowers, honey-balls, pond dogwood, swamp sycamore.

Cephalanthus: From the Greek *kephale*, "head", and *anthose,* "a flower".

Occidentalis: Meaning western, or of the western hemisphere.

Madder family: *Rubiaceae*

Buttonbush is found in most of the northeastern and eastern United States and in Cuba. Varieties are found in California, Oklahoma, and Texas. In Iowa, it grows on the edges of wetlands throughout the state, but by far most common in the southeast, often found in shallow standing water. It is in bloom in July and August.

This shrub or small tree may achieve a height of 20 feet, but normally grows 3 to 10 feet. The leaves are petioled, smooth, and opposite or in whorls of threes and fours. Leaves are firm and shining, with prominent veins, especially on the underside.

The fragrant, white flowers are tubular with long, protruding styles tipped by a prominent stigma. They are borne in spherical heads similar to those of the sycamore tree and furnish nectar to bees and butterflies. The fruits are eaten by some birds in winter. Wood ducks and pheasants are known to utilize the seeds.

This plant is in the same family as the coffee tree and the tree which furnishes quinine. Rafinesque's *Medical Flora* told that the bark, especially of the root, was made into a tonic by the southern Native Americans and French settlers for treatment of fevers. Although the seeds provide food for certain animals, the leaves contain glucoside, a poison which may affect browsing animals. Some medicines are derived from the leaves. The root bark has been used to treat diabetes.

This species can be propagated by seed, or by cuttings of ripe wood in the fall or of green wood in the spring. It makes an attractive addition to moist habitats with its striking globular flower heads and its habit of blooming in late summer.

Cottonwood: *Populus deltoides* Marsh.

Other common names: Alamo, Carolina poplar, Eastern cottonwood, eastern poplar, necklace poplar, necklace tree, river poplar, yellow cottonwood.

Populus: Classical name for the plant.

Deltoides: From the delta-shaped outline of the leaf.

Willow family: *Salicaceae*

This stately tree, one of the survivors of the plant world, enjoys wide range in eastern North America—from Quebec to the Rocky Mountains and south to Florida and Tennessee. In Iowa, it grows statewide, but is replaced in the far west by the western cottonwood, *P. deltoides* var. *monilifera*, mainly on sandy soils along the Missouri River. These are plants of wet soil, usually alluvium, but will thrive if planted in upland habitats. They do best when within 15 feet of the water level, but may be found higher on the landscape in situations where water collects. The flowering time is April.

The cottonwood grows to heights of over 100 feet, with a trunk 6 feet in diameter. The older bark is gray and thick, the younger is thin and greenish-yellow. The triangular-shaped leaves are on rather long petioles that are flattened near the blade. They are 3–7 inches long with two to three glands at the apex of the petiole. Winter buds are nearly an inch long and taper to a sharp point.

The flowers appear early in the season, before the leaves, with staminate and pistillate flowers in catkins on different trees. The female trees release large quantities of fluffy seeds that may be sufficient to clog sewers. For this reason, some cities have banned their use for planting along streets. The seeds have a relatively short germination period and must alight on wet soil to take root. The timing of seed-release often coincides with receding spring flood waters.

Male cottonwoods are planted for ornamental purposes due to their fast growth and lack of seeds to release. However, the branches are brittle and break easily and they are subject to storm damage. The wood has some value for pulp and may be used as a cheap source of packing boxes.

This tree, when older, often has cavities which are good for wildlife. It can also grow where few other trees can survive. It is the standard tree of the Great Plains.

Elderberry: *Sambucus canadensis* L.

Other common names: American elder, black-berried elder, common elder, elder blow, sweet elder.

Sambucus: Perhaps from the Latin *sambuce,* an ancient musical instrument because the stems of this species were hollowed out to make tubes and used as flutes and whistles.

Canadensis: meaning "of Canada".

Honeysuckle family: *Caprifoliaceae*

The elderberry, a shrub of wooded swamps and wetland edges, ranges from Nova Scotia and Quebec to Manitoba and south to Georgia and Oklahoma. In Iowa, it is common throughout the state in a variety of habitats ranging from the edges of marshes to woodland borders and fencerows. It is in flower in June and July. The fruits ripen in September.

This rather coarse, branched shrub may achieve a height of 10 feet and often forms a dense thicket. The pinnately compound leaves, arranged oppositely along the stem, normally have seven sharply serrate leaflets. The leaves may achieve a length of 10 inches with short-stalked leaflets, which may be 4 inches long. The stems and twigs are covered with small, warty structures. This species spreads by underground runners which may result in a dense colony forming.

The inflorescence, a head which is often 6 inches across, is composed of small white flowers less than ¼ inch across. The fruit is a small purple-black berry which contains several seeds. These fruits turn from green to purple-black in late August and September.

Native Americans used this plant extensively as food by eating the berries fresh or cooked and by concocting a beverage by steeping the blossoms in water. The fruits have been used to make pies, wine, and pancakes. It is a common food of quail, pheasant, doves, turkey, and deer, and livestock readily eat the foliage. Pioneers used this species to make tubes for collecting maple syrup. The fresh leaves, flowers, bark, and roots contain a bitter alkaloid which can produce a small amount of hydrocyanic acid (prussic acid), but this is destroyed with cooking.

Children have been poisoned by chewing on the bark of whistles which are commonly made by punching out the pith of the stem. The root is poisonous if eaten. Elder flowers have been used medicinally by the pioneers as an infusion to treat blisters, sores, and hemorrhoids. The related red elder (*S. racemosa*) is considered poisonous—but has been used by the Menomini as a powerful medicine—and only used when all other remedies failed. It has powerful purgative and emetic qualities and was used in cases of serious constipation. The Indian name for elder means "pop-gum wood".

Indigo bush: *Amorpha fruticosa* L.

Other common names: False indigo, bastard indigo, river locust.

Amorpha: From Greek *amorphos,* meaning generally "without shape", referring to the flower with only one petal.

Fruticosa: Meaning "shrubby".

Legume family: *Fabaceae (Leguminosae)*

   Indigo bush is found from Pennsylvania west to Wisconsin and Kansas and south to northern Florida and Louisiana. Its habitats are stream banks, along lake shores, and in prairie swales. It is a heterogeneous plant with many varieties throughout its range. It is frequent to common throughout Iowa and blooming occurs from late May to July.

   This shrub generally grows less than 10 feet in height but may attain a height of 20 feet under ideal conditions. The long-petioled leaves are pubescent and pinnately compound with 13 to 35 leaflets that measure about 2 inches long and 1 inch wide. The leaflets have smooth margins, a grayish green cast, and large resinous dots.

   The flower corolla consists of only the upper dilated petal called the standard, or banner. It is violet, usually 1/3 inch long, and wraps around the stamens and pistil. The inflorescence is a panicle of erect racemes, which give it a spike-like appearance. The protruding anthers are bright orange.

   The curved seedpods, which also have large resinous dots, are less than an inch long. Although each pod contains only one or two seeds, the plant is prolific and has many pods. The seeds are tiny, with an average of 60,000 per pound.

   The species was used medicinally, but the history of its uses have been lost through time. It is known that it was gathered and spread on the bison butchering ground to keep the meat clean.
   Although the plant may be poisonous to stock that graze on it, it is a good wildlife food and is valuable as a soil anchor along streams. Bobwhite quail are known to eat the fruits.

   Because it is particularly attractive when in bloom, it is valued as an ornamental, but does not survive well in shade. In northeastern United States it has been cultivated as an ornamental and will occasionally escape and persist in the wild.

   Some taxonomists separate the variety *angustifolia,* based on narrow leaves and pubescent petioles. Other members of the genus occurring in Iowa are lead plant, *A. canescens,* and fragrant false indigo, *A. nana.* Both are 3 feet or less tall; lead plant is very hairy, while fragrant false indigo is glabrous (without hairs) and both grow in dry habitats.

Meadow sweet: *Spiraea alba* DuRoi

Other common names: Bridal wreath, hardhack, muskrat-bush, narrow-leaved meadowsweet, steeplebush.

Spiraea: From the Greek *speira*, "a wreath".

Alba: Meaning "white" from the color of the flowers.

Rose family: *Rosaceae*

Meadow sweet is found from Quebec to Saskatchewan and North Dakota and south to Delaware, North Carolina, Ohio, Illinois, and northern Missouri. In Iowa, it is found statewide, but is more common in the northeast and northcentral and rare in the south and west. It is found on moist prairies, swales, fens, and edges of marshes. Its blooming time is June through August.

The erect shrub grows to 6 feet in height. The stems are yellowish brown, normally unbranched, with leaves arranged alternatively. The leaves are petioled, up to 2 inches long and ½ inch wide, finely serrate, pubescent, and pale on the underside.

The inflorescence is an elongate panicle with pubescent branchlets. There are five petals, five sepals, and the white flowers are about ¼ inch across. Several linear seeds are found in each of the five to eight follicles.

There are about 75 species in the genus in the Northern hemisphere, but only one in Iowa. It is found on most moist prairies in the northeast quarter of Iowa.

This is very closely related, possibly the same species, as the bridal wreath so commonly planted around dwellings.

In part of its range meadow sweet serves as browse for deer and has been known to be eaten by prairie chickens.

The Forest Potawatomi used this plant as one of their medicines, but the exact nature of this use has been lost. Among the early settlers, the root was used for its diuretic and astringent properties. It was also listed in the early dispensatory that the herbage was used as an astringent and diuretic. An infusion of the leaves is quite like China tea and used as a substitute for that drink. The Flambeau Ojibwa used the root to prepare a bait for trapping.

Red-osier dogwood: *Cornus stolonifera* Michx.

Other common names: Marsh flame, red dogwood, red dagwood.

Cornus: Latin name from *cornu,* "horn", alluding to the hardness of the wood.

Stolonifera: Derived from its stolon-bearing habit.

Dogwood family: *Cornaceae*

Red-osier dogwood grows from Newfoundland and Labrador to the Yukon and south to West Virginia, Ohio, Indiana, Illinois, Iowa and Nebraska. In Iowa, it is native only in the northern tiers of counties, but is widely planted in other parts of the state. Its habitat is edges of marshes, shores of ponds and lakes, and fens. Its flowering time is late May into July.

This shrub may attain a height of 10 feet and normally sends up erect osier-like branches from the prostrate branches to form a dense thicket. The young twigs are bright reddish-purple. The leaves may be 5 inches long, broadly ovate with five to seven pairs of veins.

The inflorescence is a flat-topped cyme up to 2 inches across and relatively few-flowered. The fruit is white to bluish, with individuals up to ⅓ inch in diameter, but vary widely in size.

There are some 50 species of dogwoods in the world, around 20 of which occur in North America and seven occur in Iowa. A great array of wildlife utilize the fruits and buds of red-osier dogwood. Some examples are ruffed grouse, bobwhite, wild turkey, cardinal, catbird, and grosbeak. The wood and fruits have been known to be used by beaver and cottontail, and browsed by deer.

Fruits may persist on the plants into the winter months, making it particularly useful to certain wildlife.

Because of the bright color of the stems it is often used in landscaping. It is easily propagated by cuttings either in fall or spring or by layering and using the rooted stock.

The fruits were eaten by North American Indians in the Missouri River region and in British Columbia.

This plant is one of several which the Menomini, Forest Potawatomi and other Indians call *kinnikinik* and also used for tobacco. It was sometimes added to smoking tobacco to make the tobacco more mild. To make kinnikinik, the bark was peeled off the stems and twigs. After flaking, it was roasted over a fire to prepare it for use.

The bark was also used to make a liquid hemorrhoid remedy. The Menomini also used the bark of one of the dogwood species to make a poultice to cure cancer of the face.

Riverbank grape: *Vitis riparia* Michx.

Other common names: Frost grape.

Vitis: From Latin *viti,* pertaining to the vine, specifically another member of the genus.

Riparia: From the Latin *ripa* "bank of stream or river" or *riparius* "frequenting banks of streams or rivers".

Grape family: *Vitaceae*

Riverbank grape is found throughout a considerable portion of North America—from Quebec to Manitoba and south to New England, West Virginia, Tennessee, Missouri, Texas, and New Mexico. This is a genus largely restricted to the temperate regions of the Northern Hemisphere. In Iowa, it is common throughout the state. Its habitats are floodplains, woodland edges, and along streams.

The leaves, with coarse, acuminate teeth, are up to 6 inches broad with long tapering lobes and a prolonged acuminate apex of those on the fertile branches. The fruits are small, usually around ⅓ inch in diameter, with a whitish bloom.

This species climbs on trees and other vegetation, adhering to these plants by tendrils, which are found opposite leaves on the stem. The bark scales off in long strips. In some old specimens, the stem reaches a diameter of several inches. There is a dividing membrane, called a diaphragm, located in the nodes of most grapes. In the riverbank grape, this diaphragm is noticeably thicker than in its close relatives.

The small, inconspicuous flowers are in a compound thryse. The flowers are five-parted and fall off without expanding. Some plants have perfect flowers, others have only male flowers. When in bloom, this plant emits one of the sweetest aromas in nature. This is the common "wild grape" of Iowa.

There are some 30 species of wild grapes in the continental United States. There are four species of wild grape in Iowa; the other three are rare and local.

Native Americans gathered fruits of this and related species, drying them for the winter. The somewhat acid-tasting grapes improve after a frost, when they become sweeter. The fruits of fox grape, *V. vulpina,* were in great demand for making jellies, marmalades, and preserves. George Washington Carver recommended preparation of a "leather" from a related species, *V. rotundifolia,* called muscadine, which has a large, sweet fruit. The exfoliating bark of the riverbank grape is often used by birds in nest-building.

All grape species are of value as wildlife food, but there is a marked variation in the yield—from abundant to a near total failure. Wildlife species make no distinction between wild and cultivated grapes and in some regions damage to vineyards is considerable.

River birch: *Betula nigra* L.

Other common names: Black birch, red birch, water birch.

Betula: This is the ancient Latin name for this genus.

Nigra: Meaning "black", from the dark appearance of the bark.

Birch family: *Betulaceae*

River birch is found from New York and Connecticut to Pennsylvania, West Virginia, and Ohio and west to southern Michigan, eastern Iowa, and Kansas. In Iowa, it is found along streams and in very wet bottomlands, especially in the eastern third of Iowa. It seems to do best in sandy substrate. It becomes increasingly less frequent toward the western part of the state and is rare or absent in the western third. It is in flower in April and May.

This tree may reach a height of 70 feet and a diameter of over 30 inches in Iowa. However, these large trees are found only in southeast and eastcentral Iowa, with younger trees common along streams farther north. The irregularly oval leaves are arranged alternately on the stem and the margin of the upper part of the leaves are doubly serrate. These leaves are 2½ to 3 inches long, bright green on the upper surface and grayish-white below. The young bark is salmon-colored, with strips of older bark peeling and curling. This gives the tree a shaggy appearance.

Flowers are arranged in catkins, which are dry, usually unisexual spikes. These are about 1 inch long, but the cone-like pistillate (female) catkins disintegrate when ripe. The staminate (male) catkins form in summer and open the following spring. The fruit, a nutlet, is flattened and winged and matures in May or June. Flowers appear before the leaves in spring. The wind shakes the upright cone-like catkins, scattering the seeds on the rich soil where they soon germinate.

This is a desirable ornamental tree which can grow in a variety of habitats and is often used in landscaping. The bark of this tree has a tendency to peel off into extremely thin, tissue paper-like membranous sheets. This probably accounts for the fact that the white birch, yellow birch, paper birch, and canoe birch were used more commonly for storage baskets, wigwam frames, sap buckets, and similar uses.

Sage willow: *Salix candida* Fluegge ex Willd.

Other common names: Hoary willow.

Salix: The classical name for the genus.

Candida: Meaning "white" or "bright" for the whitish cast of the twigs and undersides of the leaves.

Willow family: *Salicaceae*

This diminutive willow is found from Labrador to British Columbia and south to New Brunswick, New England, Pennsylvania, northern Ohio, northern Indiana, northern Illinois, northern Iowa, South Dakota, and Colorado. In Iowa, it is found in calcareous habitats, such as fens and other peatlands in the northeastern one-third of the state. It is in flower in April and May.

This shrub, which normally achieves a height of around 3–4 feet, is one of our most distinctive willows. It is so because of the dense white-matted hairs on the undersides of the leaves, which have rolled-under margins. The leaves are around 2–5 inches long, and normally five to ten times as long as wide. The leaves are arranged alternately along the stem. The twigs are also covered with dense white-matted hairs, but tend to become less so with age.

The pinkish to white catkins are cylindrical, densely flowered, and appear before the leaves. The flowers are unisexual. The fruits (capsules) are densely white-woolly. This species is known to hybridize with other willows such as *S. sericea* and *S. pedicellaris*, which grow in the same habitat. Sage willow is normally a solitary species but may be scattered over a wide area.

The Ojibwa boiled the thick, inner bark of the roots to prepare a decoction for treatment of cough. Some willows are important bee plants—others are used for basket-making.

Other common names: Coyote willow, gray sandbar willow, gray willow, inland willow.

Salix: This is the classical name for this widespread genus.

Exigua: From the Latin word *exiguus,* meaning "weak" or "feeble", from the small size and ease with which the branches are broken.

Interior: Meaning "inland", derived from its distribution.

Willow family: *Salicaceae*

The sandbar willow is a shrub or small tree widespread in North America, being found from eastern Quebec to Alaska and south to New England, Ohio, Indiana, Illinois, Arkansas, and Oklahoma. The typical form is also widespread in the western United States. In Iowa, sandbar willow is common throughout the state on stream banks and especially sand or gravel bars where it often is a pioneer. It flowers in May and early June.

The linear leaves, arranged alternately along the stem, may achieve a length of nearly 5 inches and are remotely denticulate. The leaves are silky pubescent or glabrous on both surfaces and taper to a short petiole. The stipules at the base of leaves in willows do not persist in this species. The plant is often multi-stemmed with multiple sprouts from the base that have large, heavily toothed, lance-oblong leaves that appear quite different from those of the adult plant.

The staminate (male) catkins are on long peduncles, up to 1 inch long, with two stamens. The female catkins are up to 3 inches long on leafy peduncles. As in the rest of the willows, these appear with or before the leaves.

This species is extensively colonial and spreads via stolons (underground stems). Because of this trait, it may become a dense thicket, particularly where the soil is sandy and moist.

There are 18 species of willows in Iowa, ranging from the beautiful drooping weeping willow planted in many of our front yards to the pussy willow, whose fuzzy catkins herald the arrival of spring, to the prairie willow that appears on many high-quality prairies throughout the state. Others, like the bog willow, *S. pedicellaris,* and sage willow, *S. candida,* are so fussy about their habitat that they only grow in peatlands, and the shining willow, *Salix lucida,* is only currently known from two sites in Iowa.

Willows have been used for 2,000 years for their pain-relieving qualities. Early settlers used the bark to make a bitter tonic, an astringent, and a treatment for certain fevers. The sandbar willow is so widespread that it was likely one of the willows used for these purposes. Fresh willow bark contains *salcin,* which forms salicylic acid in the human body. Aspirin gets its effect from a synthetic salicylic acid.

The Menomini used the roots as a spasmodic and to control colic and diarrhea. The Potawatomi boiled the root bark for a tea to stop bleeding, and the Meskwaki used the roots to prepare a tea as an enema for flux. The leaves were used as a poultice to stop bleeding and to treat colic. The bast (fibrous portion of the inner bark) has been dried and ground into flour and used as an emergency food. It is bitter and only used during dire straits.

The foliage, twigs, and bark are eaten by elk, moose, deer, and rabbits. Buds and twigs are a major staple for grouse and ptarmigans. This species performs a valuable function as a soil binder in unstable stream-side habitats.

Silky dogwood: *Cornus amomum* Miller ssp. *obliqua* (Raf.) J.S.Wils.

Other common names: Dagwood, Gray dagwood, red willow, streamside dogwood.

Cornus: From the Latin *cornu,* "a horn", from the hardness of the wood of a related European species.

Amomum: Latin name for some shrub, the identity of which is now lost.

Obliqua: Meaning "oblique", referring probably to the angle of the branches of the type.

Dogwood family: *Cornaceae*

   This shrub, which may achieve a height of 10 feet, is found from New Brunswick to North Dakota and south to New England, West Virginia, Arkansas, and Oklahoma. In Iowa, it is common in the northeast quarter, infrequent in the remainder of the state. Its habitats are moist woods, wet prairies, and floodplain marshes. Its flowering period stretches from mid-May to mid-July and it is in fruit from late May into October.

   The branches have a reddish brown to gray bark and a tawny-colored pith. As with most dogwoods, the arrangement of branches is opposite. The underside of the leaves have a fine pubescence, consisting of white appressed hairs, which results in a silky appearance, hence its common name. The leaves are simple, up to 5 inches long, rounded at the base with an abrupt tip and have four to six pairs of lateral veins.

   The inflorescences occur in open cymes with small white flowers. The fruit, which may persist on the shrub throughout the winter, is a dark blue berry.

   There are seven species of dogwoods in Iowa, ranging from the tiny dwarf cornel, *Cornus canadensis,* which grows on algific talus slopes, to the rough-leaved dogwood, *Cornus drummondii,* which may achieve the status of a small tree. Only one species, the pagoda tree, *Cornus alternifolia,* has alternate leaf arrangement.

   Silky dogwood is often planted for wildlife cover. It forms dense thickets in or near wetlands and this characteristic provides excellent habitat for an array of wildlife. The bark is quite palatable for rabbits and hares, the fruit provides food for quite a range of wildlife including ruffed grouse, sharptailed grouse, and gray partridge. In the northern portion of its range, it is browsed by moose and deer.

   The bark of several species of dogwoods were used in the preparation of an astringent. The fruits, steeped in an acidic solution, furnished an extraction used by the Menomini for treatment of pleurisy. A western species provided straight, tough wood for arrows. The young flowers were used by the Potawatomi to prepare a flavorful tea.

Silver maple: *Acer saccharinum* L.

Other common names: Creek maple, river maple, soft maple, swamp maple, white maple.

Acer: Latin name of the maple.

Saccharinum: Meaning "sugary".

Maple family: *Aceraceae*

Silver maple is found from New Brunswick and Quebec to Minnesota and South Dakota and south to Florida, Tennessee, and Oklahoma. In Iowa, it is the dominant tree on floodplains, especially in the eastern half of the state, where it is often found growing on the very edges of streams. The flowers appear very early in spring; in Iowa, it may begin to flower in late February or early March, depending on weather conditions.

The tree may achieve a height of over 80 feet, with long, pendulous branchlets. The trunk diameter can be over 5 feet. The leaves are opposite, deeply lobed and with a narrow terminal leaf base. The leaves are green above and silvery white below with greenish petioles. The twigs and buds, however, are reddish.

The bark is smooth and gray on young trees and on younger branches, but becomes ragged and flaky as the tree ages. The roots are spread widely and are often so shallow they may be seen on the surface of the soil.

The tiny flowers are red and lack petals. Pollination is by the wind and the resulting fruit is a winged samara with wings up to 2 inches. Staminate (male) and pistillate (female) flowers are normally on different branches on the same tree or on separate trees. The fruits are shed in great quantity in early June.

This fast-growing tree is widely planted for ornamental purposes. Its soft wood results in the formation of many cavities, which make it valuable as a den tree. The silver maple can withstand prolonged periods when the bases are in standing water. In the northern half of the state it is associated with American elm and green ash; in southeast Iowa the sycamore becomes a more frequent associate. Farther north, the red maple is found growing with the silver maple, but it is also found in upland habitats. In Iowa the red maple is restricted to a small area in extreme northeast Iowa.

When the wind blows on a silver maple, the tree's appearance suddenly changes from green to silver as the silvery undersides of the leaves are exposed, hence its common name.

The silver maple was sometimes used as a source of maple syrup, but the concentration of sugar in the sap is so low that it could not compete with the sugar maple. No uses of the silver maple by Native Americans are known; however, the red maple and mountain maple are known to have been used by the Ojibwa for various purposes. The wood of these maples is sometimes used as a substitute for hard or sugar maple in furniture.

Sycamore: *Platanus occidentalis* L.

Other common names: Buttonwood, plane tree.

Platanus: From the greek *platys,* "broad", from the width of the leaves.

Occidentalis: Meaning "western", from its distribution in the western hemisphere.

Plane tree family: *Platanaceae*

This distinctive and lovely tree enjoys a wide distribution in North America—from Maine to Ontario and Nebraska and south to Florida, Alabama, Mississippi, and Texas. In Iowa, it is most common on the Southern Iowa Drift Plain and diminishes in frequency northward. Along the Des Moines River, for example, it terminates its range in Boone County and is seldom found farther north. Its habitat is wet woodlands and along streams.

The bark is conspicuously mottled and scales off in broad, brittle, thin sheets. This exposes the light tan or nearly white trunk which makes it easy to pick out these trees on the landscape. The white bark of the limbs seems to gleam, especially in the moonlight, making it one of the most conspicuous and unmistakable of trees, and accounting for one of its local names—"Ghost of the Forest".

This is one of our largest deciduous trees with heights of up to 170 feet recorded, with trunks up to 11 feet in diameter. The crown may be 100 feet across. The leaves are very large—up to 9 inches across and somewhat star-shaped.

The flowers occur in ball-like clusters, with male and female flowers in separate clusters on the same tree. The fruit is a spherical structure about an inch across which hangs at the end of a long thin stem throughout the winter and in spring ruptures to free the wind-dispersed nutlets.

Sycamores are often used in landscaping but are susceptible to a fungus which inhibits leaves from forming early in the season. This is rarely fatal but detracts from the appearance. The wood, which is very hard, has been used for butcher blocks because it resists splitting, and for ox-yokes, and tobacco boxes. It has been used for veneer for furniture because of the beauty of the medullary rays in radial section. More recently, sycamore has been used for wooden ware, boxes and crates, barrels, and even pulp for making paper.

Early reports stated that pioneers used the sap for making sugar and syrup. Some ornithologists believe this tree, with its often hollow trunks, provided homes for chimney swifts prior to settlement and construction of buildings. It has been reported that the extinct Carolina paroquet preferred the fruit of the sycamore as a favorite food. These old trees also were used by early settlers as a place to smoke meat and store grain. Some were even large enough to furnish temporary shelter for pioneer families.

HERBS GROWING IN WATER: EMERGENT, FLOATING, OR SUBMERGENT

(in alphabetical order, by common name)

American lotus: *Nelumbo lutea* (Willd.) Pers.

Other common names: Duck corn, great yellow water lily, rattlenut, water chinquapin, waternut, wankapin, yackeynut, yankapin.

Nelumbo: A word of Ceylonese origin for the Asian lotus.

Lutea: From Latin for "yellow", referring to the flower color.

Waterlily family: *Nymphaeaceae*

American lotus is found from Florida to Texas and north locally to New England, New York, southern Ontario, Minnesota, and Iowa. In Iowa, it is found mainly in the backwaters of the Mississippi and Missouri Rivers, where it may form extensive beds. It has been introduced into interior lakes, such as Lily Lake in the Amana colonies and Otter Creek marsh in Tama County. It is in bloom from July through August.

The large, round leaves, up to 2 feet in diameter, are peltate—attached to the petiole at the center. The margins of the leaves are smooth and turned upward in the shape of a shallow funnel. Prominent veins radiate from the center to the outer edge, usually branching once or twice toward the margin. Leaves may be held a foot or more above the water, or they may float on the surface.

The horizontal perennial rootstock may be as long as 50 feet. In the fall, numerous tuberous enlargements store starch to provide nourishment for early growth the following spring.

Pale yellow, sweet-scented flowers resembling water lilies are held above the water. The flowers are large, often 8 inches across, and each has several rings of petals and sepals, which are similar.

An elevated receptacle stands in the center of the flower. As seeds develop, this funnel-shaped receptacle expands to as much as 5 inches across and becomes woody. Its flat top is pitted, with each pit holding a spherical, acorn-like seed which is up to ½ inch in diameter. There may be 25 to 30 seeds per receptacle. These seeds are released when the receptacle decomposes and the seeds may lie in the sediment for decades before germinating.

The seeds have long been an important source of food for American Indians in the eastern half of the United States. Eaten when half-ripe, their taste resembles chestnuts. Ripe seeds were boiled or roasted.

Growing tips and tubers along the underwater rootstock were prepared for food by boiling or roasting. Their flavor reminds one of yams or sweet potatoes. For storage, Indians cut these banana-like tubers crosswise into small sections and strung them on a basswood string. Once dried, they could be stored in a dry place for extended periods. When needed, they were soaked and cooked with meat, corn, or beans. As such, they served as an important winter food.

As long as 400 years ago, American Indians cultivated the American lotus on the Cumberland and Tennessee Rivers. Early residents of the Amana area recall groups of Indians camping by the old Amana millpond while the women and children waded waist deep to harvest the tubers.

The seeds and tubers provide a rich source of food for many birds and other marsh animals.

Arrowhead: *Sagittaria latifolia* Willd.

Other common names: Broadleaf arrowhead, duck potato, Indian onion, katniss, swamp potato, swan potato, tule potato, tule root, wapatoo, water nut, white potato.

Sagittaria: From Latin meaning "of an arrow", referring to the arrowhead shape of the leaf.

Latifolia: From Latin meaning "wide leaf".

Water plantain family: *Alismataceae*

Arrowhead is found from New Brunswick to British Columbia and south to South Carolina, Alabama, Louisiana, Oklahoma, and California. In Iowa, it is found throughout the state in wet bottomlands, marshes, and edges of ponds in shallow water, or in slow-moving streams. It blooms from July into September.

As its name implies, this plant is distinguished by its dark green leaves in the shape of arrowheads. The leaves, up to a foot long, occur mostly above the water level on petioles to 3 feet long. In deeper water, leaves may become narrower—sometimes nearly grass-like. The liquid from broken stems is milky.

The perennial root system has long runners which produce white potato-sized tubers in late summer. These tubers, typically twice as long as broad, end in a pointed tip.

Attractive flowers to over an inch across appear in whorls of two to five, mostly three, erect spike-like flower stalks. Flower parts are in threes—three petals and three sepals. Petals are rounded, usually with a small indentation. In most cases, the smaller upper flowers bear pollen while the larger lower flowers are seed producers. Individual seeds, about ⅛ inch across, develop in spherical clusters ranging from ½ to 1½ inches across.

Tubers of arrowhead provided a major food source for many American Indians. As such, they were an important commodity in trade. Some Indians sliced the boiled tubers and strung the pieces on basswood cords to dry in the sun. Once thoroughly dried, the slices stored easily and became a major winter food supply. The potato-like tubers were mostly boiled or roasted. When cooked they tend to lose their slightly bitter taste and take on the flavor of water chestnuts.

Early explorers often depended on arrowhead tubers for food. Lewis and Clark ate the tubers and referred to them as *wapatoo* in their journal records. Wapatoo was the common name applied to this species by Indians throughout the west.

American Indian women harvested tubers by entering the chilly water, supporting themselves by a hold on a canoe, and forcing the tubers loose with their toes. Thus freed, the tubers floated to the surface where they were collected. When a storage cache of a muskrat could be found, tubers were stolen—or "traded" by replacing them with a more plentiful food to avoid angering the powers that look after the welfare of the muskrat. Both fruits and tubers are food for various species of waterfowl.

A similar species, called wappate, was used for food by California Indians. The Menomini prized them enough to travel to distant lakes to find them. One such lake was called White Potato Lake because of the good supply of wapatoo to be found there. The Indian name *wapsi-piniuk*, which means "white potato", may be the source of the name for the Wapsipinicon River, because of the plentiful supply of wapatoo to be found along its banks.

Bladderwort: *Utricularia vulgaris* L.

Other common names: Greater bladderwort, common bladderwort.

Utricularia: From *utriculus,* meaning "a little bladder".

Vulgaris: Meaning "common" from the abundance of the plant.

Bladderwort family: *Lentibulariaceae*

This interesting plant is found in shallow standing water of marshes where it floats horizontally just under the surface of the water. It is widespread in North America, found from Labrador to Alaska and south to New England, Ohio, Indiana, Missouri, Texas, and Mexico. In Iowa, it is common in the lakes area of the northern part of the Des Moines Lobe, infrequent to rare elsewhere. It is in bloom in June and July.

This is a true aquatic plant which spends all phases of its life cycle submerged—except for the flower—and never forms roots. The stems may reach a length of 3 feet, normally less. The leaves are arranged alternately along the stem and may be up to 2 inches long, with sections repeatedly forking into twos or threes.

The flowers are borne on erect stems that rise above the surface of the water for a height of several inches. The flower is yellow with brown vertical stripes on the large palate, with a broad lower lip slightly three-lobed and slightly shorter than the curved spur. An individual flower stalk bears 5–20 flowers. Seeds are brown and striated.

The most astounding characteristic of the bladderwort is the presence of bladders on the leaves. The bladders, also called utricles, are hollow structures with a small aperture, closed by a flap serving as a valve. These bladders serve as traps for small animals, which are then food for the plant. The animals seem to be digested after capture, but no specific enzyme for this purpose has yet been identified.

Like many true aquatic plants, this species prepares for winter by forming winter buds, or turions, which sink to the bottom and become dormant. They float to the surface and resume growth when the water warms again in the spring. This is the principal means of reproduction in the species.

There are three other species of bladderwort in Iowa. Small bladderwort, *U. minor,* and flat-leaved bladderwort, *U. intermedia,* are found on fens in northwest Iowa. Humped bladderwort, *U. gibba,* is found in shallow water or mud banks, but has only been collected from two counties in eastern Iowa.

Bur-reed: *Sparganium eurycarpum* Engelm.

Other common names: Giant bur-reed.

Sparganium: From the Greek *sparganion* or *sparganon,* "swaddling band" in allusion to the ribbon-like leaves.

Eurycarpum: Meaning "broad-fruited", in reference to the large seed heads.

Bur-reed family: *Sparganiaceae*

Bur-reed is found throughout a considerable portion of North America from eastern Quebec to northern Alberta and southern British Columbia and south to Florida, Ohio, Indiana, Illinois, Missouri, Colorado, and California. In Iowa, it is found statewide, but most common in the lakes area and least common on the Paleozoic Plateau. Its habitat is shallow standing water or on the edges of sluggish streams. It is found in bloom in early June and the seeds are ripe in late July.

The plant may achieve a height of over 4 feet. Its leaves are stiff, keeled, and nearly flat. The plant arises from a horizontal rootstock which may form tubers which give rise to new plants. The plant reproduces principally by seeds, however.

The flower stalk bears male flowers near the tip and the wind causes these to shed pollen onto the female flowers located lower on the stem. The spherical fruiting head is sessile, 1 inch to nearly 2 inches across, and composed of numerous triangular seeds. These seeds turn brown when ripe and become easily dislodged by being shaken or by movement in the wind. The seeds fall from the head in late summer, float for a brief time, then sink to the bottom of the marsh where germination may occur, or germination may be delayed until favorable conditions are present.

This plant is a good soil binder at marsh edges and along streams. It is of importance as food for wildlife and approximately 20 species of waterfowl and marsh birds are known to utilize it. Muskrats use the entire plant for food or in building lodges.

Some plants form tubers that are especially rich in starch. These tubers, which form late in the season, were gathered and used as a starch supplement by the Klamath Indians. They are relatively small structures and not formed on all plants. Gathering them in quantity proved so difficult that the tubers never became important in human diets.

The species is easily transplanted by moving rootstocks and is easily propagated by gathering and spreading seeds.

There are around 10 species of bur-reed in northern United States and southern Canada. In Iowa, there are four species. They range from one like *S. androcladum,* which has been collected on two occasions, to *S. americanum* and *S. chlorocarpum,* which are rare or infrequent, to the present species which is found in most relatively undisturbed marshes and is an important component in marshes in north central Iowa.

Coontail: *Ceratophyllum demersum* L.

Other common names: Common hornwort, cornfile, hornwort.

Ceratophyllum: From Greek *ceras* "a horn", and *phyllon,* "leaf".

Demersum: "Submerged", from the habit of the plant.

Hornwort family: *Ceratophyllaceae*

Coontail occurs statewide and throughout North America in quiet waters of lakes, ponds, and slow-moving water of streams. The inconspicuous flowers may be found from June into September. In Iowa, it is most frequently encountered in the lakes area of the Des Moines Lobe.

This submerged truly aquatic plant has weak stems which may achieve a length of 8 feet, but normally breaks into shorter sections. The leaves are in whorls of 5–12, are forked two or three times, and are stiff with toothed margins. These leaves are easily broken from the stem and are crowded toward the growing tip—this gives rise to the common name "coontail". The plant is a perennial, totally submerged, with slender, elongated stems and numerous lateral branches.

The flowers are very small, unisexual, and each is surrounded by minute bracts. Normally one flower occurs in the axil of each leaf in a whorl. The male flower has numerous stamens which are on a common stalk. The female flower has one sessile ovary. A real perianth is not present. The fruit is a one-seeded nutlet, ellipsoid, about ⅕ inch long and black. Flowers are seldom noticed and the seeds rarely collected.

Normally, the species propagates vegetatively by the breaking off of branches or tips. Pollination occurs under the surface of the water. The mature stamens detach and rise to the surface, where they burst. The pollen, thus released, is heavier than water and sinks slowly where it contacts the stigmas of the female flowers. After fertilization and maturation, the seeds fall to the bottom of the marsh and germinate.

In fall, as the water temperatures drop, the plant forms thick lateral tips which are deep green and contain high starch levels. The stems fragment and sink to the bottom, become dormant, and gradually become covered with sediment. In spring, when the water temperature rises, new shoots develop from the branch buds which have remained dormant in the axils.

Coontail is one of our most abundant aquatic plants, often becoming so dense that other plants are shaded out. It is also one of the most significant plants because it provides habitat for small fish and insects essential to fisheries. It is readily eaten by invertebrates and the seeds are sought by diving ducks.

Curly pondweed: *Potamogeton crispus* L.

Other common names: Crisp pondweed, curly-leaved pondweed, curly muckweed.

Potamogeton: From Greek *potamos,* "a river", and *geiton,* "a neighbor".

Crispus: Meaning "crimped" from the wavy leaf margins.

Pondweed family: *Potamogetonaceae*

This perennial, herbaceous rooted aquatic is native to Eurasia, but has spread to Africa and Australia as well as North America. It was introduced into this country in the middle of the nineteenth century and is now known from southern Canada and nearly all of the contiguous states. In Iowa, it is abundant in the cool trout streams of northeast Iowa, in the backwaters of the Mississippi River, and scattered lakes, including Lake Okoboji. It grows in a variety of habitats, from clear, pristine streams to polluted bodies of standing water. Its blooming time is April to June.

The leaves are sessile, oblong to broadly linear, often reddish with toothed margins that are often crimped and undulate. Stipules unite around the stem to form a sheath at the base of the leaf. The stem is flattened, brittle, and with channels. The inflorescence, a few-flower spike, is held above the surface of the water on a slender, often recurved, peduncle. The fruits are beaked nutlets which ripen in late June and July.

Primary means of reproduction is vegetative through dispersal of winter buds formed as compact, leafy structures at the apex of a shoot. These may develop into as many as seven independent shoots. This method, plus its rhizomatous nature, makes the curly pondweed very successful. These winter buds or winter apices are high in starch and eaten by waterfowl.

This pondweed is important to various kinds of fish and game. Bass and muskies use it for shelter, and it also shelters smaller fish which provide food for predatory fish. It is frequently found in cities in salt and fresh water environments.

Occasionally this species is used in aquatic gardens—probably the source of the original introduction from Europe.

PHOTO BY DEAN ROOSA

Elodea: *Elodea canadensis* Michx.

Other common names: Canadian pondweed, choke pondweed, water thyme, water weed.

Elodea: From the Greek *elodes,* meaning "marshy".

Canadensis: Meaning "of Canada".

Frog's-bit family: *Hydrocharitaceae*

This is a submersed aquatic herb with long, weak, slender stems generally sparsely branched. It enjoys a wide distribution in the United States, growing in quiet water across Canada and south to California and South Carolina.

The lower leaves are arranged opposite on the stem, the upper are in whorls of three. These leaves are about ½ inch long, ⅛ inch wide, with minute teeth along the margins.

The female flowers are borne on long thread-like stems that reach the water surface. Male flowers are in the axils of upper leaves. The male flowers break off and float to the surface where they come in contact with the female flower. After pollination, the seed matures under water. As with many aquatic species, asexual or vegetative reproduction is far more important than that involving pollination and subsequent formation of seeds, and seeds are rarely found. This species fragments easily, and each part may become a new plant. New plants grow from creeping, thread-like stolons.

Circulation of cytoplasm and of chloroplasts within the cells is often clearly visible in this species. For this reason, biology classes often use it for laboratory studies. Stomates are unknown in this genus. This plant was introduced into Europe in 1836 and spread dramatically.

This species is of some value as a duck food. Plants root readily, making it easy for this plant to become a nuisance. This characteristic increases its value as a duck food, since it recovers and spreads rapidly. But, the fact that it rarely forms seeds limits its value as a waterfowl food. However, one redhead duck was found with its stomach filled with 600 fruits. Ducks will feed on both leaves and fruits.

Elodea is sometimes found in such large masses that it interferes with movement of boats and canoes, and can cause management problems. While normally found in shallow water, it has been known to grow in water 25 feet deep.

Flat-stemmed pondweed: *Potamogeton zosteriformis* Fern.

Other common names: Zoster pondweed.

Potamogeton: An ancient name, composed of the Greek *potamos,* "a weed," and *geiton,* "a neighbor," from the place where these plants grow.

Zosteriformis: Because of the similarity to *Zostera,* a grass-like marine herb which gets its name from the Greek word *zoster,* "a belt" from the entire, ribbon-like leaves.

Pondweed family: *Potamogetonaceae*

Flat-stemmed pondweed is a rather common, easily identified pondweed. It is found from Quebec to northern Alberta and southern British Columbia and south to Virginia, Ohio, Indiana, northeast Illinois, Nebraska, Montana and northern California. In Iowa, it is frequent in the northern part of the Des Moines Lobe, rare or absent elsewhere.

The length achieved by this plant depends on the depth of water but may reach a length of slightly over 3 feet. The stem is flattened, up to ⅛ inch wide, freely branched, leaves alternate, a little wider than the stem, and may reach a length of 2–8 inches. There are no floating leaves.

The flowering spike is held above the water where pollination is by wind. It is around ¼ inch long, held aloft by a peduncle about 1 inch long. The achene (seed) is small—about ⅛ inch long.

This species grows from a slender rhizome. It forms winter buds which are dense or tightly clustered leaves that break free from the parent plant as it disintegrates late in the season. These buds lie on the marsh or pond bottom throughout the winter. In the spring, they send out new rhizomes and a new stem. This is the method by which this plant survives year to year. The winter buds, high in protein, are eaten by waterfowl. They can also be carried from wetland to wetland by ducks to form new populations.

The seeds serve as food for waterfowl and the winter buds are eaten by a variety of marshland animals.

Some pondweeds are notoriously difficult to identify. This species, with its distinctive flattened stems, is unmistakable. It is an important component of Iowa's wetlands and a good starting place to learn to identify members of this interesting family.

Greater duckweed: *Spirodela polyrhiza* (L.) Schleiden

Other common names: Big duckweed, water flaxseed.

Spirodela: From the Greek *speira*, "a cord", and *delos*, "evident".

Polyrhiza: Meaning "many rooted".

Duckweed family: *Lemnaceae*

Greater duckweed is a common floating plant, found in most marshes and in many small sluggish streams, but not as common as lesser duckweed. Its range in North America is from Nova Scotia to British Columbia and south to North Carolina, Alabama, Texas, and California. This species flowers in June, but is rarely observed in flower or fruit. In Iowa, it is found throughout the state.

This duckweed, only slightly larger than lesser duckweed, is found floating in masses on the surface of marshes, often in the company of lesser duckweed, star duckweed, and water meal. The fronds are up to ⅓ inch in diameter. This species is distinguished from other duckweeds by having a purple underside, and several rootlets, each with a conspicuous root-cap.

Flowers, when produced, occur in pouches on the edge of the frond.

Duckweed forms special shoots at the arrival of cold-water conditions. These shoots, or turions, are of great importance to the species since seeds are so rarely set. The turions are smaller than the normal summer frond and somewhat kidney-shaped. The air spaces are reduced and the cells are packed with starch, causing them to become heavier than water and sink. In the spring, lateral fronds grow out, absorbing starch from the parent; these develop normal air spaces and float to the surface.

Reproduction is principally by vegetative division which may be quite rapid under good conditions. Plants in the duckweed family can inhabit badly polluted waters and have been used to purify such areas.

Duckweeds are an important waterfowl food, sometimes constituting a substantial part of the diet, although some authors have speculated that ingestion of invertebrates found among the duckweeds may be of equal or greater importance.

This is a common member of the Iowa wetland flora, often being found in pure stands. It can be separated from lesser duckweed by the purple undersides of the fronds and the presence of multiple rootlets.

Many marsh and pothole plants can filter and help purify water that is polluted. This might help control water pollution in the future.

Lesser duckweed: *Lemna minor* L.

Other common names: Duck's meal, toad spit, water lentil.

Lemna: The name of a water plant mentioned by Theophrastus.

Minor: Meaning "small" or "smaller".

Duckweed family: *Lemnaceae*

Lesser duckweed is a very common plant of the quiet water of marshes, sluggish streams, and backwaters of rivers. It is found in quiet waters throughout most of the contiguous United States. In Iowa, it is found throughout the state, probably in every county. It is in flower in June and July, but flowering is a rare event and rarely observed.

This tiny plant floats on the surface of the water and has a single thread-like rootlet produced from the underside. The fronds are flattened, round to elliptic-ovate, only about ⅛ inch in diameter and obscurely three-veined. The fronds are green above and below.

Reproduction is chiefly vegetative, with new fronds budding from the older ones and quickly separating. This division progresses rapidly and in a short time these plants can cover the entire surface of a pond.

When present, the flower is in a small pouch on the edge of the top of the frond. It consists of three flowers—two male flowers made up of a single stamen; the other, a female flower, is represented by a single pistil. The entire inflorescence is surrounded by a spathe.

The duckweeds are very important as food for waterfowl and of lesser value to herbivores, like muskrats. Some of the food value, however, may be in the invertebrate fauna ingested with the duckweeds.

This constant member of the aquatic flora of Iowa is often associated with watermeal (*Wolffia* sp.) and greater duckweed (*Spirodela polyrhiza*).

At the approach of cold weather, the older fronds may freeze, become water-logged and sink, taking with them the younger fronds. In this manner, they survive the winter and in spring begin to photosynthesize and float to the surface.

Long-leaved pondweed: *Potamogeton nodosus* Poiret

Other common names: Knotty pondweed.

Potamogeton: An ancient name, from the Greek *potamos,* "a river" and *geiton,* "a neighbor".

Nodosus: Meaning "knotty".

Pondweed family: *Potamogetonaceae*

This pondweed is widely distributed in North America—from New Brunswick to southern Quebec and southern Ontario to British Columbia and south to Alabama, Texas, and Mexico. It is also found in South America, Eurasia, and Africa. In Iowa, it is common in the lakes area of the northern part of the Des Moines Lobe, frequent in the remainder of the state. It is in flower in July and in fruit in August and September. Its favored habitat is shallow standing water. It often is found in the shallow water at the edges of farm ponds.

The plant produces two types of leaves—those which are entirely submerged and those which float on the surface. The submersed leaves are elliptic to lanceolate, up to over an inch wide with an acute tip and tapering to a petiole which is from 1 to 5 inches long, and with 7–15 nerves per leaf. The floating leaves are oblong, rounded at the base, leathery and thicker than the submersed leaves and have long petioles.

In the northern portion of its range, this species hybridizes with three other pondweeds to produce intermediates which makes for a confusing complex. The species is so widespread and prolific that it is very important as a wildlife food.

As pondweeds go, long-leaved pondweed is easy to identify and sufficiently common that it is available to wetland enthusiasts statewide. It is a good place to begin gaining familiarity with this large and interesting family.

PHOTO BY DEAN ROOSA

Pickeral weed: *Pontederia cordata* L.

Other common name: Marsh blue.

Pontederia: Named for Guilio Pontedera, a professor of botany at Padua in the early 1700s.

Cordata: From the shape of the leaves which have cordate (heart-shaped) bases.

Pickeral weed family: *Pontederiaceae*

Pickeral weed is found from Prince Edward Island to southern Ontario and south to New England, northern Florida, Missouri, and Oklahoma. In Iowa, it is infrequent to rare throughout the state, although it grows in the shallow water of marshes and backwaters of the Mississippi River. Although it is not a common plant in Iowa, when found, it is often in large colonies. Part of the reason it is uncommon is that it cannot tolerate the extreme fluctuations in water level which is often the result of marsh management for waterfowl. It has a long blooming period, beginning in June.

The thick and glossy leaves are soft, up to 10 inches long, possess broadly cordate bases, and taper to a point. The petiole of the leaf is about 2 inches long.

The flowers are violet-blue, ephemeral, and arranged in a dense spike. However, new flowers are produced continuously and some may be found freshly blooming most of the summer. The flower is two-lipped, with three upper lobes, and three lower lobes. The length of the flower is about ¾ inch long and bears a distinct yellow-green spot. This is one of our most striking aquatic herbs when observed in full bloom.

This species is a prolific seed producer. Fruits are about ½ inch long and crested with toothed ridges. Seeds are ⅓ to ½ inch long. The seeds mature and fall from the plant and for a time float on the surface of the water. They later sink to the bottom and germinate late in the summer. The rhizome is thickened and spreads horizontally, resulting in a dense colony.

The seeds are often eaten by ducks, and muskrats use the leaves and rhizomes as food. Some sources state that the seeds, when taken from the more mature spikes, are starchy and taste somewhat nut-like. The seeds can be eaten as they come from the plant, or dried and used in making cereals and breads.

Other plants in this family are mud plantain, *Heteranthera dubia,* found in shallow water or on mud in most Iowa marshes, and the infamous water hyacinth, *Eichhornia crassipes,* which has become such a nuisance in the southeastern United States.

Red-head pondweed: *Potamogeton richardsonii* (A. Benn.) Rydb.

Other common names: American pondweed, red pondweed.

Potamogeton: An ancient name composed of the Greek *potamos* "a river", and *geiton,* "a neighbor", from the habitat in which the plant is found.

Richardsonii: Named for its discoverer, Sir Johnathan Richardson, 1787–1865.

Pondweed family: *Potamogetonaceae* (some use the name *Zosteraceae*)

This distinctive pondweed is found from Labrador to Alaska and south to Quebec, New England, Pennsylvania, Ohio, Indiana, northern Iowa, Nebraska, Colorado and California. In Iowa, it is found fairly commonly in the lakes area, sparingly in the remainder of the northern portion of the state. Its habitat is shallow water of lakes, ponds, and marshes. It hybridizes freely with several other taxa. Its blooming period is from July into September.

This species and others in the genus are rooted in the lake or stream bottom and produce leaves on the submersed portion of the stem. In some species, the plant produces floating leaves of a very different texture from the submersed ones.

The plant branches freely and is densely leafy. The leaves, all submerged, are lanceolate to nearly linear, one to four inches long and up to an inch wide. These leaves are sessile and clasp the stem, have cordate bases and three to five prominent nerves.

The peduncle is about as thick as the stem, 1–4 inches long and supports a dense flowering spike 1–2 inches long. The flowers, which lack a perianth, are very inconspicuous and are wind-pollinated.

The only other pondweed in Iowa with which this plant could be confused is *Potamogeton praelongus*, a plant which is quite rare and has keeled leaves.

There are 19 species of pondweeds in Iowa, ranging from one known from a single station to one which is found in most shallow water habitats. They range from those which can be identified at a glance to those which need a scope and good keys. They are important in the food chain of many marshes and provide excellent cover for a variety of inhabitants of marshes and lakes.

This species cannot tolerate prolonged periods of dry conditions or prolonged pollution. Its presence in a marsh is a sign that the marsh is in a healthy condition and the water level is not manipulated for waterfowl management.

Sago pondweed: *Potamogeton pectinatus* L.

Other common names: Sago, fennel-leaved pondweed.

Potamogeton: An ancient name, composed of the Greek *potamos*, "a river", and *geiton*, "a neighbor", from the place where these plants grow.

Pectinatus: Meaning "comb-like".

Pondweed family: *Potamogetonaceae*

Sago pondweed has a wide range in North America, growing from Newfoundland to British Columbia and south to Florida, West Virginia, Missouri, Texas, and Mexico. It also occurs in South American, Eurasia, and Africa. In Iowa, it is found growing in most marshes. It grows best in water 2–5 feet deep, but has been reported growing in water 15 feet deep. It seems to display a wider ecological tolerance than most pondweeds. It can grow in saline, alkaline, or polluted waters. It is in bloom from June to September.

The stem is nearly thread-like and branches repeatedly, giving the plant a bushy appearance. The leaves are very narrow and bristle-like with parallel sides but with tapering points. The stipules are joined to the bases of the leaves, making a sheath for them. Tubers are borne on a horizontal stem at the base of the plant, just below the soil surface.

The flowers are borne on short spikes and occur as two to six whorls separated by a space. These flowers are held above the water surface and pollination is accomplished by wind. Copious seeds are produced on these spikes. Each fruit has a short beak and occurs in up to six well-separated whorls. Each fruit is about ⅛ inch long, compressed, rounded on the back and with poorly defined ridges on the sides.

The tubers are abundant on the horizontal stem which is anchored in the soil of the marsh. These tubers are readily eaten by waterfowl and may be used to introduce this species into new habitats. Pondweeds are probably the most important waterfowl food, and sago is probably the most important of the pondweeds for this purpose because of the copious production of seeds and tubers. One plant under cultivated conditions produced over 63,000 seeds and over 36,000 tubers in six months. Its wide range makes it important as a food plant for migrating waterfowl. It often forms the dominant cover in Iowa marshes where open water is found. Sago pondweed seems to grow in polluted water better than any other pondweed found in Iowa. It also grows well in clear, unpolluted water.

This species and about five other pondweeds have tubers which are considered edible. However, harvesting them is some times a difficult task.

Spatterdock: *Nuphar luteum* (L.) Sibth. and Sm.

Other common names: Beaver root, beaver lily, bonnets, bullhead lily, cow lily, dog lily, frog lily, yellow pond lily, yellow waterlily.

Nuphar: From an ancient Arabic common name for this species.

Luteum: From Latin, meaning "yellow".

Waterlily family: *Nymphaeaceae*

This attractive aquatic plant is found from Florida to Texas and Mexico and north to New England, Pennsylvania, Ohio, Michigan, Wisconsin, and Nebraska. In Iowa, it is found sparingly throughout the state, mainly in ponds and marshes in the northern part of the Des Moines Lobe. It is in bloom from May into October.

The flat smooth leaves are broadly oval, sometimes more than 1 foot long and 9 inches wide. Leaf margins are smooth, usually with a deep narrow notch to the petiole attachment. The leaves have more of a mid-rib than other waterlilies. They usually float on the water surface, but may be submerged or held above the surface. The leaf petioles are flattened above with a ridge extending from the mid-rib of the leaf.

The thick, spongy perennial rhizome is an irregular cylinder that may be 3 or 4 inches thick and more than 4 feet long.

Bright yellow cup-like flowers up to 2 inches high and over 3 inches wide may show a greenish or purplish tinge on the outside. Individual petals are small and numerous. The outer sepals are green while the others have bright yellow edges shading to purple or maroon toward their bases. The central disk is green or yellowish.

The mature fruit is a ridged egg-shaped structure, approximately 2 inches long and 1 inch thick. It contains many seeds which resemble popcorn. However, they increase in size without bursting the outer skin when roasted.

Native Americans ate the root roasted or boiled with meat. The taste is described as bland and sweetish. The seeds were also parched or ground into flour. The Sioux pulverized dried roots into a powder which they used to arrest external bleeding. Pioneers used a root preparation to treat diarrhea and leucorrhea. Indian women sometimes waded into the water and dislodged the rhizomes with their toes, or dived to the bottom to dislodge the roots which floated to the surface and were easily harvested. An easier method was to raid a supply of roots stored by muskrats as a winter food supply. Some did this as the animals were hunted. Others merely borrowed the spatterdock rhizomes and replaced them with food that was more plentiful in order to avoid angering whatever powers looked after the welfare of the muskrats.

Records show that spatterdock roots provided food for moose, deer, beaver, muskrats, and porcupines.

Star duckweed: *Lemna trisulca* L.

Other common names: Forked duckweed, ivy duckweed, ivy-leaved duckweed.

Lemna: The name of a water plant mentioned by Theophrastus.

Trisulca: Meaning "three furrowed", for the three obscure nerves of the branching fronds.

Duckweed family: *Lemnaceae*

Star duckweed is found in shallow water at the edges of marshes. Its range in North America is from Nova Scotia to New Jersey, south to Texas, and west to the coast. It is practically worldwide in its distribution, being found in Australia, Africa, Europe, and Asia. In Iowa, it is statewide wherever shallow standing water is common. The plant flowers in July, but this is a rare event and rarely observed.

This minute, stemless plant floats just below the surface, often in tangled masses. It forms an irregular net of branching fronds, each up to ⅖ inch long, with the offshoots remaining connected. The fronds are green above and below, often with rootlets; when these are present, they are single short strands lacking vascular tissue.

Flowering is rarely observed; when it occurs, the flower is borne in a sac at the margin of the frond. The flower consists of two stamens and a pistil.

Reproduction is principally by vegetative division. The new fronds tend to remain together.

When cool weather approaches, the tangled masses of this plant disintegrate and segments sink to the bottom where they remain throughout winter. In spring, these are among the first to photosynthesize and float to the surface.

The duckweeds in general are very important as wildlife food. They are also noted for their ability to divide rapidly and cover a pond or marsh. In this regard, they are often used in the classroom for models of vegetative reproduction.

Water hyssop: *Bacopa rotundifolia* (Michx.) Wettst.

Other common names: Round-leaf hyssop, southern hyssop.

Bacopa: Thought to originate from an aboriginal South American name.

Rotundifolia: Meaning "round leaved" from the nearly circular shape of the leaves.

Figwort family: *Scrophulariaceae*

The range of this species is from Mississippi to Texas and north to Indiana, Illinois, Minnesota, North Dakota, and Montana. In Iowa, it is infrequent in the southcentral and southeast parts to rare in the northern half of the state. It appears periodically, usually in very wet years, in shallow pools in the Sioux Quartzite in extreme northwest Iowa. Its Iowa habitats are shallow water and muddy shores. The genus is principally tropical in distribution and Iowa is near the northern edge of its range.

Water hyssop is a creeping plant that roots at the nodes and forms floating mats or mats on muddy banks. The leaves are thin, nearly orbicular, and with narrowed, clasping bases. These are oppositely arranged, palmately many-nerved and around 1 inch to 1½ inches across.

The flowers are axillary, white with yellow throats, bell-shaped, and about ¼ inch long. There are four petals, three or four stamens. Pollination is by insects during its flowering time, from May into September. The fruit is a capsule with numerous seeds.

This species can grow entirely submerged, but is then sterile. This characteristic makes it useful as an ornamental plant in tropical aquaria.

The foliage and seeds are known to be of value to wildlife, especially waterfowl. It appears to be an annual, propagating by seeds.

The figwort family, to which water hyssop belongs, is represented by over 50 species in Iowa. It is an important and diverse family with beautiful showy members and inconspicuous members, some of which grow in the driest habitats, and some in water.

This is one of those plants that offers a challenge to Iowa naturalists. There are only scattered Iowa records. Judging by information from nearby states and the habitats where it grows, it should be far more common here than our records indicate. Because of its inconspicuous nature, perhaps we are overlooking it. Look for it in southeast and southcentral Iowa in shallow standing water or on muddy shores.

Other common name: Water pepper.

Wolffia: Named for Johnson Friedrich Wolff, 1788–1806, who published on Lemna in 1801.

Columbiana: Meaning "of Columbia".

Punctata: Meaning "dotted", from the character of the plant.

Duckweed family: *Lemnaceae*

Watermeal is found from Florida to Texas and north to New England and southern Canada. Both species occupy approximately the same range. These tiny plants are commonly found floating on quiet waters of marshes and backwaters throughout Iowa. These plants rarely flower and few people have seen this event.

These are the smallest flowering plants known and appear as tiny green dots floating on, or just below, the surface of the water. They produce no roots. The plant body is spheroid to ellipsoid, about one and one-half times as long as wide, and up to about ½5 inch long.

Reproduction is principally by vegetative division because flowering is apparently a rare event. Vegetative reproduction may be very rapid under favorable conditions. This method of reproduction is so successful that the need for sexual reproduction is diminished.

The microscopic flowers are on the upper surface of the thallus, or burst through the upper surface. Two flowers occur on the upper surface of the plant, one flower is a single stamen, the other a globular ovary with a short style and depressed stigma.

These two species appear very similar and are virtually indistinguishable if not in fresh condition. *W. punctata* is brown-dotted and has a flattened upper surface; *W. columbiana* lacks dots and is strongly convex above. The latter is somewhat more common in Iowa.

The plants have been reported as being good duck food and are of interest because of their rapid rate of vegetative reproduction. They have also been reported as muskrat food.

At the approach of cooler water conditions, the tiny plants increase in starch content and sink to the bottom of the marsh, where they spend the winter. In spring, when the water warms, the plants begin to photosynthesize and float to the surface.

Often five minute members of our wetland flora (3 duckweeds, 2 watermeals) are found floating together at the edges of Iowa marshes.

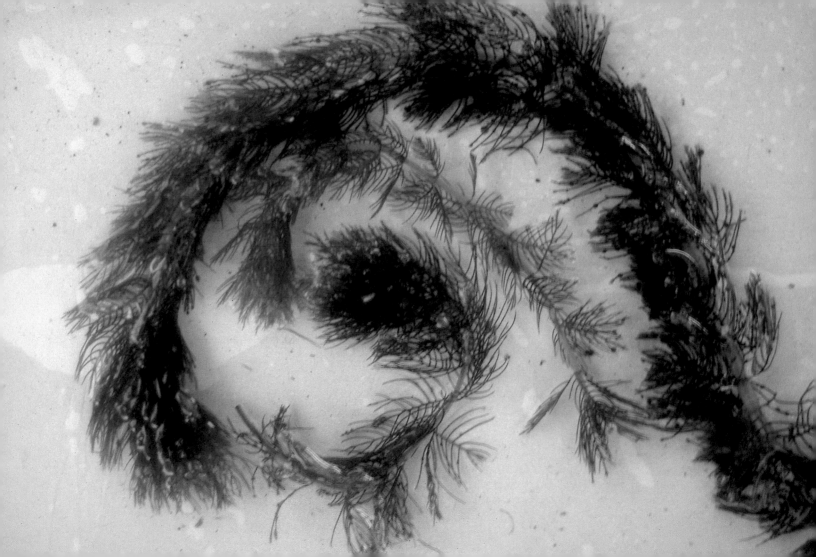

Water milfoil: *Myriophyllum exalbescens* Fern.

Other common names: Milfoil, pale milfoil.

Myriophyllum: From the Greek *myrios,* "numberless" and *phyllon,* "leaf" alluding to the innumerable divisions.

Exalbescens: Meaning "becoming pale", referring to the whitish color the plant becomes upon drying.

Water milfoil family: *Haloragaceae* (sometimes *Haloragidaceae*)

Water milfoil is found from Labrador to Alaska and south to Newfoundland, New England, West Virginia, Ohio, Indiana, Illinois, Minnesota, Kansas, Oklahoma, Arizona, and California. In Iowa, the plant is found in quiet water in marshes and shallow lakes nearly statewide but most common in the northcentral and rare in the southwest part of the state. It has a long blooming period, beginning in July and extending through September.

It is an aquatic, perennial herb. The purple stems are weak and may reach a length of several feet, depending on the depth of the water. The leaves occur in whorls of four or five around the stem and are highly dissected into six to ten thread-like divisions.

The flowers occur in a spike held above the water surface several inches and are surrounded by a whorl of very short leaves. The flowers, which occur in the axils of the leaves, are inconspicuous and lose the four petals early. The lower flowers are pistillate, the upper staminate and depend on the wind for pollination. The nut-like fruit is very small, about 1/10 inch long and deeply four-lobed. The plant is shallowly rooted and easily dislodged.

One method of reproduction in this species is by the formation of turions, or specialized dwarf shoots. These shoots become detached as the parent plant decomposes in late fall and spend the winter on the bottom of the marsh. In early spring, the dwarf leaves spread away from the axis, roots are produced from the basal nodes, and a new plant is formed. This is not an uncommon occurrence in aquatic plants and explains why some members of this genus can become a nuisance in some bodies of water.

Its value to wildlife derives from its shelter for many insects that are food for fish. A related species, *M. brasiliense,* is sold as an aquarium plant.

This plant is a native of North America but is found in waters of Europe and Asia. European water milfoil, *E. spicatum,* a related species, was introduced into eastern United States a half-century ago and has spread dramatically, choking lakes and hampering fishing and boating. It has become a nuisance in Minnesota and has been collected from several Iowa lakes in recent years.

Water milfoil is a normal component of Iowa marshes, lakes, and ponds, and one that all students of Iowa wetlands should get to know.

Watershield: *Brasenia schreberi* Gmel.

Other common names: Deer food, frogleaf, little waterlily, purple wen-dock, water target.

Brasenia: Genus name of uncertain origin.

Schreberi: Named for Johann Christian Daniel von Schreber, botanist, 1739–1810.

Waterlily family: *Nympheaceae*

Watershield is widespread in North America—from southern Canada south to Oregon, Minnesota, and northern Iowa—also in Tropical America, Asia, Africa, and Australia. In Iowa, it is exceedingly rare, reported only from Black Hawk, Buchanan, Hancock, and Worth counties since 1950. Flowering time in Iowa is June and July.

In Iowa, it grows in shallow standing water; in other parts of its range, it may be found in sluggish streams. Leaf blades are oblong, measuring around 4 inches by 2 inches and are peltate (stem connected to the underside of the leaf at the middle). Leaf stalks are arranged alternately along the stem and are usually covered with a gelatinous substance, as are the undersides of the leaf and the stem.

Flowers are small, up to ¾ inch long, with three or four red or purplish petals—quite modest in comparison to other waterlilies in the state. Flowers float on the surface of the water, or occasionally are held above the surface by the stem. Fruits are a cluster of club-shaped pods—small and inconspicuous. The slender rootstock, buried in the silt, is freely branched.

Tuberous, starch-filled roots were collected by Native Americans in California in autumn and early spring to be eaten as a salad. The starchy roots could be baked, boiled, or eaten raw. In Asia, the young, mucilage-covered leaves were collected and served with vinegar as a salad. The rhizomes have been used by the early settlers for treating dysentery and phthisis.

Watershield is an important waterfowl food throughout its range, but of outstanding importance along the gulf coast, where it is reported to be one of the four most utilized foods for ducks, especially diving ducks.

Water stargrass: *Heteranthera dubia* (Jacq.) MacM. (Some taxonomists prefer *Zosterella dubia*)

Other common name: Mud plantain, water starwort

Heteranthera: Name from the Greek *hetera*, "different", and *anthera*, "anther", from the dissimilar anthers of the original species.

Dubia: Meaning "doubtful", probably in reference to the difference in appearance of the various forms.

Pickeral weed family: *Pontederiaceae*

This species is widespread in North America—from Florida, Texas and Mexico north to southern Quebec and Ontario, Idaho, and Oregon. In Iowa, it is rare to infrequent in slow-moving streams and standing shallow water statewide. It is in flower in late summer into October.

This is generally a submersed grass-like herb, that may achieve a length of many feet, but sometimes gets stranded on a mudbar. Under these conditions, it may be quite dwarfed or spread out into a mat that roots at the nodes. These plants growing on wet soil are known to some botanists as *forma terrestris*. The leaves are linear, translucent, and sessile; they are finely parallel-veined without a distinct mid-vein and may achieve a length of 6 inches.

The flower is pale yellow, less than an inch long, and exposed above the water on the end of a long, thread-like tube.

Water stargrass provides food and shelter for fish. It also serves as a valuable waterfowl food in certain parts of its range. This is an inconspicuous member of the family when compared to such relatives as water hyacinth and pickeral weed.

There are three species in the genus in eastern North America and all three occur in Iowa. In addition to mud plantain, there are *Heteranthera limosa,* a very rare plant with records from Fremont, Lyon, and Muscatine counties, and *Heteranthera reniformis,* a plant known in Iowa only from Red Haw Lake in Lucas County.

White waterlily: *Nymphaea tuberosa* Paine

Other common names: Castalia, pond lily, sweet white waterlily, water cabbage, water nymph.

Nymphaea: From Greek and Roman mythology, probably referring to the attractive and playful water nymphs of similar habitat.

Tuberosa: From Latin meaning "with tubers".

Waterlily family: *Nymphaeaceae*

This gorgeous plant is found from Quebec to northern Ontario, Minnesota and Nebraska and south to Ohio, Indiana, Illinois, and Arkansas. In Iowa, it is found widely scattered throughout the state, but mainly in shallow standing water in the northern half. It begins blooming in early June and continues until frost.

The large round leaves, up to a foot across, float on the water surface above a submerged fleshy horizontal perennial rootstock. These leaves are dark green above, light green or purplish beneath. The smooth leaf margins have a single indentation to their center where the petiole is attached. Each petiole usually has four main air channels which are easily visible when cut in cross section.

Showy white flowers with yellow centers may float on the surface or may be held above. Some are distinctly fragrant while others are only slightly so. This is the basis for separation into different species, according to some authorities.

Numerous petals in the shape of narrow ovals may have a pinkish cast and diminish in size toward the center. The four sepals are green outside, whitish inside. Flowers are up to 6 inches across. One Native American legend tells that the waterlily was created from a falling star, an appropriate testimonial to the showy beauty of this flower.

Flowers of each *Nymphaea* species tend to open at a particular time each day. They follow this pattern for three or four days, then bend over or coil downward so the seeds can ripen beneath the water surface. When mature, in six to ten weeks, the pods burst open and release seeds which float for several hours. Action of the waves and wind disperse seeds to other areas. This ensures survival of the species.

Early pioneers, but apparently not Native Americans, used the root as a treatment for dysentery, a gargle for sore throat, and a wash for sore eyes. Sometimes the root was powdered and combined with crushed seeds of flax or slippery elm to make a poultice for skin sores and other irritations.

The Ojibwa cooked the flowerbuds for food. The seeds, rich in digestible protein and oil, were also eaten. The tubers served as a substitute for potatoes.

Waterfowl and many other forms of wildlife feed on the seeds or tubers.

Wild celery: *Vallisneria americana* Michx.

Other common names: Eel grass, tapegrass, water celery.

Vallisneria: Named for the Italian botanist Antonio Vallisneri, 1661–1730.

Americana: Meaning "of America".

Frog's-bit family: *Hydrocharitaceae*

Wild celery is found widespread in eastern North America—from New Brunswick to North Dakota and south to Florida and the gulf states. In Iowa, it is found mainly in the deep lakes of the northern portion of the Des Moines Lobe and in the Mississippi River. It is in flower in June into August.

This is an entirely submerged plant with long flexible leaves which may reach 6 feet and less than 1 inch wide. Given good water conditions, it may grow in water up to 20 feet deep. The stems are buried in the mud but produce clusters of leaves which resemble long, pale-green ribbons. The common names eel grass and tape grass are a reflection of the morphology of the leaves. The stem freely forms roots at the joints. Through the growing season, tapegrass spreads by producing rosettes; near the end of the growing season, the production of these rosettes ceases and winter buds form in the axils of leaves. These buds remain in the sediment during the winter and emerge the following spring.

Plants are either male or female. The female flower floats on the surface of the water on the end of a long, coiled stem. Male flowers break loose and rise to the surface where they float about, and eventually they may touch and pollinate the female flower. After pollination, the coiled stem contracts, drawing the pistil and fruit below the surface where it matures. Mature fruits are found in September and October. These fruits are 3–7 inches long and contain 250–300 seeds which are shed in a mass of gelatinous material.

Fruits, buds, and underground buds provide waterfowl food, particularly for the canvasback duck. This association is shown by the scientific name of the canvasback, *Aythya valisineria*. Apparently this food preference gives an excellent flavor to the meat and makes the canvasback highly prized. Wild celery is so important in waterfowl management that wildlife managers transplant the plant into new habitats by gathering winter buds or portions of rootstocks and scattering them in wetlands. It is eaten also by fish, muskrats, and many other species of waterfowl.

Wild rice: *Zizania aquatica* L.

Other common names: Northern wild rice, folle avoine, menomin, water-oats.

Zizania: Adapted from the Greek *zizanion,* a weed of wheatfields.

Aquatica: Meaning "aquatic".

Grass family: *Poaceae (Gramineae)*

Wild rice is found from New Brunswick to Minnesota and south to New England, Massachussets, New York, Pennsylvania, Indiana, and northern Iowa. In Iowa, it is found in scattered locations in the northern half of the state at the edges of potholes, slow-moving streams, or in shallow standing water. It is in anthesis in July into August.

This is an annual species which may achieve a height of 10 feet. Although a rare plant in Iowa, it grows in a variety of aquatic habitats. Because it is widely planted, it is difficult to determine if the remnant Iowa populations can be considered native.

The leaves are up to 2 inches wide and may be 3 feet long. The root system is shallow and easily dislodged.

The inflorescence is a large panicle up to 2 feet long. The pistillate flowers are located on the top of the panicle, with the staminate flowers below. The fruits are enclosed in thin, papery, roughened scales. The lemma has a long awn.

There seem to be two varieties in Iowa: var. *interior,* a midwestern species which includes most of the Iowa material, and var. *angustifolium,* an eastern species which is shorter.

This is an important food for wildlife and is often sown for a waterfowl food crop. The seeds can be scattered in fall or early spring. In parts of its range, it is food for moose, muskrats, and some songbirds. Wild rice is an important commercial crop in the northern portion of its midwest range. In Iowa, the fruits seem mostly parasitized by a weevil, which prevents large amounts of seed from being produced.

The Menomini derived their name from the Native American word for wild rice—and it was one of their most important foods. The wild rice harvest was conducted according to definite customs and rituals.

Wild rice grows best in clear water that has a slight current. It will grow in deeper water, but prefers water about 2 feet deep or less, with a mucky or silty bottom. Because of its suitability as food for both humans and wildlife, it has been cultivated extensively.

Yellow water crowfoot: *Ranunculus flabellaris* Raf.

Other common names: Threadleaf buttercup, yellow water buttercup.

Ranunculus: From Latin meaning "a little frog". Also, a name applied by Pliny to these plants—apparently because they grow where frogs abound.

Flabellaris: Meaning "fan-like", referring to the shape of the leaves.

Crowfoot family: *Ranunculaceae*

Yellow water crowfoot is found from Maine to southern British Columbia and south to North Carolina, Louisiana, Kansas, and California. In Iowa, it is frequently encountered in the lakes area of the northern portion of the Des Moines Lobe and in central Iowa, but rare in much of the remainder of the state. It grows on muddy shores and in shallow standing water. It is in bloom in May and June.

This perennial is normally rooted on the bottom of the marsh, but can grow out of water on a mud bank that is permanently wet. When this happens, the plants are quite different in appearance, being reduced and often with clustered, long-petioled leaves.

The submerged leaves of this species are finely divided which accounts for a common name—threadleaf buttercup.

The leaves alternate up the stem and while quite variable, are usually divided into thread-like segments. This is a heterophyllous species—that is, it forms different shapes of leaves in response to environmental conditions such as the depth of water or nature of the substrate. The lower nodes often form new roots.

The flower petals of many species of buttercups have a waxy patina which makes the petals appear varnished. They are bright golden yellow and ¼–½ inch long. Fruits are numerous, numbering 50–75 achenes in a cylindrical head.

Yellow water crowfoot is a normal component of Iowa's marshes and probably occurs in every sizeable marsh or prairie pothole. Livestock are said to have been poisoned from eating this buttercup, but this is rare and somewhat circumstantial.

Abscission layer. A layer of special cells at the base of an appendage that allows the appendage to separate from the rest of the plant.

Achene. A small, dry, hard, one-seeded fruit.

Alterative. A substance that gradually changes a condition.

Analgesic. An agent that reduces or controls pain.

Annual. A plant that completes its life cycle in 1 growing season.

Anodyne. A substance that relieves pain.

Anthelmintic. A substance that expels or kills intestinal worms.

Antihysteric. A substance that lessens the state of nervous instability and hysteria.

Antiperiodic. A remedy that prevents the return of periodic diseases, such as certain fevers.

Antirheumatic. An agent that helps to relieve pain in the joints.

Antisyphilitic. A substance that supposedly relieves or controls syphilis.

Aperient. A laxative.

Astringent. A substance that contracts body tissue and blood vessels, checking the flow of blood.

Awn. A slender, bristle-shaped appendage; usually used in describing fruits of grasses.

Bifid. Forked; divided by a cleft.

Biome. Large, easily recognizable community unit.

Bract. A modified leaf subtending a flower or flower cluster.

Callus. A hard protuberance; in grasses, a tough swelling at the point of insertion of the palea and lemma.

Calyx. The sepals of a flower, considered collectively.

Carminative. A substance that relieves gas and colic.

Carpel. A simple pistil, or one member of a compound pistil.

Cholagogue. A substance that increases the flow of bile.

Ciliate. Marginally fringed with hairs.

Claw. The narrowed base of some sepals and petals.

Corolla. All the petals of a flower, taken collectively.

Culm. The stem of a grass or sedge.

Cyme. The cluster of flowers in which each main and secondary stem bears a single flower.

Decoction. An extract produced by boiling a substance in water.

Dentate. With pointed teeth, as on the margins of leaves.

Diaphoretic. A substance that increases the flow of perspiration.

Diuretic. A substance that increases the flow of urine.

Emmenagogue. A substance that induces menstrual flow.

Epispastic. A substance that produces blistering.

Escharotic. Tending to produce a dry scab resulting from a burn or corrosive substance.

Expectorant. A substance that causes mucus to be expelled from the respiratory tract.

Genus. A large assemblage of plants, usually made up of numerous species. The first name of a scientific name and always capitalized.

Glabrous. Smooth, without hairs or glands.

Glume. The husk or chaff-like bract of grasses.

Herb. A non-woody plant.

Heterogeneous. Differing or opposite in structure or quality.

Hydric soil. A soil that is saturated long enough for reduction and oxidation of manganese to occur and form bands or layers of high chroma inclusions.

Hydrophytic vegetation. That which grows in hydric soils and can grow in a reducing atmosphere.

Indehiscent. Remaining closed at maturity.

Inflorescence. The flower cluster of a plant.

Infusion. A substance made by steeping a plant material in a liquid without boiling.

Laciniate. Having a torn appearance.

Lemma. The lower of two bracts enclosing the flower of a grass.

Ligule. The small structure where the grassblade meets the stem.

Monotypic. A plant community consisting of a single species.

Moxa. A soft, woolly mass made from stems, used as a cautery.

Muck. A soil consisting of partially decomposed plant material.

Native. A species indigenous to an area.

Nerve. A vein on the leaf of a plant, especially grasses.

Peat. A soil consisting of partially decomposed plant material wherein the species can still be identified.

Pedicel. The stalk of a single flower.

Perennial. A plant that lives for three or more years.

Perigynium. A papery structure that surrounds the ovary in the genus *Carex*.

Petiole. The stalk of a leaf.

Phthisis. A wasting away of any part of the body; especially tuberculosis.

Pubescent. A soft hairiness on the surface of a plant.

Punctate. Dots or glands that appear as dots on the plant surface.

Ray. A strap-shaped marginal flower in the aster family.

Receptacle. An enlargement at the summit of the flower stalk in the aster family.

Recurved. Structure of a plant that is curved backward.

Rhizome. An underground stem, normally grows horizontally.

Scabrous. A roughness on the surface of a plant.

Sessile. Lacking a stalk to support a leaf.

Stamen. The male organ of a flower; that which bears pollen.

Stipule. A clasping structure at the base of a leaf in grasses.

Wetland. An area with hydric soils where anaerobic conditions persist long enough for hydrophytic vegetation to become established.

Whorl. Three or more plant parts that surround a node.

SELECTED BIBLIOGRAPHY

The following references, in addition to providing technical information for this book, are designed to aid those interested in pursuing the study of wetland plants and wetland communities.

Anderson, W. A. 1943. A fen in northwestern Iowa. *Amer. Midl. Nat.* 29:787–791.

Angier, B. 1978. Field guide to medicinal wild plants. Harrisburg, Pa.: Stackpole Books.

Bailey, L. H. 1963. The standard cyclopedia of horticulture. New York: MacMillan.

Baker, R. G., D. G. Horton, J. K. Kim., A. E. Sullivan, D. M. Roosa, P. M. Witinok, and W. P. Pusateri. 1987. Late Holocene paleoecology of southeastern Iowa: Development of riparian vegetation at Nichols Marsh. *Proc. Iowa Acad. Sci.* 92:78–85.

Beal, E. O. 1954. Aquatic monocotyledons of Iowa. *Proc. Iowa Acad. Sci.* 60:89–91.

Beal, E. O., and P. H. Monson. 1954. Marsh and aquatic angiosperms of Iowa. *Univ. Iowa Stud. Nat. Hist.* 19(5):1–95.

Bishop, R. A. 1981. Iowa's Wetlands. *Proc. Iowa Acad. Sci.* 88:11–16.

Bishop, R. A., and A. G. van der Valk. 1982. Ch. 9 *in* Iowa's Natural Heritage, T. C. Cooper (ed). Iowa Nat. Heritage Found. and Iowa Acad. Sci.

Bishop, R. A., R. D. Andrews, and R. J. Bridges. 1979. Marsh management and its relationship to vegetation, waterfowl, and muskrats. *Proc. Iowa Acad. Sci.* 86:50–56.

Carter, J. L. 1960. The flora of northwestern Iowa. Ph.D. dissertation, Univ. of Iowa, Iowa City.

Clambey, G. K., and R. Q. Landers. 1978. A survey of wetland vegetation in north-central Iowa. pp. 32–35 *in* D. C. Glenn-Lewin and R. Q. Landers. *Proc. Fifth Midwest Prairie Conf.,* Ames: Iowa State Univ. Extension.

Conard, H. S. 1952. The vegetation of Iowa. *Univ. Iowa Stud. Nat. Hist.* 19(4):1–166.

Conservation Foundation. 1988. Protecting America's wetlands: An action agenda. Washington, D.C.: Conservation Foundation.

Coon, N. 1974. The dictionary of useful plants. Erasmus, Pa.: Rodale.

Cooperrider, T. S. 1958. The flora of Clinton, Jackson, and Jones counties, Iowa. Ph.D. dissertation, U. of Iowa, Iowa City.

Correll, D. S., and H. B. Correll. 1972. Aquatic and wetland plants of the southwestern United States. Washington,

D.C.: U.S. Supt. of Documents, U.S. Gov't. Printing Office.

Cowardin, L, V. Carter, F. Golet, and E. LaRoe. 1979. Classification of wetlands and deepwater habitats of the United States. Washington, D.C.: U.S. Dept. of Interior.

Currier, P. J., C. B. Davis, and A. G. van der Valk. 1978. A vegetation analysis of a wetland prairie marsh in northern Iowa. pp. 65–69 *in* D. C. Glenn-Lewin and R. Q. Landers. *Proc. Fifth Midwest Prairie Conf.*, Ames: Iowa State University Extension.

Davidson, R. A. 1959. The vascular flora of southeastern Iowa. *Univ. Iowa Stud. Nat. Hist.* 20(2):1–102.

Davis, C. B., and A. G. van der Valk. 1978a. The decomposition of standing and fallen litter of *Typha glauca* and *Scirpus fluviatilis. Can. J. Bot.* 56:662–675.

Davis, C. B., and A. G. van der Valk. 1978b. Litter decomposition in prairie glacial marshes. pp. 99–113. *In* R. Good, D. Whigham, and R. Simpson. Freshwater wetlands: Ecological processes and management potential. New York: Academic Press.

Davis, C. B., and A. G. van der Valk. 1978c. Mineral release from the litter of *Bidens cernua* L., a mudflat annual at Eagle Lake, Iowa. *Proc. Internat. Assoc. Theor. Appl. Limnol.* 20:452–457.

Densmore, F. 1974. How Indians use wild plants for food, medicine, and crafts. New York: Dover Press.

Eggers, S. D., and D. M. Reed. 1987. Wetland plants and plant communities of Minnesota and Wisconsin. U.S. Corps of Engineers, St. Paul district.

Eilers, L. J. 1971. The vascular flora of the Iowan area. *Univ. Iowa Stud. Nat. Hist.* 21(5):1–137.

Eilers, L. J., and D. M. Roosa. 1994. The vascular plants of Iowa: An annotated catalog and natural history. Iowa City: Univ. of Iowa Press.

Errington, P. L. 1960a. Wetland saga. *Nat. Hist.* 69:8–15.

Errington, P. L. 1960b. The wonder of an Iowa marsh. *Iowan* 8(7):41–45.

Errington, P. L. 1961. Muskrats and marsh management. Harrisburg, Pa.: Stackpole Press.

Errington, P. L. 1963. Muskrat populations. Ames: Iowa State Univ. Press.

Fassett, N. C. 1966. A manual of aquatic plants. Madison: Univ. of Wisc. Press.

Fay, M. J. 1953. The flora of southwestern Iowa. Ph.D. dissertation, Univ. of Iowa, Iowa City.

Fernald, M. L. 1950. Gray's manual of botany, 8th ed. New York: American Book Co.

Fernald, M. L., and A. C. Kinsey. 1943. Edible wild plants of eastern North America. Cornwall-on-Hudson: Idlewild Press.

Fielder, M. 1975. Plant medicine and folklore. New York: Winchester Press.

Freese, E. L., and W. J. Platt. 1991. Vascular flora of Arend's Kettlehole, Freda Haffner Kettlehole State Preserve, Dickinson County, Iowa. *Jour. Iowa Acad. Sci.* 98:102–107.

Gilmore M. R. 1977. Uses of plants by the Indians of the Missouri River region. Lincoln: Univ. of Nebraska Press.

Grant, M. L., and R. F. Thorne. 1955. Discovery and description of a *Sphagnum* bog in Iowa with notes on the distribution of bog plants in the state. *Proc. Iowa Acad. Sci.* 62:197–210.

Hartley, T. G. 1966. The flora of the "driftless area". *Univ. Iowa Studies in Nat. Hist.* 21(1):1–174.

Hayden, A. 1943. A botanical survey in the Iowa Lakes region of Clay and Palo Alto counties, Iowa. *Iowa St. Coll. J. Sci.* 17:277–415.

Hedrick, V. P. (ed.) 1919. Sturdevant's edible plants of the world. New York: Dover.

Holte, K. 1966. A floristic and ecological analysis of the Excelsior Fen complex in northwest Iowa. Ph.D. dissertation, Univ. of Iowa, Iowa City.

Kingsbury, J. M. 1964. Poisonous plants of the United States and Canada. Englewood Cliffs, N. J.: Prentice-Hall.

Krochmal, A., and C. Krochmal. 1973. A guide to medicinal wild plants. New York: New York Times Book Co.

Lammers, T. G., and A. G. van der Valk. 1977. A checklist of the aquatic and wetland vascular plants of Iowa: I. Ferns, fern allies, and dicotyledons. *Proc. Iowa Acad. Sci.* 84:41–88.

Lammers, T. G., and A. G. van der Valk. 1979. A checklist of the aquatic and wetland vascular plants of Iowa. II. Monocotyledons, plus a summary of the geographic and habitat distribution of all aquatic and wetland plants in Iowa. *Proc. Iowa Acad. Sci.* 85:121–163.

Magee, D. W. 1981. Freshwater wetlands: A guide to common indicator plants of the northeast. Amherst: Univ. of Mass. Press.

Mann, G. E. 1955. Wetlands inventory of Iowa. Washington, D.C.: Office of River Basin Studies, Fisheries and Wildlife Service.

Martin, A. C., H. S. Zim, and A. L. Nelson. 1951. American wildlife and plants—a guide to wildlife food habits. New York: Dover.

Medsger, O. P. 1957. Edible wild plants. New York: MacMillan.

Mohlenbrock, R. H. 1976. Sedges: *Cyperus* to *Scleria*. Carbondale: Southern Illinois University Press.

Monson, P. H. 1959. Spermatophytes of the Des Moines lobe in Iowa. Ph.D. dissertation, Iowa State Univ., Ames.

Muenscher, W. C. 1957. Poisonous plants of the United States and Canada. New York: MacMillan.

Nekola, J. C. 1990. Rare Iowa plant notes from the R. V. Drexler herbarium. *Jour. Iowa Acad. Sci.* 97:55–73.

Novacek, J. M., D. M. Roosa, and W. P. Pusateri. 1985. The vegetation of the Loess Hills landform along the Missouri River. *Proc. Iowa Acad. Sci.* 92:192–212.

Palmer, E. L., and H. S. Fowler. 1975. Fieldbook of natural history. New York: McGraw-Hill.

Pearson, J., and M. Leoschke. 1992. Floristic composition and conservation status of fens in Iowa. *Jour. Iowa Acad. Sci.* 99:41–52.

Peck, J. H., and D. M. Roosa. 1983. Bibliography of Iowa aquatic and wetland plant literature. *Proc. Iowa Acad. Sci.* 90:72– 77.

Peck, J. H., and M. M. Smart. 1985. Bibliography to Upper Mississippi River aquatic and wetland plant literature. *Proc. Iowa Acad. Sci.* 92:78–84.

Prior, J. C. 1991. Landforms of Iowa. Iowa City: Univ. of Iowa Press.

Pusateri, W. P., D. M. Roosa, and D. R. Farrar. 1994. Habitat and distribution of plants special to Iowa's Driftless Area. *Jour. Iowa Acad. Sci.* 100:29–53.

Rogers, D. J. 1980. Edible, medicinal, useful, and poisonous wild plants of the Northern Great Plains, South Dakota region. Sioux Falls: Biol. Dept., Augustana College.

Roosa, D. M. 1981. Marsh dynamics: The role of historical, cyclical, and annual events at Goose Lake, Hamilton County, Iowa. Ph.D. dissertation, Iowa State Univ., Ames.

Roosa, D. M., L. J. Eilers, and S. Zager. 1991. An annotated checklist of the vascular plant flora of Guthrie County, Iowa. *Jour. Iowa Acad. Sci.* 98:14–30.

Roosa, D. M., M. J. Leoschke, and L. J. Eilers. 1989. Distribution of endangered and threatened vascular plants. Des Moines: Iowa Department of Natural Resources.

Sculthorpe, C. D. 1967. The biology of aquatic vascular plants. London: Edward Arnold.

Shaw, S., and C. G. Fredine. 1971. Wetlands of the United States. Circular 39. Washington, D.C.: U.S. Dept. of Interior, Fish and Wildlife Service.

Sievers, A. F. 1930. American medicinal plants of commercial importance. Washington, D.C.: USDA, Pub. 77.

Smith, H. H. 1923. Ethnobotany of the Menomini. Milwaukee, Wis.: Bull. of the Milwaukee Public Museum.

Smith, H. H. 1928. Ethnobotany of the Meskwaki Indians. Milwaukee, Wis.: Bull. of the Milwaukee Public Museum.

Smith, H. H. 1932. Ethnobotany of the Ojibwe. Milwaukee, Wis.: Bull. of the Milwaukee Public Museum.

Smith, H. H. 1933. Ethnobotany of the Forest Potawatomi. Milwaukee, Wis.: Bull. of the Milwaukee Public Museum.

Smith, P. E. 1962. An ecological analysis of a northern Iowa *Sphagnum* bog and adjoining pond. Ph.D. dissertation, Univ. of Iowa, Iowa City.

Smith, P. E., and R. V. Bovbjerg. 1958. Pilot Knob bog as a habitat. *Proc. Iowa Acad. Sci.* 65:546–553.

Steffeck, D. W., F. L. Paveglio, Jr., and C. E. Korschgen. 1985. Distribution of aquatic plants in Keokuk Pool (Navigation Pool 19) of the Upper Mississippi River. *Proc. Iowa Acad. Sci.* 92:111–114.

Stern, W. T. 1966. Botanical Latin. New York: Hafner.

Swanson, S. D., and S. H. Sohmer. 1978. The vascular flora of Navigation Pool 8 of the Upper Mississippi River. *Proc. Iowa Acad. Sci.* 85:45–61.

Thompson, C. A., and E. A. Bettis III. 1994. Age and developmental history of Iowa fens. *Jour. Iowa Acad. Sci.* 101:73–77.

Thompson, C. A., E. A. Bettis III, and R. G. Baker. 1992. Geology of Iowa fens. *Jour. Iowa Acad. Sci.* 99:53–59.

Thompson, J. R. 1992. Prairies, forests, and wetlands—the restoration of natural landscape communities in Iowa. Iowa City: Univ. of Iowa Press.

van der Valk, A. G. 1981. Succession in wetlands: A Gleasonian approach. *Ecology* 62:688–696.

van der Valk, A. G. (ed.). 1989. Northern prairie wetlands. Ames: Iowa State Univ. Press.

van der Valk, A. G., and C. B. Davis. 1976a. Changes in the composition, structure, and primary production of plant communities along a perturbed coenocline. *Vegetatio* 32:87–96.

van der Valk, A. G., and C. B. Davis. 1976b. Seed banks of prairie glacial marshes. *Can. J. Bot.* 54:1832–1838.

van der Valk, A. G., and C. B. Davis. 1978a. The role of seed banks in the vegetation dynamics of prairie glacial marshes. *Ecology* 59:322–335.

van der Valk, A. G., and C. B. Davis. 1978b. Primary production of prairie glacial marshes. pp. 21–37. *In* R. Good, R. Whigham, and R. Simpson. Freshwater wetlands: Ecological processes and management potential. New York: Academic Press.

Van Dyke, G. D. 1972. Aspects relating to emergent vegetation

dynamics in a deep marsh, northcentral Iowa. Ph.D. dissertation, Iowa State University, Ames.

Weller, M. W. 1981. Freshwater marshes: Ecology and wildlife
management. Minneapolis: Univ. of Minn. Press.

Weller, M. W., and C. S. Spatcher. 1965. Role of habitat in the
distribution and abundance of marsh birds. *Iowa Agric.*
Ames: Iowa State Univ. Home Econ. Expt. St. Spec. Rept.
43. 31 pp.

Winterringer, G. S., and A. C. Lopinot. 1966. Aquatic plants of
Illinois. Springfield: Illinois State Museum and Dept. of
Conservation.

ABOUT THE AUTHORS

SYLVAN T. RUNKEL, best known as "Sy," was the senior natural historian and interpretive naturalist in Iowa. Long before it was the "in" thing, he was an advocate for Iowa's woodlands, prairies, and wetlands. His special skill in interpreting nature to people of all ages has left a legion of admirers throughout Iowa.

Sy Runkel spent a lifetime telling and showing, lecturing and explaining, planning and guiding, sitting on boards, developing trails and outdoor classrooms, and quietly gaining supporters to help save the native remnants he loved. Sadly, he passed away in January, 1995, after the bulk of this book was completed.

Runkel willingly devoted time to service on boards and committees. He was president of the Iowa chapters of the Soil Conservation Society of America, the Society of American Foresters, and the Wildlife Society. As chair of the State Preserves Advisory Board and board member of the Iowa chapter of the Nature Conservancy, he was instrumental in protecting numerous natural areas.

Throughout his life, Runkel was given awards for his devotion to conservation. They included Iowa Conservationist of the year, Federal Civil Servant of the year, Iowa Conservation Hall of Fame, The Nature Conservancy's Oak Leaf Award, the Frudden Award of the Iowa chapter of the American Foresters, the Silver Beaver Award from the Boy Scouts, and the Hagie Award from the Iowa Natural Heritage Foundation. He was a fellow of the Iowa Academy of Science, the Soil Conservation Society of America, and the Society of American Foresters. Morningside College, in Sioux City, awarded him the degree of Doctor of Science. In June 1996, a portion of the Loess Hills wildlife area near Onawa was dedicated as a state preserve in memory of Sylvan Runkel.

Along with Alvin Bull, Runkel wrote *Wildflowers of Iowa Woodlands, Wildflowers of Illinois Woodlands,* and *Wildflowers of Indiana Woodlands.* With Dean Roosa, he wrote the *Wildflowers of the Tallgrass Prairie.*

Except for five years as a glider pilot in World War II, the focus of Runkel's forty years with the federal government (mostly in the Soil Conservation Service) was conservation of natural resources.

Along with Dean Roosa, Sy was honored by the establishment of the "Runkel–Roosa award" of the Iowa Natural History Association: a fund established to aid students in conducting research projects.

DEAN M. ROOSA was State Ecologist for Iowa from 1975 to 1992. He worked with the State Preserves Advisory Board to establish a statewide system of natural, historical, geological, and archaeological sites to be given special protection under the Code of Iowa.

Roosa served as board member of the Nature Conservancy and the Natural Areas Association, chair of the Iowa Natural History Association, president of the Iowa Ornithologists' Union and is a fellow of the Iowa Academy of Science. He has distinguished service awards from the Iowa Academy of Science and the Nature Conservancy; an honorary Doctor of Science degree from Grinnell College; and the Alumni Achievement Award from the University of Northern Iowa. Along with his friend, Sy, he is honored by the Runkel–Roosa Award of the Iowa Natural History Association.

After a master's thesis in ornithology at the University of Northern Iowa, Roosa wrote a doctoral dissertation on wetland ecology at Iowa State University. He is one of the authors of *Iowa Birds* and of *Iowa's Natural Heritage*. With Sy Runkel, he wrote *Wildflowers of the Tallgrass Prairie*, and with Larry Eilers, *The Vascular Plants of Iowa*. Roosa's principal research interests are raptor biology and the status of Iowa's wetland plants. Before embarking on a career in conservation and preservation, Roosa taught in high schools and community colleges in Iowa.

With his wife, Carol Jacobs, Roosa lives in a rural area near Ames and operates an antique mall and an environmental consulting firm.